John Chrysostom and the
Transformation of the City

# John Chrysostom and the Transformation of the City

*Aideen M. Hartney*

**Duckworth**

First published in 2004 by
Gerald Duckworth & Co. Ltd.
90-93 Cowcross Street, London EC1M 6BF
Tel: 020 7490 7300
Fax: 020 7490 0080
inquiries@duckworth-publishers.co.uk
www.ducknet.co.uk

A catalogue record for this book is available
from the British Library

ISBN 0 7156 3193 4

Typeset by e-type, Liverpool
Printed and bound in Great Britain by
Biddles Ltd, *www.biddles.co.uk*

# Contents

# Preface

Any study of John Chrysostom's work is both rewarding and intensely frustrating. It is rewarding because of the eloquence of this fourth-century Christian leader, and the constantly surprising insights into life in this period of the Roman Empire that can be uncovered in his work. But it is frustrating because the sheer size of the body of work that is ascribed to this man means that only a small portion of it can be examined in any detail at any one time. In this book I have tried to shed some light on Chrysostom's preaching, but even here it has been necessary to be selective. As a result I have narrowed the discussion to those sermons preached by John on the Pauline Epistles, which do indeed give us a valuable insight into the preacher's methods and philosophies. It has been necessary, however, to maintain a narrow focus in the interests of keeping this study to a manageable length, and being able to complete it in a single lifetime! Readers will understandably feel therefore that there is still almost everything to be done on Chrysostom, with a variety of angles for future study remaining unexplored.

A number of people have been kind enough to read some or all of this manuscript in various stages of its incarnation. They have all made valuable suggestions for directions the study might take, and for useful areas of expansion and comparison. In some cases, due to these constraints of time and space, it has not been possible to do full justice to these suggestions in this work. I can only hope to have a chance to revisit Chrysostom on a future occasion in an effort to redress this situation. So I would like to thank Gillian Clark, Mark Humphries, Averil Cameron, John Davies, Theresa Urbainczyk and Peter Garnsey for taking the time and trouble to share their ideas with me throughout this project. Any errors or omissions are mine alone, and I hope they will forgive me for leaving so many tantalising areas of discussion as yet untouched.

I would also like to take this opportunity to thank friends and family for their continued support. My parents and siblings have been extremely enthusiastic and encouraging throughout – my gratitude to Maura, Anthony, Fiona and Shane – while special thanks must go to Simon Spence for his constant friendship and assistance. I am also grateful to Bernadette Toal, Pat Murphy, Malcolm Latham, Mark Simpson, Maeve Eogan, Joan O'Shea, Mary Saunderson, Tim Healy and Rory McDonnell for always taking an interest in this project, and thereby keeping my spirits from flagging. My thanks go to all concerned.

A.M.H.

For my family

# 1

# Pagan and Christian Cities

'Well, my lad, and what may you want up here?' 'I wanted to know where the city of Christminster is, if you please.' 'Christminster is out across there, by that clump. You can see it – at least you can on a clear day ... The time I've noticed it is when the sun is going down in a blaze of flame, and it looks like – I don't know what.' 'The heavenly Jerusalem,' suggested the serious urchin ... The boy strained his eyes also; yet neither could he see the far-off city.

Thomas Hardy, Jude the Obscure, ch. 3

## Introduction

Even his earliest commentators saw the fourth-century Antioch-born preacher John Chrysostom as a complex, often difficult, and yet enormously influential individual. Socrates, writing of Chrysostom in his *Historia Ecclesiastica* as one of the most prominent figures in church and state politics at the end of the fourth century, declares:

> He was a man who in his enthusiasm for virtue was over-bitter, and given to wrath rather than to modest dealings; from the uprightness of his life he took no thought for the future, and from his simplicity of character acted without deep consideration. He used unmeasured freedom of speech with those whom he encountered and as a teacher greatly benefited his hearers; but was considered by those who did not know him to be arrogant in his behaviour.[1]

It is this 'unmeasured freedom of speech' that will be the focus of this book, for it is a seam that can be deeply mined for a large number of resources relevant to the study of antiquity. It is perhaps surprising that so little excavation has been done in this regard to date, but an exploration of the themes of John Chrysostom's preaching, and of his own career, shows us a picture of a society struggling with changing ideals and structures at a key moment in history. From a group of publicly preached sermons, we can see the importance of this period in late antiquity for members of the Church hierarchy, but also for the ordinary members of the public who attended these spiritual lectures on a regular basis. Information that can be uncovered ranges from the interesting but small facts about personal grooming, to the larger theological anxieties that were prevalent at the time. John Chrysostom lived and worked during an exciting period of Church and Roman history alike, and his own preaching style is a fitting reflection of this state of ferment.

'Chrysostom' ('golden mouth') is a posthumously bestowed nickname, given to the more properly named John of Antioch as a tribute to his oratorical prowess. He has long been acknowledged as one of the leading lights of the early Greek Church, with an enormous body of work extant today. It is perhaps the very size of this corpus that has led to the relative neglect of this figure in comparison to other Church fathers such as Augustine or Jerome. Chrysostom's prolific nature and the polished nature of his Greek have meant that large portions of his work have gone untranslated and unstudied. And yet his surviving texts show an exciting, and even radical, approach to pastoral ministry and to Christian living.

## Chrysostom studies

One of the main problems facing anyone interested in the life or the work of John Chrysostom is the limitation of the source material and existing scholarship. The Migne collection of the works of the Greek Church Fathers is often the only place where Chrysostom's homilies can be found, and in many cases there has been no further attempt to provide a critical edition of his works. The Sources Chrétiennes series has begun to bridge this gap in recent years, but until now most of its attention has been focused on Chrysostom's written texts rather than his orally delivered sermons. This can leave the English-speaking scholar at something of a disadvantage, with only the nineteenth-century translations provided in the Nicene and Post-Nicene Fathers series to fall back on. These translations are often stilted and archaic, and there is little in the way of critical annotation. It is therefore perhaps understandable as to why many have steered clear of conducting detailed studies of Chrysostom's work for so long.

Until very recently any writing on John Chrysostom has been largely biographical in nature. This was the case even in antiquity, as early Church historians confined themselves to factual commentary on this illustrious career, and his equally spectacular fall from grace. Socrates and Sozomen, for example, were both writing comprehensive histories of the early Church, but some of the theological debates stirred up during Chrysostom's ministry were too sensitive to allow them to linger for too long on the details of Chrysostom's philosophy of Christian living, or on his recommendations to his flock. Indeed Chrysostom's career was the last event of any note covered by these historians, as anything following his deposition and death must have seemed too close to their own times for comfort. Socrates and Sozomen therefore restricted themselves to a relatively simple retelling of the main occurrences of Chrysostom's career in the course of their history.[2] Even a close supporter of Chrysostom, the biographer Palladius, was more interested in uncovering a perceived conspiracy against his subject than in discussing the content of any of Chrysostom's work.

In more modern times we have had extensive study of the life and career of Chrysostom, with Chrysostomous Baur's exhaustive and admiring two-volume exposition of this accomplished Church figure, first published in the late 1950s. More recently, J.N.D. Kelly has been less obviously devotional, but nevertheless focused on Chrysostom's rise and fall, to the exclusion of any detailed study of the preacher's work. Other studies, such as those completed by Liebeschuetz and Elm, have dealt with Chrysostom's political career, with the emphasis primarily on the way in which he fell foul of so many of those in positions of authority in the course of his ministry at Constantinople. As such, they are accounts that concentrate for the most part on the enmity of the Bishop of Alexandria, Theophilus, for Chrysostom, and on the controversy surrounding the Affair of the Tall Brothers which was the catalyst for Chrysostom's final deposition.[3] Once again there is little analysis of individual works by Chrysostom. And yet it is in this body of work that we can see so many of the clues to his unpopularity with secular and Church authorities alike, and to his ultimate downfall.

Two new directions for Chrysostom studies to take have been uncovered in the last few years. The first of these acknowledges the massive and important contribution to the study of late antiquity that analysis of Christian preaching can make. Based in Australia, Pauline Allen and Wendy Mayer have begun construction of an exhaustive database of John Chrysostom's sermons. The intention is to extend this to a group of preachers operating in Constantinople over a period of time. But for now, every reference made by Chrysostom to an aspect of life in a late Roman city has been uncovered, catalogued and cross-referenced. This work is a perfect illustration of the kind of information that can be obtained from Christian sermons on a range of subjects, from women's dress to artisan's working hours, to literacy levels of the congregation. Certainly this project is a fitting counter-argument to A.H.M. Jones' decision that little of value about ancient society could ever be learnt from the homiletic tradition:

> I soon decided to abandon theological treatises and commentaries on the Scriptures and secular belles-lettres.... There are a few grains of wheat in these, but the quantity of chaff (from my point of view) is overwhelming.... I next, after reading a fair sample, abandoned sermons, having discovered that most consisted of exegesis of the Scriptures or of vague and generalised moralisation.[4]

While this work by Allen and Mayer is both vital and fascinating, it is perhaps more useful to those interested in the broader canvas of late antiquity than it is to those who are interested in John Chrysostom as a product of this antiquity. Indeed, while their research provides a richness of detail about life in the ancient city largely derived from Chrysostom's sermons, there is almost everything still to be done on the thematic content of these works.[5]

It is here that the work done by Blake Leyerle helps to fill a gap. She has approached the work of Chrysostom from a thematic point of view, identifying some of his key preoccupations, and demonstrating how these are the natural results of his cultural upbringing, as well as a subtle reworking of this heritage. In this way, Leyerle has shown how some of Chrysostom's writings can illustrate many of the tensions that are at the heart of the consolidation of Christianity within Roman society, and it is in this vein that much of my own discussion will proceed. However, Leyerle's analysis of Chrysostom's homilies has been brief as yet, with most of her focus being directed at his ascetic treatises. She discusses two of these treatises – those on the *subintroductae* – as texts composed according to a model familiar from ancient comedy, and which would therefore appeal to an audience on an entertainment level as well as a spiritual one.[6] Leyerle's discussion of Chrysostom's homilies has touched on some very important themes in those of Christian preaching on children and on wealth as projected in these sermons, but her analysis has of necessity been brief and wide-ranging.[7]

R. Wilken is the only other scholar who has chosen to analyse a specific series of Chrysostom's sermons for their thematic content, when he discusses the anti-Semitic sentiments expressed by the preacher in a series of homilies preached against the Jews. In this case it is a prevailing climate of anti-semitism in the later Roman empire that Wilken concentrates on, and so his work is quite specific in its range of discussion. He demonstrates that accusations of anti-Semitism levelled against Chrysostom are in fact the result of reading this series of sermons out of context. The individuals Chrysostom speaks out against are in fact 'Judaisers' rather than Jews, indicating that it was a very definite course of action that aroused the preacher's ire, rather than a simple prejudice against Jews.[8] In addition to these few thematic studies, the Oxford Patristics Conference in recent years has thrown up some very interesting work in its panels on the Greek Church Fathers, and on Chrysostom himself, but this is the only forum where such consistent discussion of the preacher's work and motivation has taken place. There is therefore almost unlimited scope for a study of Chrysostom's sermons as important aspects of both his own career, and the process by which Christianity came to institutional status.

It is also worth remembering at this stage that much of the scholarship to date dealing with the writings of any of the Church Fathers, has as its focus the rise of the ascetic movement, and the extent to which the ecclesiastical authorities tried to win converts to this way of life. The dramatic actions of some of the foremost ascetics have captured the minds of commentators, leading to work concentrated on attempting to explain the place of this phenomenon within the changing order of late antiquity.[9]

Yet it has also been acknowledged that we know comparatively little of the ordinary men and women who did not feel inclined to renounce their sexuality or their worldly lifestyles. And it is precisely from the sermons of any of these church preachers that some information of this sort can be gleaned. Preaching in the Christian tradition was a predominantly urban phenomenon, and the city was not the ideal location for the practice of asceticism. Therefore, the audience of a Christian homily would, by its very nature, be comprised of those individuals who had chosen to adopt the Christian religion, but practise it within the boundaries of everyday living, and so the words of the orator would be tailored, at least to some extent, to the worldly nature of his audience.

## Preaching as a Christian innovation

Studies of Church Fathers and their works often fail fully to appreciate how revolutionary church preaching was as an oratorical tool in antiquity. It is not that similar discourses had not existed before Christianity, since we know the practice of expounding on a piece of text was popular both in the Jewish tradition of worship and in the more secular environment of the Roman classroom, where schoolboys were expected to be able to comment and expand on a passage from any of the authors on the curriculum. It is rather that the nature of the audience shifted profoundly between the Roman secular model of public exposition and the model instigated by the Church. While audiences of Roman oratory were primarily comprised of members of the middle and upper classes, themselves possessors of a considerable education and almost always male, Christian congregations were remarkable by virtue of their inclusiveness. Men, women and even children could regularly attend church, regardless of social class or level of education. The Christian homily was therefore radically expansive in its target audience.

It is this fact that makes the study of Church preaching such a rewarding one. Since anyone who wished within ancient society could have access to Church teachings in this way, a fantastic opportunity existed for Christian authorities to disseminate their own ideals and philosophies, which were often in conflict with those already established within the society. Many preachers made the most of this opportunity, and the result was some impassioned public oratory on a wide range of subjects, as these men of God struggled to impose their view of a Christian world order on their congregations. And it is in this forum that John Chrysostom comes into his own, as his nickname might suggest.

An accomplished speaker from his youth, Chrysostom employed his talents throughout his career to a very specific end. This was the remodelling of the ancient city along the lines that he considered appropriate for a Christian community. We shall see much more of this as we proceed. But his is a career that shows the clash of spiritual and secular particularly well, at the same time as trying to influence the most fundamental human relationships in his society.

Chrysostom believed in working change from the bottom up, and so addressed his flock at the most basic level at which they would understand him. He spoke of their households and the human interaction that went on there. He worked to reorder relations between husbands and wives, fathers and children, patriarchs and servants. The next stage was to have any changes effected here spill over into the larger community, thus moving upwards and outwards. Chrysostom's ultimate aim was a re-ordered city, one that reflected and embodied the central tenets of Christianity, and his rhetorical skill was constantly being stretched in an effort to achieve it.

### Tolling the death knell of the ancient city?

The ancient Roman city was a vibrant and activity-filled place. It was also a place with a number of structures and systems that both identified and maintained the civic unit. The theatre, sports arenas, the forum, financial dealings and political interactions all served to define the Roman city as such, and also to define its citizens.

Those who wished to consider themselves citizens of the urban unit were conscious of the importance of taking part in those activities that were an intrinsic aspect of city living. It was almost a demonstration of belonging to attend the theatre or sporting events at the hippodrome. It was also an indication of citizenship to engage in financial or political deals with fellow inhabitants of the city. And so a man could both make a public display of his civic spirit on an individual basis at the same time as helping to maintain the overall urban structure through his activities.

Not surprisingly, pagan and Christian thinkers had opposing views on this version of the urban community. We will see throughout this work the extent to which John Chrysostom wished for a transformation of the ancient city into a recognisably Christian community, involving a substantial alteration in the behaviour of its inhabitants. It was a common Christian anxiety at this time that participation in the daily activities of the ancient city might somehow disqualify people from heavenly salvation, indicating the strength of the belief that urban living was incompatible with true devotion.

But pagan thinkers of the day had their own anxieties about the city structure. They perceived their world as under threat from the encroaching forces of Christianity, which called into question structures and traditions that they had held dear for centuries. The writings of the orator Libanius are an excellent example of this kind of feeling, as he spoke of the changes he saw occurring around him on a daily basis and which he saw as undermining the traditions of the ancient city, and by extension his own role as a leading citizen in such a community.

Libanius was a skilled orator with experience in some of the leading cities of the Roman empire. Throughout his career he spent time in Athens and Constantinople before returning to his native Antioch to take up the chair of rhetoric there. He took his duties seriously, presenting superbly crafted speeches on any occasion of civic importance in Antioch, as well as educating many of its younger citizens in this subject area. Chrysostom himself was a student of Libanius, but it was common practice for any family who could afford it to send their sons to a rhetorician during their young adulthood in order to finish their education. The skill of public speaking was seen as essential to the male character in the Roman empire, and as a result it was taken seriously by most members of the middle and upper classes.

Libanius was exceedingly fond of his native city and its traditions, and composed a number of orations singing its praises. But he also watched it changing before his eyes with considerable anxiety. At times Libanius feels that the advance of Christianity is to blame for the shifting attitudes of the Antiochenes. He speaks derisively of the black-robed, shabby monks he can see coming down from the mountains to mingle with the townspeople, spreading their doctrine of abstinence and celibacy. Libanius feels that this kind of preaching sparks unrest among his fellow citizens, and he reserves some of his most cutting language for Christian ascetics as a result. Libanius also feels that the observance of a religion can be a private affair, whereas Christians demand a demonstrable and communal system of worship.[10] These monks are the most obvious of all, given their altered appearance and their radical message.

The monks and ascetics to whom Libanius objects so strongly embodied a philosophy that was entirely alien to that of the rhetorician. While he appreciated the importance of self-discipline and restraint in living, and indeed advocated it in a number of his orations, Libanius objected to a degree of abstinence that would undermine the very foundations of the city. Such ascetics as he describes in his works were those who felt that the only way of truly worshipping God was to withdraw from urban life completely, and to embrace celibacy to such an extent that the very population of the city could eventually be threatened. Libanius believed that one of the key duties of a Roman citizen was to perpetuate the family line, so that the ranks of the nobility could be constantly replenished, allowing the city to flourish and survive – maintained by those who understood its structures and had its best interests at heart. The ascetic philosophy seemed completely at odds with this, and the prominent and noticeable presence of monks on the streets of Antioch was naturally interpreted by Libanius as a threat to all he held dear.

However, it was not just Christianity that threatened to rewrite the philosophies and structures of the ancient city. Libanius was also concerned about the changing attitudes of his fellow Antiochenes. He noticed an increased interest in power, in political intrigue, and most of all in the accumulation of wealth. And while financial transactions were still important aspects of the civic community, Libanius felt that greed and ostentation had become the driving forces behind peoples' business deals, instead of a sense of civic pride and duty. The ideal citizen of the ancient

city was supposed to conduct his business so as to keep the city in existence, and so as to transmit any wealth accumulated in this way to future
generations of his family. Euergetism was also a cornerstone of this philosophy, whereby an honourable citizen would use some of his own wealth in
order to support the institutions of his native city. This could be done by
means of sponsoring entertainments or civic events, maintaining civic
buildings and public places, or simply helping to contribute to the upkeep
of the urban unit. It was a means both of proving one's citizenship and of
celebrating the city itself.

Libanius, however, sees many of his peers as becoming more interested
in presenting themselves as wealthy individuals than as dutiful and noble
citizens. And so he criticises their wealth, the kind of greed that leads to
the non-payment of his own fees, and the rise in vulgar ostentation on the
streets and in the villas of Antioch. Large houses were being built on all
available land in Antioch, crowding out more humble dwellings, and even
depriving them of natural light due to the offensive size of the newer
structures.[11] Sacrifices and festivals were being neglected in favour of
lavish dinner parties, on which vast sums of money were 'squandered'.[12]
He accuses those at fault in this respect of forgetting their duty as inhabitants of the city, and of actually bringing its continued existence into
doubt. The rhetor's anxiety on this score leads to some acerbic outbursts
as he struggles to remind his audiences of the traditional values which
made their city great, and which need to be rediscovered if it is to continue
to hold such a prominent position in the Roman empire. As a result his
fellow citizens often complained against his public orations and his opinions, calling him tiresome, and ridiculing his views:

> The complaint is that I am constantly praising and longing for what
> is dead and gone, denouncing the present day, harping on the past
> prosperity and the present misery of the cities, and that this is my
> tale, everywhere, every day. Some complain about this and are
> annoyed at my comments, but they are those who have benefited
> from the present situation.... So to these *nouveaux-riches* I am inor-
> dinately displeasing and tiresome with these remarks ... [13]

As part of the same oration Libanius complains that citizens are no longer
willing to serve on the curial councils, that the burden of taxation has
impoverished many leading lights of society, and that even the temples and
sacrifices are neglected in the current atmosphere. The military might of
the empire is also being compromised. Soldiers are not being paid properly,
and as a result they have lost their interest in protecting their homeland:
'Their glory is to get drunk, fetch up their food and start off at once on
another round of eating and swilling.'[14]

Libanius is not the only pagan author to have such concerns regarding
the state of the ancient city. Ammianus Marcellinus, writing about Rome
itself, was also anxious about the ostentation, the vulgarity, and the care-

lessness of wider consequences that he saw enacted around him on a daily basis. He paints a number of pictures of rich citizens indulging themselves and pampering their senses to such an extent that they have forgotten their privileged position within the civic structure, and have forgotten what they owe to this structure in return:

> Some, dressed in gleaming silk, go about preceded by a crowd of people, like men being led to execution or, to avoid so unfortunate a simile, like men bringing up the rear of an army, and are followed by a throng of noisy slaves in formation.... If one tries to greet these people with an embrace they turn their head to one side like a bad-tempered bull, though that is the natural place for a kiss, and offer their knee or their hand instead, as if that would be enough to make anyone happy for life.[15]

Sycophants congregate around men of means and pressure them to make a will from which they might benefit. Wives and husbands nag each other to similar ends, forsaking marital harmony in the interests of financial gain. Religious observances have become trivialised to the extent that a rich man or woman will not step outside their front door without consulting horoscopes and diviners, but traditional rites and temples are neglected. Even theatrical performances have become vulgar and tasteless, with most people concerned more with the gambling and brawling opportunities presented by sporting events. And underlying all of these vices, according to Ammianus Marcellinus, is an overriding sense of gluttony.[16]

The tone of both of these pagan authors is urgent enough to conjure up a picture of a rapidly changing society, with constant clashes between old and new creeds, lifestyles and systems of morality. Their answer to this perceived 'crisis' is to invoke images of a former time, when cities were justifiably regarded as the pinnacle of human community living, and when the values espoused by citizens both defined and bolstered the urban unit. And so their writings emphasise a traditional way of life, and the accompanying value system, in an attempt to remind readers and audiences of the importance of remembering one's duty to the city in which one lived.

What is also interesting to note, however, is the extent to which their anxieties and their concerns mirror those of Christian authors, Chrysostom in particular. Chrysostom too has reason to reprimand the citizens of Antioch, and later Constantinople, for focusing on money to the exclusion of their religious obligations, or even to the neglect of the proper raising of their offspring. He is also concerned about the distractions posed by an increasingly worldly city, and by a perceived breakdown in order and morality. But other Church Fathers were similarly suspicious of the values of the ancient city, and took every opportunity to preach against its distractions and its non-Christian characteristics.

In the ideal Christian city the clergy would be the leaders of their flocks in a new style of living. It would a restrained lifestyle, with the emphasis on prayer, fasting and almsgiving as the best way of worshipping God. Priests and bishops saw themselves as opinion leaders and patrons in this system, and in most cases played their parts with the utmost seriousness. Whereas previously it would have been a prominent politician or businessman who acted as patron to a limited group of 'clients', within the Christian Church the bishop would be patron to his entire diocese. And the influence wielded by the Christian bishop would be spiritual rather than social or financial. With attention focused largely on the afterlife, even suggestions that parishioners should give alms were more about safeguarding the souls of those in question rather than on any substantial redistribution of wealth within the community.

Chrysostom was just one of these new Christian patrons. Other Christian leaders also played a similar part, and probably played it a great deal more effectively. The Cappadocian fathers, for example, were generally quite reasonable and open in their approach to those in their care – recognising and making allowances for human frailties. But even Basil found himself ground down by the political dimension to his job, and retired from Constantinople to a more sedate administrative post near his home. Others, such as Ambrose and Augustine, found themselves to be more skilled at balancing the worldly and spiritual demands of a bishopric. Indeed Ambrose took on the emperor of the day and won an ostensible victory, by forcing Theodosius I to acknowledge the superiority of God's representative as he did penance for ordering the massacre at Thessalonica, thus straddling the pagan and Christian civic systems better than most.

Within the newly postulated Christian city therefore, the clergy could almost replace the traditional leaders of society and become patrons and protectors par excellence. Not only would they instruct their charges as to how to improve their lives, but they would also guarantee to represent their interests in front of the highest authority there was – that of God himself. The spiritual benefits accrued in this way would surpass any temporal advantages achieved through the traditional patron-client system.

Chrysostom took the representative side of this role very seriously indeed. He was constantly anxious about those souls which might be lost under his care, and for which he would be answerable on the day of Final Judgement. He was also eager to educate his audience in the new style of living that he felt to be most appropriate to them as Christians. But he was less concerned with the political dimensions of this job, feeling they were somehow at odds with his Christian ethics. And this 'short-sightedness' ultimately led to his downfall. More skilled political movers such as Ambrose or Augustine therefore, were able to interact with the temporal world without compromising their Christian duties. It was this sense of compromise that Chrysostom never quite seemed to grasp, and which could have done much to bring his idealised Christian city closer to realisation than all his rhetoric ever achieved.

It has been suggested by Peter Brown that Chrysostom's preaching sounded the death knell of the ancient city, in that the preacher worked to undermine everything that the traditional Roman citizen held dear.[17] Brown feels that the radical nature of many of Chrysostom's recommendations regarding the lifestyles of his congregants was aimed at bringing about the swift and sudden demise of the ancient city. Under Chrysostom's tutelage citizens would cease to conduct financial transactions, would cease to demonstrate their allegiance to the civic unit by means of public participation in communal events, and above all, would cease to procreate – thus stopping the replenishment of the ranks of the nobility for generations to come. It would seem that Brown bases much of this judgement on the ascetic content of much of Chrysostom's work. Chrysostom was indeed fervent in his praise of a life of strict renunciation, and dedicated in his own pursuit of such a way of life. But it would be a mistake to think that his preaching energies were devoted to encouraging his congregations to retire from urban life and adopt asceticism in all its extremes in the deserts or mountains outside of their cities. If such calls were to be found in Chrysostom's sermons, we might indeed consider his preaching to be a grave threat to the ancient order. Certainly Chrysostom attacks civic institutions such as the theatre, municipal games, and the Roman obsession with transmitting familial wealth through the generations. But he does not demand that his audience abandon these traditional structures in favour of a subsistence life in the desert. Instead he asks for a reinterpretation of existing models in a Christian framework. In fact, much of Chrysostom's preaching is directed at keeping the ancient city alive and thriving. The only difference is that it would be a demonstrably Christian city in all its components. Chrysostom hopes that eventually the city would cease to be a place from which ascetics felt compelled to flee, and would become a place where their Christian vocations could be realised unhindered. It would therefore seem a little dramatic to talk of Chrysostom sounding a final toll for this way of life. Nor would it seem to be what Chrysostom himself wanted. As we can see from the pagan authors mentioned above, there is much to suggest that the ancient city was already in a state of change and flux, and that the advent of Christian philosophy was only a single element of this. Chrysostom's more subtle ambitions for the city – rather than its complete destruction – and the way in which he worked to realise them is the substance of this work.

What Chrysostom did insist on was that those in his spiritual care would behave in such a way as to obviously proclaim their Christianity. As with many of the Church Fathers during this key period in Church history, John Chrysostom worried that members of his flock would simply fade into the background of the ancient city. No longer persecuted for their faith, there was little to mark Christians out as unusual or different within their society. Church authorities felt that this was a contradiction of the central tenets of their faith, which called on everyone to allow every aspect of their daily lives to be imbued by their faith. If such an ideal could be achieved, what would occur would be a reinterpretation of ancient society and its citizenship. In this way Chrysostom uses his preaching skills for innovative and radical ends, moving beyond the simple theological or biblical education presented by other Christian orators in their sermons. Chrysostom advocates a lifestyle as well as expounding on Scripture, and this coupled with his entertaining style means that he stands out among his more restrained, or more theologically concentrated peers. And according to those historians closest to him in time, he was not altogether unsuccessful in his aim to re-create the ancient city:

> As the result of these reforms, the Church put forth daily more abundant blossoms; the tone of the whole city was changed to piety, men delighting their souls with soberness and psalmody.[18]

## Gender roles in the Christian city

Chrysostom's opinions regarding the classical city and his aims for reform can be seen throughout much of his written work, along with his respect for the ascetic lifestyle. But written texts were not his only, or even his most effective, means of persuasion. In order to reach the majority of his flock, Chrysostom took care to incorporate his message into his sermons for regular dissemination from the pulpit. It is for this reason that Chrysostom's public preaching is the focus of this work. For it is in the public forum that he worked to change the lives of his audience by appropriating the accepted discourse of the day for Christian purposes. The Christianisation of the classical city could only be accomplished through appealing to the inhabitants of that city – and as broad a range of citizens as possible. This Chrysostom managed in his rhetorically skilled preaching, thus reaching many people who would never normally have been exposed to such philosophies or theories. Whereas Chrysostom's letters and written treatises can be seen as directed to a select, educated, and socially well-off group of people, his homilies were aimed at all classes, at all levels of education and at large numbers. They therefore show a difference of approach from Chrysostom's more private discourse, while maintaining many of the same aims and opinions.

Chrysostom's purpose in his public ministry was the transformation of the city. However he chooses to promote this aim from a somewhat oblique angle within his sermons. Rather than simply denouncing civic institutions and hoping to achieve his goal through blunt prohibition from a position of superiority – although we will sometimes see him resort to this too – he works to appeal to his congregation by means of their daily interpersonal relationships. By altering the way Christians interacted with each other on this most basic scale, his reforms can thus spread outwards and upwards rather than from the top down. Indeed many historians suggest that this was the way Christianity itself spread through society in its early years. This approach shows a high degree of observation and intelligence on the part of the preacher and explains why representations of gender and sexuality are so prominent in some of his rhetoric. His is a practical approach rather than one concentrated on esoteric or theological concepts.[19]

One of the key human-relations models in Roman society was that of gender interactions. As will be seen, fixed parameters of behaviour for both sexes were established within the urban community, both to underpin relations between the sexes, and to define suitable citizens of the late antique city. It is important to emphasise at this stage that ancient perceptions of sexual differences were by no means as firmly based on physical appearance as they are today. Until very recently our own concepts of gender were almost entirely appearance-related. The increase in obvious transvestism and sex changes has muddied the waters somewhat, with such activities being offhandedly described as 'gender-bending'. But it is only now that we are faced with such potential confusion and even embarrassment that we can arrive at some understanding of the state of play in Roman society. Then it was a person's publicly perceived behaviour that identified their gender rather than their anatomical appearance. Thus a male who was somewhat effeminate in appearance could, nevertheless, dispel doubts as to his gender by ensuring that he was obviously seen to behave in ways classed as traditionally male. The public persona was what an individual was defined by in this society. This is something that has been examined with regard to first- and second-century sophistic culture in the Roman empire.[20] There has also been some analysis of the issue as alluded to in Jewish texts.[21] But as yet there has been little discussion of gender as an obvious and acknowledged performance in the later empire.

However, Chrysostom is concerned with outward behaviour at all times, whether as a definition of faith, spirituality or sexuality. And just as the ancient city was inextricably bound up with public display, so the addressing of the display that was integral to everyone's life – the gender display – was a way into the civic structure, and a tool for organising change.[22] The preacher's concerns with such matters of gender and sexuality in his own private life and in his written treatises, have been well examined to date.[23] The presentation of such sensitive issues, and the ultimate purpose of their presence within his public preaching, is as yet, however, a new field of study.

It has been suggested, again by Peter Brown, that Chrysostom's discussions of gender, sex and the body function simply as set pieces, common to many of the Church Fathers of this period. Brown would argue that such pieces are merely conventions, and that Christian concerns regarding human sexuality become almost akin to rhetorical tropes – included and expected at regular intervals. Brown suggests that, in spite of some virulent outbursts on the evils of sex and the weakness of women, what is really important in Chrysostom's sermons is the preacher's efforts to achieve a new city of the poor, who are his real concern. Certainly

Chrysostom was deeply disturbed by the gap between rich and poor that he witnessed in so many aspects of life in late antiquity. But I believe that his preaching on gender was a key means of resolving this disparity, and therefore achieving his Christian city, rather than a separate or purely conventional line of thought. In this way, Chrysostom regards the relationship between the sexes as the foundation of society, and therefore a logical place to start the process of change.

This was actually quite a traditional approach, since from Aristotelian thought, the concept that any community was made up of a series of much smaller units or relationships had become incorporated into the consciousness of the ancient city. The most basic human relationship was that which was formed between a man and woman. From this starting point a family and subsequently a household could grow, and when a number of these *oikoi* gathered together and agreed on a division of labour and a certain system of organisation, the basic *polis*, or city state, came into being.[24] As we move on, we will frequently see echoes of Aristotelian thought in Chrysostom's approach. In his work to alter the appearance of the *polis* he began by targeting the basic unit of this community, the household, using it as his primary tool for change. This in turn required considerable discussion of the hierarchy within this household, which was almost entirely gender-based. Within the Christian discussions, however, the writings of St Paul ostensibly replaced Aristotle as Chrysostom's blueprint for this system, as the traditional reference systems for household and human relations were relentlessly Christianised.

### 'The Blessed Paul' – exegesis on the Pauline epistles

As Christianity began to establish itself as the official religion of the State, Church authorities needed new models of philosophy and oratory to replace traditional pagan models. The process by which these models were created and presented has been well documented in recent years and has become known as the Christianisation of discourse. In this way the language and symbols that formed the basis for all cultural references became overlaid with a Christian tone and flavour. The logical extension of this process was that the discourse of power within society would also become Christianised, allowing the Church to present itself as the automatic and only power-base within the empire.[25]

In order to begin this process and provide the Christian cultural references that would replace existing structures, the Scriptures were the obvious place to turn. The writings of St Paul in particular were guidelines for the establishment of early Christian communities, offering advice and remedies for the various problems that arose as this new religion negotiated its path in Roman and Jewish societies. As such, their style and content was well suited to later Church leaders, who faced similar complexities in their attempts to create a recognisably Christian empire. Paul was also a missionary Christian, and his proselytising was a useful alternative to the persuasive words of Graeco-Roman philosophers who were traditionally revered in this society. Christian commentators liked to boast of Paul's relative lack of education, compared to the sophisticated philosophers and orators gone before him such as Plato, Aristotle and Josephus. This made his achievement seem all the more remarkable, as well as facilitating the replacement of traditional philosophers with an equally meretricious substitute.

Considering the importance attached to Paul by early Church leaders, John Chrysostom's homilies on his epistles are especially worthy of study. These sermons also richly repay anyone interested in the issues of gender appearance and behaviour. Modern perceptions of the early Church's attitudes to gender roles, and specifically to portrayals of femininity, tend to view St Paul as the instigator of anti-female doctrines. And indeed the Apostle did have much cause to teach and write about the appropriate behaviour of Christian women.[26] It would be a mistake, though, to interpret his many and varied instructions to the earliest Church communities as evidence of a coherent or unified policy on gender issues. Paul's epistles were constructed as replies to queries and anxieties on the part of those churches under his guidance and patronage. Responses were issued according to specific needs as they arose, and as Paul deemed them to be important. Indeed accusations of misogyny are born out of a reading of Paul's letters in corpus form, a manner in which they were not originally written or intended to be read. Much of Paul's rhetorical skill was directed at demonstrating himself to be as close as possible to his congregation in thought and deed, rather than at laying down spiritual truths for the subsequent church body.[27] The letter to the Galatians, for example, was written in reply to accusations faced by Paul himself that he was supporting the Jewish Law in contravention of the doctrines of Christianity. Both letters to Timothy are pieces of advice to a younger colleague of Paul's with particular instructions as to how best he could lead a Christian community and safeguard the souls of his charges. The Corinthians had been experiencing instability and contradictory voices in their struggle to lead appropriately Christian lives, hence the two epistles dispatched to them, filled with advice, reprimands and encouragement. We must remember therefore, that each reference to women or broader gender issues within Paul's work occurred within a specific context.

It is the interpretation of such discussions out of their context that has led to Paul being branded as a narrow-minded misogynist. But some blame must also be laid at the door of earlier commentators on the Apostle – of whom John Chrysostom was possibly the most systematic and prolific. The exegetical homilies on Paul's texts which were preached in a public forum and then preserved for posterity, led to the understanding of Paul as a man with a definitive philosophy to propound. We have seen that this was not actually the case, but scholars such as Chrysostom treated the words of Paul as second only to those of Christ on a doctrinal level. With the dissemination of this viewpoint through the public discourse that was church preaching, the spontaneous advice of Paul in relation to an individual problem was literally treated as 'gospel'. The close exegesis of his epistles contained in such homilies led to a thorough expounding of his opinions, which were then received by the audience as doctrine, regardless of the original context or motivation for their writing.

Aside from the considerations of gender and discourse, Chrysostom's homilies on the Pauline epistles form a unique body of work in the ancient Church. His discussion of the letters is detailed and complete, and in his work he saw himself as opening the eyes of his congregation to one of the greatest saints ever to have lived. This led to a polished level of style that has prompted commentators to flag certain series as his best work, while back in the ancient world Isidore of Pelusium was to write:

> I think that if the divine Paul had wished to expound his own writings, he would not have spoken otherwise than this famous master; so remarkable is his exposition for its contents, beauty of form, and propriety of expression.[28]

### John Chrysostom's life and work

It is hardly necessary to embark on a detailed account of Chrysostom's life here, given the comprehensive biographical work of Kelly and Baur. But for those who may not be familiar with the preacher, a brief survey might serve as an introduction to his personality and his priorities.

John – later nicknamed Chrysostom in tribute to his oratorical abilities – was born in Antioch around 349.[29] His family belonged to what could be called Antioch's upper middle classes, and although John's father died while he was still very young, his mother, Anthousa, ensured that he obtained the best education money could buy – even using funds from her own dowry. In this late antique city, as throughout the Roman empire, such an education automatically consisted of a study of the Classical Greek literary heritage and of extensive training in rhetoric, while philosophy might also form part of the curriculum. Although it has recently been questioned, it is generally agreed that in rhetorical matters, the young John was a pupil of the famed orator Libanius.[30] Under his tutelage, John himself became skilled in oratory, enhancing his compositional skills, his eloquence and his talent for argumentation. Libanius and Chrysostom held each other in high regard in spite of their religious differences, and thematic and stylistic similarities can be traced in the work of both men.[31] John stemmed from a devout Christian family, while Libanius regarded the spread of Christianity – especially in his native Antioch – as a source of great anxiety, perceiving it as an attack upon his own culture. He had after all been an admirer and extoller of the virtues of the pagan emperor, Julian. Nevertheless, the rhetor's paganism did not prevent him from recognising his pupil's oratorical expertise. It is in fact reported that Libanius, while on his deathbed, suggested that John would have been an appropriate successor to his chair of rhetoric, 'if only the Christians had not stolen him from us'.[32]

And indeed in his youth, the tenets of the ascetic side of Christianity pulled John far more strongly than the attractions of a secular career in the civil service or the law courts. He and a few of his peers seem to have created their own, informal equivalent of a monastic community within the bounds of the city – congregating about the bishop of the day, Meletius, and diligently studying the Scriptures. While Antioch was known as one of the most cultured and entertaining cities in the empire at the time, with many of its citizens more concerned with temporal pleasures than with their spiritual welfare, it was nevertheless a city that was also proud of its strict ascetics who lived in the surrounding mountains and who gathered many admirers by virtue of their devout austerity. From an early age, these monks exercised a strong hold on John's imagination, and he was eager for the time to come when he might be able to join them in the wilderness. Even as a youth, therefore, he seems to have decided that the ascetic lifestyle was the means by which he would best achieve closeness to God. His membership of the informal *asketerion* around Meletius was merely a transitional state until he could pursue the 'real thing'. This *asketerion* seems to have been a small gathering of devout young men, who chose to spend their time studying Scripture and endeavouring to live a modified form of the ascetic life within the boundaries of the city, while attending the bishop as part of his staff. Chrysostom's close friend Basil was also a member of this micro-community. The zeal of Chrysostom to join a recognised ascetic community, however, was temporarily halted by the pleas of Anthousa, who begged him not to leave her a widow a second time by thus departing to the mountains.[33]

Priding himself on being a dutiful son, John agreed to stay put for a time, but he was evidently chafing at the bit – even to the extent of enacting an elaborate deception to avoid involuntary ordination some time in 371 or 372 AD. He and his friend Basil were targeted by the authorities for elevation to the priesthood, but such a promotion would end the companions' dreams of dedicating themselves to the ascetic life, since at this time in the church community there was often a sharp divide between those deemed capable of public ministry and those ascetics who were merely 'holy'. Filled with consternation, John and Basil agreed that whatever road they would go down, they would at least travel it together. John, however, modestly felt certain that, while he was utterly unfit for a life of public ministry, Basil was eminently qualified. He therefore left town and ensconced himself in the middle of an ascetic community, and so finally achieved his long-held goal. The unfortunate Basil was seized and ordained while under the mistaken impression that John had already submitted to similar treatment. When he was disabused of this idea he confronted his friend, but John did not seem to view the matter in the same doleful light as Basil, congratulating himself rather on having enacted an admirable scheme:

No sooner had he [Basil] opened his mouth than he was prevented from utterance by grief cutting short his words before they could pass his lips. Seeing then his tearful and agitated condition, and knowing as I did the cause, I laughed for joy, and seizing his right hand, I forced a kiss on him, and praised God that my plan had ended so successfully, as I had always prayed it might.[34]

John was thus freed to pursue his own ascetic goals undisturbed, and did so with an untempered zeal which will soon become apparent as one of his defining characteristics. An elderly monk resident in the mountains educated and guided him in the basics of ascetic living, and for four years he lived as part of a monastic community in the mountains overlooking Antioch. Although it does not seem to have been a rigidly organised or regulated grouping, later on in his career Chrysostom would look back on this lifestyle with approval and something like nostalgia. At the time, however, he was not content to stop there, and John continued to exercise increasingly rigorous discipline on his body and his mind. Leaving his small group of fellow ascetics he journeyed further into the wilderness and spent the next two years entirely isolated from human company and under the most austere of circumstances. He fasted continually, denied himself sleep, and refused to sit down at any stage during this time.[35] Throughout, he devoted himself to the task of learning the Scriptures thoroughly, thus providing for himself an alternative literary and philosophic corpus to those classical texts that had formed the core of his original education, and which he would turn to constantly in the course of his subsequent preaching career. We will see when we turn to the sermons themselves that Chrysostom was at all times able to refer to passages of either Testament for illustrative purposes or support of an argument, building up an impressive system of cross-referencing, doubly impressive if we accept that he preached extempore.

Not surprisingly, such extreme self-mortification caused irreparable damage to John's physical health. His digestive system nearly ruined and his kidneys on the verge of failure, he had no choice but to return to civilisation, evidently feeling confident that God had more in store for him than death on a mountain-top. Palladius rejoices at this piece of good fortune for the Church:

As he could not doctor himself, he returned to the haven of the Church. And here we see the providence of the Saviour, in withdrawing him by his infirmity, for the good of the Church, from ascetic toils, and compelling him by this obstacle of ill health to leave the caves.[36]

Church authorities were delighted to see John back, and he was quickly appointed as a lector and as right hand man to the bishop of Antioch. Here his duties required that he deliver the readings at church services, and be responsible for some of the secretarial business of the diocese. Finally, in 386, he confirmed his reintegration to the urban and conventional church by now accepting ordination. From this point onwards, John's career was unequivocally public in its nature, not least because he chose to occupy a prominent position in the people's consciousness via his blunt outspokenness and seeming fearlessness in all areas of his ministry. With his usual reformer's zeal, he decided that since he now had an official post within the Church, he would make the most of it in order to win as many people over to the path of salvation as possible. Initially his system of reform seems to have been essentially ascetic in nature. His early Church career shows a remarkably prolific period of writing in which John churned out letters, pamphlets and treatises, many of which were on the topics of virginity, widowhood and the advantages of monastic living, and generally show an overriding concern with the renunciation of sexuality.

John's preaching career, however, really took off in 387, following the event in Antioch that became known as the Riot of the Statues. Enraged by the emperor's latest series of tax demands, the people rioted, defacing statues of the imperial family displayed throughout the city. Government displeasure was swift and severe; Antioch was stripped of its status as a recognised city of the empire, while its public theatres and the hippodrome were closed. The cowed citizens feared that still worse was to come, and their current bishop – Flavian – set out for Constantinople to plead for clemency. In his absence John was left in charge of the spiritual health of the Antiochenes and took his role very seriously indeed. Throughout the season of Lent he preached sermon after sermon both comforting his congregations and exhorting them to turn to God for help in their hour of need. He also made the most of this opportunity to recommend a more obviously Christian lifestyle to those who appeared to care too much for secular concerns, even claiming that the emperor had done them a favour in closing the theatres, since they were places of temptation and immorality. And when news came that the edict against the city had finally been lifted, John continued to preach, now extolling the mercy of God and the merits of gratitude.

From this point onwards, John was firmly established as the favoured preacher of the Antiochenes. He preached regularly, and it would seem that he always tried to provide 'value-for-money' for his congregation, educating them by means of his skilful rhetoric and his ability to hold the interest of his flock – even when discussing Scripture or knotty theological problems. Ancient historians rated his skills highly, not least because of his own obviously virtuous behaviour:

Many of those who heard the discourses of John in the church, were thereby excited to the love of virtue, and to the reception of his own religious sentiments. But it was chiefly by the bright example of his private virtues, that John excited his auditors with emulation. He produced conviction the more readily, because he did not resort to rhetorical artifices, but expounded the Sacred Scriptures with truth and sincerity. Arguments that are corroborated by actions always commend themselves as worthy of belief; but when a preacher's deeds will not bear investigation, his words, even when he is anxious to declare the truth, are regarded as contradictory. John taught, both by precept and example: for while on the one hand his course of life was virtuous and austere, on the other hand he possessed considerable eloquence and persuasiveness of diction. His natural abilities were excellent, and he improved them by studying under the best masters.[37]

Such a gifted and popular preacher was bound to attract the attention of the high-ranking imperial eunuch – Eutropius – who visited Antioch as part of a tour of this region of the empire. Such was the impression he made on this influential official, that when the bishop of Constantinople – Nectarius – died in 397, John Chrysostom was nominated as his successor. It is said that he was lured out of Antioch by night and spirited across the empire under armed guard for fear of the reaction of the Antiochenes, such was the extent of his popularity.[38]

Constantinople, as imperial capital of the eastern empire, provided a great challenge for Chrysostom's reforming instincts. It was a cosmopolitan and sophisticated city, with much political intrigue going on just beneath the surface and certainly a great emphasis laid on the possession and display of wealth on the surface. As will become increasingly apparent as we progress, such ostentation was anathema to John, and he set about reordering things and curtailing these excesses within the city. The ecclesiastical administration was the first institution targeted, in the course of which shake-up recalcitrant clergy found themselves dismissed and others warned to be more disciplined in their lifestyles, while the finances of the See came under drastic scrutiny. In a radical step, Chrysostom cut back on the ostentation of the Church itself, thus scaling down many of the entertainment and hospitality functions a bishop was expected to provide. Funds freed up in this exercise were rerouted to the care of the poor and the sick, thus putting many noses out of joint in clerical circles.[39] Chrysostom also continued his regular preaching, in which the laity too, were encouraged to alter their style of living to a more Christian mode. Such 'rough' reforming alienated many of John's clergy and many of his flock.

However, aside from this, the very fact of John's appointment had also enraged the bishop of Alexandria – Theophilus – who had hoped that a more malleable candidate of his choosing would be elevated to the one bishopric that challenged his own position of authority. Theophilus, therefore, was constantly alert for a way to end the career of John Chrysostom, and an opportunity came when John granted asylum to a group of refugee

Origenist monks fleeing from Theophilus himself. The Alexandrian prelate was quick to challenge John's actions and skilfully avoided a trial in which he was to be held accountable for his own behaviour in putting the monks to flight, swiftly turning the tables so that John should be the one called to account. This is a very brief sketch of events surrounding the so-called Affair of the Tall Brothers, but more detailed accounts can be found in those works more concerned with Chrysostom's political career than I am here.[40]

This scheme to discredit the bishop would probably not have been so successful had Chrysostom himself not amassed a considerable number of enemies, among whom was the empress Eudoxia. A woman very sensitive to her own position of respect and authority, she had become enraged at certain sermons of John's which she felt to be overtly critical of her in her capacity both as a woman and as an empress. Eudoxia had a strong sense of the power and symbolism of the role of empress, but this could not co-exist with Chrysostom's concepts of ecclesiastical authority for very long.[41] The loss of imperial favour was the final straw for Chrysostom and he was deposed and exiled in 403. This exile, his first, lasted no more than a day, for Eudoxia was alarmed by an earth tremor in the city which seemed to her to indicate the Almighty's disfavour at her treatment of his represen-tative, and so the order for Chrysostom's recall was sent out. He was initially cautious about re-entering the city, but a month later he was back preaching to his jubilant followers.

Behind the scenes Theophilus had not ceased his intriguing, and continued to work to bring Chrysostom to trial on a medley of charges, ranging from the wrongful dismissal of a cleric, to eating his meals alone, to diverting the funds of the Church into his own coffers. Faced with such hostility, John would have done well to maintain what support he had in the city, but he stubbornly refused to abandon his blunt outspokenness and his exhortations towards a different way of life for those professing to be Christians. And yet again he infuriated Eudoxia, this time supposedly comparing her to Herodias – at whose instigation John the Baptist was beheaded – following the unveiling of a silver statue of her near the church amidst much revelry and unseemly display.[42] Losing all patience with such constant wrangling, and being forced to decide between two sides of the same ecclesiastical hierarchy, the emperor Arcadius ordered a second and final exile for Chrysostom, and he left Constantinople for the last time in June 404.

Proof that it was not simply the offending of Eudoxia that led to Chrysostom's fall from grace lies in the fact that her death in that same year did not lead to his recall or even a relaxing of the hostility towards him. Indeed so strong was the enmity of some against him that his followers were continually persecuted in Constantinople and John himself was frequently removed to yet more remote spots within the empire.[43] Such travelling exacted a heavy toll on his already fragile health, and by 407 Chrysostom was seriously ill. This won him no sympathy from his armed guard, however, and John Chrysostom died that September on route to a still more barren spot for his exile. He was only 'rehabilitated' in Constantinople and his holiness officially recognised in 416.[44]

# *Nolo Episcopari* and the Transformation of the City

> He soon found the means to make his addresses, in express terms, to
> his mistress, from whom he received an answer in the proper form,
> viz., the answer which was first made some thousands of years ago,
> and which hath been handed down by tradition from mother to
> daughter ever since. If I was to translate this into Latin, I should
> render it by these two words, *nolo episcopari*, a phrase likewise of
> immemorial use on another occasion.
>
> Henry Fielding, *Tom Jones*, bk I, ch. xi

It is quickly apparent from any study of his life and his career that John
Chrysostom had many issues of contention with the antique city.
Paradoxically, however, it was in the urban setting that he won popularity
and most of his influence. His congregations were mostly comprised of city
dwellers, and many of his administrative duties involved the integration of
the Christian church with the civic structures of a Roman city. But this
immersion in urban matters went hand in hand with his own personal
desire to shun the city and all its activities as distractions from a truly
Christian lifestyle.

Chrysostom was born at a time in the fourth century when asceticism
was becoming an ever more popular expression of Christian beliefs. With
the acceptance of Christianity as a legitimate religion, and its subsequent
privileging by imperial authorities, flamboyant displays of faith through
martyrdom were no longer necessary or even possible. In many ways
therefore, asceticism became the new martyrdom as men and women
turned their backs on the comforts and conveniences of everyday life in
favour of a stringent existence of self-denial and mortification of the body.
The more strict the practice, the further those who practised it advanced
on the road to salvation. But they also became more noticeable in the
society of the day by virtue of the extreme nature of their lifestyle. This,
then, was a means by which Christianity could be announced and
displayed to all. And indeed entire communities and social movements
grew up around some of these ascetics, to the extent that villages could get
into the habit of turning to them for arbitration, advice and counsel on a
variety of subjects. The most famous example of this was the case of

Simeon Stylites, who spent forty years on a pillar in the Syrian desert, becoming a magnetic figure for towns and villages across the region.[1]

Asceticism was therefore a movement which captured the imagination of many – even those who were not themselves willing to embrace it as a lifestyle. The growing popularity of the hagiographic tradition indicates this, providing audiences with romanticised accounts of sanctity which they could admire at a safe distance. Ascetics could be intriguing and even romantic characters by virtue of their isolated existence, their often masochistic habits, and their perceived closeness to God. Chrysostom was not the first young man to be drawn to the idea of such a life.

In order to achieve his ascetic dream, however, Chrysostom had to turn his back on everything that had heretofore been part of his life. Having been raised in Antioch, Chrysostom's early education and training were directed towards a career within the city – as either an orator, or a lawyer, or perhaps some kind of civil servant. However, he began to direct his attention more towards the mountains and asceticism in his early adulthood, although he was initially prevented from following his ambitions by his mother's pleas not to be left alone in her old age. But filial piety was only so effective in keeping Chrysostom within city confines at this stage in his life. In fact it was attempts to harness his obvious religious devotion in a structured and urban ecclesiastical ministry that succeeded in driving him away from the city for a number of years, turning away from pastoral service to an ascetic life of denial.

What Chrysostom evidently felt he could not manage was the combination of his own religious ambitions with an urban ministry. Surrounded by the daily activities of a large city and the temporal concerns of a largely urban congregation, Chrysostom was sure that his own spiritual well-being would be severely compromised. And so this stage of his career marks a complete avoidance of all the trappings of a 'civilised' or conventional lifestyle. He ate rarely, slept only when he could no longer keep awake, compelled his body to remain standing for days on end, and trained his mind to study and memorise almost the entire body of Scriptures. He spent some four years in this region, and the last two were almost entirely solitary. Nothing further from the city life he was brought up in could be imagined.

Later in his career, on preaching on the Pauline Epistles to Timothy, Chrysostom had occasion to look back on his monastic experiences as part of an effort to persuade his congregation into more restrained living. He does not describe his own individual activities in doing so, but his description of the daily routine in an ascetic community shows an in-depth knowledge of such a lifestyle, and, I believe, a strong degree of nostalgia:

> Going to the monastery of a holy man is almost to pass from earth to heaven. You do not see there the kind of thing you might see in a private house. The people there are free from all impurity. There is silence and profound quiet there. The words 'mine and yours' are not used by them. And if you stay there for a whole day, or even two, you

will enjoy even greater pleasure. There, as soon as it is day, or even before day, the cock crows, and you do not see the kind of things there that you would find in a private house, with the servants snoring, the doors shut, and everyone sleeping like the dead, while the mule herder rings his bells outside. There is none of this. Everyone, immediately shaking off sleep, rises reverently when their Leader calls them, and forming themselves into a holy choir, they stand, and lifting up their hands sing the sacred hymns all together. For they are not like us, who need many hours to shake off sleep from our heavy heads. For we, as soon as we are awakened, sit for a while stretching our limbs, we answer the call of nature, then we wash our face and our hands; next we get our shoes and clothes, and a huge amount of time is wasted. It is not like this in the monastery. No one calls for his servant, for each person waits on himself: nor does he need many clothes, or need to shake off sleep. For as soon as he opens his eyes he is like someone who has already been awake and collected for some time…. Then at the third, sixth and ninth hours, and in the evening, they perform their devotions, having divided the day into four parts, and at the conclusion of each part they honour God with psalms and hymns. And while other people are dining, laughing and revelling, and bursting themselves through over-indulgence, they are occupied with their hymns. For they have no time for the table, nor for the indulgence of the senses…. They do not dread the magistrates, or lordly arrogance, there is no fear of slaves, and no disturbance caused by women or children, no great number of treasure chests, no excessive storing of clothing, no gold or silver, guards or sentinels, and no store-house. There is nothing of any of these things, but instead all is full of prayer, hymns and a spiritual atmosphere. There is nothing carnal here.[2]

Such a carefully drawn portrait points to a man both very familiar and very comfortable with the ascetic lifestyle. Indeed such was Chrysostom's enthusiasm for the life that he permanently damaged his health in its pursuit. The cold, self-starvation, and uncomfortable posture combined to leave Chrysostom's digestive system fragile and his kidneys on the verge of failure. And it was at this point that he decided to return to the city that he had shunned for so long. Palladius puts such a change of heart down to divine intervention, convinced that God had more in store for Chrysostom than death on a mountain-top. Whatever the reason, Chrysostom returned to Antioch in 382 after four years in the wilderness, and set about re-integrating himself with civic society.

Thus the man who once practised an elaborate ruse to avoid being ordained as a city priest was eventually to accept just such an ordination in 386. His writings from this period show an interesting ambivalence, with some of them encouraging members of his congregation to embrace ascetic living, as in his treatise *On Virginity*, and yet others being somewhat less than flattering about the qualities of a typical hermit. A study of Chrysostom's work during this period is a study in his own efforts to come to terms with his new vocation and its impact on his own ascetic leanings.

Shortly after his ordination, Chrysostom wrote a long document entitled *On the Priesthood* (*De Sacerdotio*). The treatise seems to be his attempt to come to terms with the conflicting ambitions in his life. He structures it as an imaginary dialogue with his friend Basil – who had failed to avoid ordination when Chrysostom first escaped to the mountains. In it he explains why he had once seemingly run away from the office which he now holds. And so he details the qualifications required of such a priest if he is to properly safeguard the souls in his care. In this document Chrysostom declares quite baldly that simple asceticism by no means renders a man either worthy or able to lead a congregation to salvation. He comments that he himself has known many men who were undeniably devout and holy when left to themselves in a solitary course of asceticism. When entrusted with the spiritual welfare of other, more ordinary, people, however, they instead emerged as incompetent, and more likely to jeopardise their own sanctity than work any good among the laity. He also suggests that while social standing, useful contacts, and wealth should by no means be used as indices for the suitability of a priestly candidate, an ability to interact comfortably with secular society is nevertheless essential. Indeed the list of qualifications required by Chrysostom for such a ministry demands a well-nigh impossible combination of dignity with humility, compassion with sternness, an aura of command with amiability, strength with gentleness. Obviously few of the predominantly rural and uneducated ascetics who won renown by virtue of their very simplicity, would possess such qualities necessary for the effectual leadership of an urban and diverse flock. And it would seem that Chrysostom would like to claim that he was once similarly unqualified for such a role, hence his previous reluctance.

It is difficult of course to decide whether Chrysostom was being genuinely modest and reluctant in his efforts to escape ordination. There is much to suggest that such humility might actually have become both a behavioural and a rhetorical trope at this time, with many of the leading Church Fathers pleading inadequacy for such a great task. St Augustine is said to have wept throughout his ordination ceremony, convinced of his own unworthiness; St Martin of Tours ran away and hid, and had to be forcibly removed from a barn; St Jerome somewhat grumpily consented to ordination on the strict understanding that he was to be given no pastoral responsibilities.[3] Was Chrysostom simply conforming to these behavioural expectations as he retold his own efforts to avoid the priesthood? Later writings and events in his career would seem to indicate that he was indeed less suited to such a role than some of his peers.

But whether a real humility or a rhetorical stance, this reluctance is no longer a viable position for the newly ordained Chrysostom. Now he must demonstrate to his flock and his ecclesiastical authorities that he is going to embrace his new duties with enthusiasm and vigour. And so

Chrysostom's detailed list of demands from anyone who wishes to fill a pastoral role within the Church in fact serves two quite different ends. In the first instance it acts as an explanation for his original refusal to adopt such a role, since there were those within the Church establishment who felt that he was merely being self-indulgent in retiring to the mountains. By emphasising the many skills a good pastor should have, Chrysostom adds weight to his previous cries of unworthiness. At the same time, however, by considering these skills in contrast to those of a solitary ascetic, Chrysostom manages to convey the idea that he is now adequately qualified for his new priestly position. In this work he distances himself from those ascetics who failed to understand the demands of a lay congregation, being instead entirely wrapped up in their own austere form of devotion. It is a clever move on the part of Chrysostom, and it means that *De Sacerdotio* is a text that looks in two different directions as he tries to signal his new-found devotion to his secular flock at the same time as explaining his original ascetic fervour. But this text also signals a fundamental tension between these two career paths that was to remain throughout Chrysostom's life and probably does much to explain his later fall from grace. A further complication is added when we consider that this presentation of the priest or bishop as superior to the individual ascetic was itself an established rhetorical trope, employed by the Church historian Theodoret among others, as part of the efforts to consolidate the authority of the orthodox and traditional church over independent ascetic communities.[4]

A look at how Chrysostom's career progressed will show that on many occasions he failed to keep enough distance between himself and the ascetics with whom his heart really lay for the liking of his peers and those influential within his society. The remainder of this book will focus on the ways in which his preaching reflects these ascetic leanings and tries to make them relevant to those in his jurisdiction. Indeed themes of self-restraint and self-denial in the interests of a spiritual salvation are common in Chrysostom's written and spoken work. The early years of his ministry are particularly noticeable for this trait as he struggled to adjust to the difference between the rigorous life he had just returned from, and the more indulgent priorities of his congregation. As a newly ordained priest he promulgated many texts on the subject of sexual renunciation and discipline of the body. In *De Virginitate*, for example, the spiritual rewards arising from the devout practice of celibacy are dwelt on at length, while a careful argument is constructed against second marriages. Like his contemporary St Jerome, Chrysostom regarded marriage at best as a refuge from fornication, and thus presented his view of it as a lesser state for the weaker members of society. A letter to a recently widowed noblewoman (*Ad viduam juniorem*), also dating from this period, presents similar arguments, although it should probably be interpreted at least in part as a rhetorical exercise intended for a wider audience than the young widow in question. There is much to suggest that the paired treatises on the *subintroductae*, in which Chrysostom spoke out indignantly against those ascetics who believed they could combine ascetic intentions with cohabitation between the sexes, also had their first airing at around this time. It is likely that this pair of treatises had a second airing when Chrysostom first to came power in Constantinople and found himself facing a clergy grown weak and ineffectual through over-indulgence in the pleasures of the flesh. All these works share an ascetic theme as well as a distinctly impassioned tone that indicates that in the first few years of his public ministry Chrysostom's thoughts were still directed firmly towards austerity and discipline with a view to a heavenly reward.

This privileging of celibacy and a solitary existence over marriage and the pleasures of the flesh are common themes in the writings of many fourth-century church figures. The Cappadocian Fathers were alike in their insistence that the most effective way of reaching salvation was to deny the needs of the body where at all possible. Even Gregory of Nyssa who was once married himself, regarded this temporal union as a barrier to attaining true closeness to God. In the Western half of the empire Jerome was almost virulent in his claims that asceticism was the only way in which a complete heavenly reward could be attained. Marriage gradually whittled away at the heavenly portion to be assigned to each person, so that a married woman could only expect to receive a thirty-fold reward from God as opposed to the hundred-fold which would be the lot of the committed virgin. Slightly later than all of these authors, Augustine was so eager to renege on his youthful indulgences with regard to sex and marriage that he became one of the most vocal proponents of celibacy and disapprovers of sexual activity, with a strong influence on the subsequent attitudes of the Church body as a whole on these matters.

Chrysostom's austere writings are by no means unusual in this context, and perhaps all the more understandable when we consider how abruptly his own pursuit of asceticism was forced to come to an end. It may be that these texts and others like them are simply an expression of his thwarted ascetic ambitions in the only practical way that remained to him. Gregory of Nyssa had disadvantaged himself through an early marriage, and so wrote extensively on the subject of virginity almost as a means of compensation. Perhaps Chrysostom's approach was part of a similar process.

John Chrysostom is worthy of note in this respect, however, because his ascetic leanings were far more than an individual preference, but instead became part of a blueprint for living for an entire congregation. Not content to simply exhort the advisability of self-denial and celibacy, Chrysostom had definite ideas as to how these aims might be realised within the urban environment. These texts therefore show how he intended to realise his own ascetic ambitions through his newly acquired congregation. But it was in his preaching that this process can be seen to its fullest extent. Church preaching by its nature was a medium that was more broadly accessible than the written texts of the day. Since the Christian religion was adamant that all its adherents attend regular services of worship, it followed that the

sermons preached at these services would have an audience of unprece-
dented breadth. Men, women and children were all in attendance,
regardless of social class, and even slaves would have access to these
Christian teachings, if only because they were brought to church to attend
on their owners. Chrysostom would therefore have had a regular and
captive audience for his message of social reform in which he strove to bring
about an ascetic revolution within the walls of the city.

Chrysostom's position as the favourite preacher of the Antiochenes was
firmly established after the affair of the Riot of the Statues in 387, and he
seems to have preached regularly from this point forward. An examination
of his sermons demonstrates the way in which he used the preaching
medium as a way of bringing his ascetically loaded message to his congregation. Just as he did with his written texts, Chrysostom used his homilies
as a way of encouraging self-discipline and frugal living in his flock as he
hoped that they would see the lasting benefits of such an approach for
their immortal souls. If this was his aim, however, he must have known
that his success could only have been limited in an environment such as
Antioch. This particular city had won a considerable reputation for itself
as a place where all manner of worldly experiences could be pursued and
enjoyed.[5] Theatrical spectacles and horse races regularly won greater
attendance numbers than more spiritually beneficial church services, and
Chrysostom was by no means unaware of this. Indeed he had regular occasion to reprimand his congregation for such frivolity of spirit. The
Antiochenes seem to have treated Chrysostom as merely another form of
entertainment – cramming the church body for the duration of his
sermon, applauding at well-argued or exciting passages, yawning at what
they had heard before, and trooping back out of the church in large
numbers at the conclusion of the discourse, not even waiting for the
Eucharist. An astute observer such as Chrysostom would have been very
aware that only a tiny minority of his congregation could be persuaded to
abandon the joys of secular living in favour of a stint of austerity on the
mountainside. He nevertheless doggedly pursued his favourite themes,
perhaps with a subtly different aim in mind.

Since the inhabitants of the late antique city demonstrated themselves
to be particularly reluctant to give up the activities that characterised
urban living, Chrysostom seems to have decided that it was the nature of
civic behaviour itself that needed changing. To this end much of his
preaching and writing targets the institutions defining the ancient city.
Thus the theatre or the races at the hippodrome were attacked not only
because of the distractions they offered to Christians who should have had
their minds on higher things, or even because their noise interrupted
Chrysostom's own performances – although these were important considerations – but because they were institutions which sustained and fostered
the prosperity of the classical city. So much that informed ancient notions
of the city and citizenship was bound up with public gatherings and social
events, the distribution and display of wealth, and the giving of gifts. The

ancient theatre was seen to perform all of these functions to a greater or lesser extent,[6] hence Chrysostom's deep distrust of it. His attacks on the theatre and other civic institutions, which we will see so often as we progress, were not however motivated by a simple desire to bring the classical city crashing down, as has been suggested by some, including Peter Brown. His intention, rather, was to rewrite the boundaries of the ancient urban community, so that a recognisably Christian environment could be created.

The pursuit of his grand scheme to restructure the ancient city according to a Christian model was, I believe, what finally allowed Chrysostom to reconcile his ascetic leanings with his public ministry and to accept his ordination as no very bad thing. The reordered city, should he succeed, would indeed have marked similarities to the monastic communities that existed outside the civic boundaries. The priorities and spiritual concerns would be much the same, and Chrysostom hoped that he could persuade his audience to adopt a more unworldly attitude, thus bringing them closer to the holy men and women who had their thoughts fixed almost entirely on a heavenly rather than temporal community. And this is perhaps why, on his sudden promotion to the episcopate of Constantinople, we hear no more murmurings from Chrysostom as to his unfitness for the task. It is in fact more likely that the See of an imperial capital presented a great and exciting challenge to the preacher. To establish his own Christian city in the very epitome of the secular city, and one as particularly worldly as Constantinople, would be an achievement indeed. It may be that here Chrysostom actually displays a measure of personal as well as spiritual ambition.

From the brief survey of this part of Chrysostom's career presented in the opening chapter, we can see the way in which his enthusiasm for reform and restructuring in the ancient city led him to fall foul of several groups of interested parties, leading ultimately to his deposition and exile. In many ways it seems that Chrysostom misjudged the extent of his influence in Constantinople, for his tremendous zeal did not have the same impact in the capital of the eastern empire as it had in the more provincial Antioch, but in fact did much to work against him. In addition to this, at Antioch Chrysostom had been a mere priest, albeit a very persuasive one. His recommendations regarding a radical change in the urban lifestyle would not, therefore, have been perceived by those wielding secular power as overtly threatening. The Antiochene congregation was also quite partisan, since there survived strong pagan, Jewish and heretical factions within the city, all of which needed to be opposed. Constantinople, on the other hand, had been, at least in name, a Christian city from its very foundation, and so its inhabitants may not have recognised the same urgency in Chrysostom's crusade as had the Antiochenes. But, as a bishop who possessed a considerable amount of the power and status available within the Eastern church, Chrysostom suddenly had the practical power necessary to implement his reforms, and he proceeded to do so without due concern for tact or diplomacy. The extreme nature of his recommendations now had the potential to be very threatening indeed to influential members of society, while his blunt manner merely served to increase their hostility and distrust. Chrysostom thus forfeited the goodwill which was so necessary for the maintenance of his career, which began to falter and fail.

Many of the charges brought against him at the Synod of the Oak in 403 attacked his frugal and disciplined lifestyle as anti-social and unsuited to a man in his position. In *De Sacerdotio* he complained of the onerous social duties incumbent upon a holder of public ministry with a palpable tone of exasperation and frustration. A bishop was expected to interact regularly with his flock, visiting the sick and even those with nothing wrong with them, but who wished to be perceived as important enough to merit the attention of the prelate. It was evidently important to keep the rich and influential citizens happy, even if doing so was to run the risk of being labelled a flatterer and a sycophant.[7] In *De Sacerdotio*, Chrysostom had dismissed this complex social activity as merely an irritation which endorsed all his earlier reluctance to accept ordination. Although he was a newly ordained priest when this text was penned, in so speaking he heralds his intention to refuse to occupy the role of patron as a bishop was expected to do, this being a function deemed vital in the organisation of Roman civic society.[8] A good patron not only upheld one of the foundations of a Roman urban community, but also demonstrated his own masculine abilities in doing so. On both counts, therefore, it was a vitally important role, and not one to be dismissed lightly. In speaking so scornfully of the duties of such a patron, and in obviously failing to perform them, Chrysostom did much more than refuse to comply with communal expectations; he called into question an entire institution and its attendant traditions. Even when wrapped up in the duties of his episcopal ministry, he continues to carp about these social expectations:

> He [the bishop] is distracted on every side and is expected to do many things that are beyond his power. If he does not know how to speak effectively, there is much complaining; and if he can speak, then he is accused of being vainglorious. If he cannot raise the dead, he is worthless, they say: such a person is pious, but this man must not be. If he eats a moderate meal, he is accused on this account, and they say that he ought to be strangled. If he is seen at the bath, he is greatly criticised. In short, he should not even look at the sun![9]

Charges brought against Chrysostom during his final trial show that this unwillingness to pander to the expectations of those who were influential in his society had merely served to alienate many who would otherwise have supported him. The wilful misunderstanding of his own disciplined approach was what led to his downfall, and it is likely that much of the reason for these misunderstandings arose from the inordinately high standards Chrysostom expected of his flock. His streamlining of the Church's finances was read as a lining of his own pockets, his habit of dining late and alone as an indulgence in hidden gluttony, and his dismissal of disobedient clergy as evidence of an irascible temper.

In this way the constant influence of the ascetic philosophy can be seen in Chrysostom's work. Again and again he can be heard to preach against over-indulgence in food, wine, sensual pleasures and public spectacles. Chrysostom worried that such practices would lead his congregation into sin, thus jeopardising their immortal souls. Perhaps there was an element of incomprehension in his attitude also. As a man who had hardly indulged in the need to sit down for two whole years, he may have found it difficult to understand why his flock were unable to moderate even their wilder excesses, let alone practise active self-denial. Such a breakdown in communication led to some acerbic public outbursts on his part, and his congregation are on record as often voicing their disapproval and offence at such repeated rebukes. It would seem, therefore, that in hindsight Chrysostom was right to be doubtful of his own suitability for public office. His innate austerity and extreme holiness were bound to create a distance between him and his more pedestrian congregation – a gulf which widened as he rose through the ranks and struggled to impose his own vision of Christianity on the ordinary inhabitants of the late antique city.

I will now turn to a detailed exploration of just how Chrysostom used his publicly preached sermons to present this vision to his congregations, and how he believed there was a carefully allotted role for everyone to play – male and female – in realising God's Kingdom on earth.

# Christian Preaching and its Audience

Incommunicative as he was, some time elapsed before I had an opportunity of gauging his mind. I first got an idea of its calibre when I heard him preach in his own church at Morton. I wish I could describe that sermon: but it is past my power. I cannot even render faithfully the effect it produced on me. It began calm – and indeed, as far as delivery and pitch of voice went, it was calm to the end: an earnestly felt, yet strictly restrained zeal breathed soon in the distinct accents, and prompted the nervous language. This grew to force – compressed, condensed, controlled. The heart was thrilled, the mind astonished, by the power of the preacher.

Charlotte Bronte, *Jane Eyre*, ch. 30

Before we examine representations of gender in Chrysostom's homilies on the Pauline epistles, and discuss the theory that instructions regarding gendered behaviour might be read as part of a larger process of effecting change within society, it is important to spend some time considering the more general tradition of preaching within the Christian Church. The importance attached to the homiletic mode by the ecclesiastical hierarchy cannot be overlooked, since there was much about it that fostered the dynamic growth of a Christianised discourse within society. As a form, the regularly preached homily was also employed by ecclesiastical authorities to educate the faithful and consolidate the population base of the Church. A brief examination of the logistics of Christian preaching can do much to shed light on this process, as we see how sermons were prepared, delivered and preserved for future reference.

## The Christian homily and classical rhetoric

Almost from the start of the Christian liturgy, the homily held a central place within services of divine worship. It took place in the first half of the liturgy, following on from the opening prayers and Scripture readings.[1] After the preaching of the sermon the Eucharistic part of the service would begin. At this point catachumen were instructed to leave the church, since the uninitiated were not considered fit to witness the central divine mystery of Christianity. It is very interesting to note, however, that the unbaptised were permitted and encouraged to attend the sermon. This

signals the keen perception on the part of Church leaders that preaching
had a measurable impact on public behaviour.

Technically defined as an informal discourse, and even described by
some modern commentators as being among the lower forms of ancient
literature and oratory,[2] the placing of the homily in such a prominent and
central place in the liturgy clearly points to the importance the Christians
themselves attached to it. As Cameron points out, as a religion
Christianity gave great attention to 'verbal formulation' as the means by
which it sustained itself, but also made itself accessible to the outside
world.[3]

Although during the very earliest stages of the Christian development
devout congregants may have been permitted to select and perform the
readings of the day, this activity as well as preaching very quickly became
the sole prerogative of the clergy, and sermons were expected to be of a
certain length. It is even thought that very few priests were permitted to
preach homilies, such an important task being the preserve of the bishop
of the region.[4] This was again due to the Church perception of the key role
of the homily in the articulation of Christian beliefs and the directing of
the behaviour of the laity. Such a heavy responsibility was assigned in
many places only to those with authority and the maturity to wield it properly. An untrained preacher could work more harm than good, simply
through not considering his words carefully enough, or not having enough
experience with the doctrinal problems that constantly threatened to
confuse his flock. Thus the Christian obsession with verbal dissemination
becomes ever more clear.

In format the Christian liturgy quickly developed with clear echoes of
its Jewish predecessor. It consisted of two parts, the first concerned with
the circulation of God's word, followed by the ceremony of the Eucharist
for those fully baptised into the Church. The new persuasive requirements of the Christian homily, however, greatly influenced the form such
sermons took. In order to safeguard the spiritual well-being of the
faithful, the Christian preacher had to take his task very seriously
indeed. It was not often an easy job – Christianity had at its heart many
complexities and points of conflict with other aspects of society. Even St
Paul found the transmission of the faith to be an exercise in advanced
public relations:

> While the Jews demand miracles and the Greeks look for wisdom,
> here are we preaching a crucified Christ; to the Jews an obstacle that
> they cannot get over, to the pagans madness, but to those who have
> been called, whether they are Jews or Greeks, a Christ who is the
> power and wisdom of God.[5]

Preaching therefore became essential to the public presentation of the
Faith within the *polis*, and it was largely an urban phenomenon. Rural
populations were less likely to have a well-educated pastor, and so were

more likely to turn to their local holy hermits and to stories of miracles and wonders for their spiritual guidance. More worldly audiences in the towns and cities were less easily convinced, and indeed often did not have the same access to such living hagiography, and so skilled presentation of God's word became of vital importance to convince the city faithful, and indeed the not so faithful, of God's power.

Church preachers therefore developed their own individual approaches to this challenge. In order adequately to instruct his congregation, the Church preacher must be able to guide them in what is right, and alert them to what is wrong. The sermon becomes a highly interactive process in which opponents are won over and convinced, the less conscientious members of the faithful reawakened in fervour, and the ignorant instructed in all aspects of the religion.[6] Thus any Christian homily could be read and understood at several levels, and when it was presented orally, the assembled congregation would presumably adopt whichever interpretation best suited their position within the ranks of the faithful. In order to function adequately in such a multi-layered guiding role, the Christian preacher needed particularly advanced yet subtle powers of public persuasion. It was a task not necessarily suited to all members to the clergy, and indeed not even assigned to all.

It began to emerge that someone accustomed to and accomplished in public speaking was really very necessary to lead the ordinary Christians to their awaiting salvation. Chrysostom strongly believed that a prelate who was unable to speak persuasively ran the risk of being derelict in his duty. When doctrinal questions arose, or heresies threatened, the preacher must have the oratorical means at his disposal to guide his flock away from such murky depths:

> In short, to overcome all these obstacles, there is no assistance given but the power of speech, and if anyone is without this skill, the souls of those who are put under his care (I mean of the weaker and more meddlesome kind) are no better off than ships which are continually storm tossed. So the priest should do all that he is able, to acquire this means of strength.[7]

He goes on to claim that elevated style is not the priority here, but rather clarity of thought and delivery on matters of dogma – a statement that is ironic given his own rhetorical accomplishments! Basil of Caesarea proclaimed a similar stance, declaring that 'The style of teaching proper to God knows nothing of the rules of panegyric.'[8] Yet such a blunt warning could indicate that the contemporary audience did indeed expect to hear God's Word preached in an elevated rhetorical style. It would seem that simplicity of speech aside, the best way of attracting a congregation's attention and then disseminating the message of Christianity was to use the modes of public persuasion already established within the Classical tradition. This meant that Church preachers would be most effective if they adopted the trends and patterns of secular rhetoric and combined a skilled use of this medium with their obvious devotion to the Christian creed. In order to avail himself of this rhetorical skill, the prospective cleric would find himself immersed in the literature and intellectual heritage of classical paganism – still the only real education available within late antique society – and a situation anxiously debated by Christian authorities.

Some members of the clergy felt that all classical literature should be regarded as anathema given its immorality and its polytheistic under-pinnings, while others felt that the style of such writing was vastly superior to their own Christian texts, and preferable for that very reason. St Jerome and St Basil of Caesarea illustrate both sides of this argument. Jerome purported to believe that a true Christian should avoid the trappings of classical rhetoric, feeling instead that simple faith should suffice. This stance is somewhat ironic considering the high rhetorical standards of his own writing. Basil of Caesarea had a slightly different approach. He felt that a classical education had much to offer young Christian men from the point of view of style and rhetorical training. He did suggest a compromise, however, recommending that such young men should sift through the classical texts for what was useful to them, ignoring the examples of immorality that might harm them as they went.[9] Chrysostom liked to ignore classical literature unless he was mocking its baseness and immorality. In his treatise on the appropriate education for young Christian boys he underlines the importance of a Biblical education transmitted within the home. Thus Scripture becomes the new literary corpus for a devout Christian. A little boy should be told of Cain and Abel, or Daniel in the lion's den, rather than of battles at Troy or of weak and fickle gods. That said, Chrysostom does not advocate an alteration in the traditional school curriculum – almost entirely based on these pagan texts. His new Christianised education is solely for transmission within the domestic sphere.[10]

Augustine too felt that a classical education could be harnessed to Christian needs, and in this we return to the emerging function of the Church homily. Since we have established that the persuasive aspect of preaching was fast becoming a priority within Christianity, the best and most effective means of public persuasion should be adopted. Late antique society responded to the traditional tropes of rhetoric, and so Augustine advises the aspiring preacher to meet these expectations if he wishes to be heeded:

> The power of eloquence – so very effective in convincing us of either wrong or right – lies open to all. Why, then, do not the good zealously procure it that it may serve truth, if the wicked, in order to gain unjustifiable and groundless cases, apply it to the advantages of injustice and error.[11]

Not only could a classical education be used for good, it was considered well-nigh essential for anyone hoping to be responsible for a congregation of immortal souls. Knowing how to speak persuasively was of paramount importance in working to mould the behaviour of a whole society. Practical considerations called for a compromise with the traditions of the secular world. Thus Augustine, in his instruction manual for the aspiring cleric, could call for a careful consideration of the substance of God's message to coincide with an acquired skill at speaking in anyone who hoped to be entrusted with the spiritual welfare of a congregation.[12]

## Composing and delivering homilies

Given the importance attached to the homily as the means of propagating and strengthening the faith within society, it might be presumed that those entrusted with the task of preaching spent a great deal of their time constructing their sermons in advance, preparing for its vital persuasive element. This is an area where the opinions of scholars are divided. It has been argued by some that most preachers prepared their sermons in advance, even writing them down in order simply to read them out before the congregation.[13] But others suggest that the homily was the only spontaneous element of the entire liturgy, a position supported by the fact that the definition of the word 'homily' means an informal discourse or conversation.[14] On a practical level it is unlikely that some of those preachers whose work survives extant would have had the time to write in advance the many sermons that remain today. Chrysostom's homilies alone number in the hundreds, while Augustine, Jerome and the Cappadocian Fathers each have a great number of homilies ascribed to them. It has been suggested that the time allotted to a usual sermon was one Roman hour – a unit of time which could range from forty-four to seventy minutes, depending on the time of year. A useful rule of thumb is to take each column of a *Patrologia Graeca* text to represent around ten minutes of speech. Such a lengthy period of preaching would require many written pages of preparation, and some priests offered several homilies a week. Considering that each of these individuals had numerous other duties besides preaching to perform in the care of their congregations, the time necessary to conduct such extensive advance preparation would have been scarce indeed.

Practical considerations aside, many of our surviving homilies from each of these authors contain internal references that suggest spontaneous preaching. Augustine provides various examples of this phenomenon in his sermons; reprimanding his audience for inattention and shuffling, asking for greater concentration on particularly knotty points, or declaring that the discourse will conclude sooner than intended since it is obvious to him that the audience are growing bored. Chrysostom too has many similarly off-the-cuff remarks and quick changes in his content or style of preaching. We see him plead with his congregation to bear with him for just a few more minutes as he finishes up his train of thought:

> But come now, rouse yourselves, as though I were just beginning my discourse, and pay attention to me with fresh minds. I would like to break off the discourse, but it will not allow me.[15]

Elsewhere he wonders bemusedly how this train of thought should become so far distracted from its origins in the course of his sermon: 'Yet indeed I do not know how I was led so far in this way of speaking ... .'[16] He frequently has cause to object to the applause of his listeners at some point they found particularly well argued,[17] on one occasion spending an extra few moments describing why such spontaneous expressions of approval merely serve to disturb him. He is only human, he declares, and so hearing the sound of applause and the murmurings of admiration from those gathered before him cannot help but raise his spirits and make him feel proud. Such satisfaction is only temporary, however, since he soon remembers that while they are busy clapping they are missing the import of what he says next, and so when he returns home he feels only sorrow that his labours have been wasted and that he should have failed to improve the moral standing of his flock. Those who are applauding are in fact applauding only the external accomplishments of the sermon – its fine rhetoric, its skilful turn of phrase – not its true message. They are focusing on the wrong thing: 'Did you applaud here? No, this is not the time for compliments; but in what comes next it is the time – for applauding, I say, and for imitating too.'[18] It has been somewhat humorously suggested by Richard Miles that Chrysostom added these comments to the transcribed versions of his sermons when preparing them for publication, in order to make himself appear popular.[19] All things considered, however, I believe many other factors besides mention of applause will support the argument for extempore preaching.

In spite of his seeming modesty and unwillingness to accept the plaudits of his congregation, Chrysostom is constantly aware of the necessity of retaining the attention of his audience in order for his message to be effectively transmitted. He complains that a sermon is sometimes treated like a public spectacle such as the games, since the audience must be won over and engaged in the same way while the preacher struggles to remain indifferent to their praise:

> For to begin with, the majority of those who are under the preachers' charge are not willing to behave towards them as towards teachers, but disdaining the part of learners, they assume instead the attitude of those who sit and look on at the public games.... For the public are accustomed to listen not for profit, but for pleasure, sitting like critics of tragedies, and of musical entertainments, and that ease of

skilled speech which we declaimed against just now, now becomes desirable, even more than in the case of barristers, where they are obliged to contend one against the other.[20]

We see him note the boredom of his listeners as he begins a discussion they have heard too often before and his often sudden introduction of some striking imagery or new arguments to bolster their flagging interest: 'But now do not become drowsy, for I still want to solve that other question.'[21] We also see him react quickly to some outbursts on their behalf: 'Did you let out a great shout?'[22] On one occasion – perhaps unwisely as it turned out – Chrysostom decided to speak on the subject of silver chamber-pots, condemning those women who commissioned them out of such vanity that they desired that even their excrement should be honoured. Of course speaking of such vulgar subjects in a church aroused the indignation of his well-bred listeners and he acknowledges this:

> I know that you are shocked at hearing this; but those women who make these things ought to be shocked, and the husbands that minister to such distempers.[23]

Even the next day, however, Chrysostom still feels that his audience must be appeased, and so he continues to defend his shock tactics, arguing that he has been entrusted with the task of teaching these people and so his means justify his ends.[24] In this example we can see the way in which audience reactions can prompt extempore comments and even shifts in direction on the part of the preacher.

These in-sermon asides are not, of course, necessarily incontrovertible proof of extempore preaching, but neither is their absence sufficient evidence of prior preparation. It has been suggested, as noted above, that when sermons were being prepared in advance, or subsequently revised for publication, the authors added in such comments to give the sense of spontaneity. Even Cicero was not above using these tactics when preparing some of his orations. While this is a possibility, I would feel that it is a remote one. It would not always be practicable for a preacher to accurately predict audience reaction and respond to it in advance to the extent we see Chrysostom do. And if we consider the question of revisions for publication purposes another issue arises. I find it hard to accept that Chrysostom would have meticulously gone through his homilies to add in those little asides and pretended interactions with the audience, and yet leave untouched the many inconsistencies of argument, the contradictions, and the tangential ramblings that remain in the texts.[25] Such complex narratives point clearly to off-the-cuff speaking, signalling a speaker who utters an idea off the top of his head only to find in the midst of its development that it does not suit his overall argument, or in another situation becomes so enamoured of this idea that he pursues it until the allotted time for the sermon has long past. This regularly happens with

Chrysostom, and some of his sermons seem to be twice as long as others preached at around the same time of the liturgical year and on the same texts. When this strikes him he generally breaks off the discourse quite abruptly, perhaps feeling like Gregory of Nazianzus that ' ... too great length in sermon is as much an enemy to people's ears as is too much food to their bodies'.[26]

This 'chaotic form' as it has been dubbed,[27] is very evident to us who have the benefit of reading the texts thoroughly and at our leisure. A contemporary audience, however, may not have even noticed that their preacher had contradicted himself unless he actually chose to draw their attention to the fact. Listening to an oral presentation means that the listener can only follow the sequence of ideas in the same order and at the same pace as the speaker. Most of Chrysostom's sermons therefore indicate such a spontaneous presentation of ideas. A late biographer of his remarks on how the congregation were regularly awe-struck by the way in which he could arrive at the pulpit with not even a scrap of paper with some scribbled notes, and yet proceed to hold forth on the relevant Biblical passage with his customary skill and polish.[28]

Augustine, in his *De Doctrina Christiana*, also urges extempore preaching as being particularly useful in the didactic function of the cleric. Since it is his duty to instruct his congregation in the Word of the Lord, he must take constant pains to ensure that he is actually being understood. Interaction with the audience is necessary for this, since he must watch their faces and movements that indicate whether they have comprehended his meaning or are as yet entirely at sea. If the listeners still appear unhappy or mystified, the speaker must continue to reiterate his message with a variety of approaches and expressions until the light of comprehension dawns on their faces:

> Those who are delivering what they have previously prepared and memorised word for word cannot do this. However, as soon as the speaker makes himself understood, he should either end his discussion or pass over to other matters. For, just as a speaker is pleasing when he makes clear things that should be learned, so he is irksome when he keeps emphasising facts that are already known.[29]

In this approach it seems clear that within the overall context of the persuasion of listening Christians to a more devout way of life, their entertainment was of paramount importance as the means to this end, and the rhetoric of secular society was harnessed for religious purposes.

If we therefore accept the above arguments in favour of extempore preaching, how is it that the sermons survive in a written form? It would seem that those preachers who won a name for themselves as particularly accomplished or especially holy attracted *notarii* – or scribes – to their churches. These stenographers sat at the back of the congregation and recorded the entire homily in shorthand.[30] This would explain the pres-

ence of such extempore remarks mentioned above if we imagine the
scribes simply scribbling down every word of the speaker, working too
hard at keeping up with the pace of the rhetoric to conduct on the spot
editing. But not all preachers had their sermons transcribed indiscrimi-
nately. A contemporary censorship exercise took place in which homilies
and orators were judged on their rhetorical merits, and if found wanting
were simply ignored by the stenographers. Socrates tells us of one Atticus
of Constantinople, who does not seem to have had a natural facility for
public persuasion:

> Formerly, while a presbyter, he had been accustomed, after
> composing his sermons, to commit them to memory, and then
> recite them in the church; but by diligent application, he acquired
> confidence and made his instruction extemporaneous and
> eloquent. His discourses, however, were not such as to be received
> with much applause by his auditors or to deserve to be committed
> to writing.[31]

It would seem that no amount of rhetorical training could compensate for
a lack of innate performance ability. And the greatest mark of a successful
preacher was one who did not have to struggle to *ad lib* his sermons.

The homilies of Chrysostom that remain to us today are organised in
series based around each Scriptural text. As a result his sermons
preached on each Pauline epistle read like a continuous commentary.
Some scholars believe that they were preached or structured by
Chrysostom in this very way, and it has led to them assigning each
series *en bloc* to either the preacher's Antiochene years or his time in
Constantinople, based on internal evidence in one or two individual
homilies.[32] Thus a reference to monks in mountain regions in a homily
delivered on the letter to the Ephesians, has been seized upon as proof
that Chrysostom was referring to the ascetics living specifically around
Antioch, and so this entire series is ascribed to the period of his
Antiochene priesthood.[33] References to imperial power and display in
another sermon lead to claims for a Constantinopolitan provenance.[34]
Indeed many scholars believe that most of Chrysostom's preaching
output stems from his Antiochene period, since as a bishop, he would
presumably have had less time to compose and deliver sermons as he
had while merely a priest at Antioch. Pauline Allen and Wendy Mayer
have done extensive work on this issue and they argue very convinc-
ingly that the evidence assigning one particular homily to a certain
location does not automatically match the entire series to that location.[35] Indeed it is very dangerous to assume that these sermons were
preached in serial order in any case. They also warn against claiming an
'episcopal tone' for various sermons of Chrysostom's, where some
commentators seize upon his use of the 'we' pronoun as evidence of his
position of authority in the ecclesiastical hierarchy, or his advice to

those entrusted with the leadership of a flock as proof that he was as yet only a priest himself. The analysis of a 'tone' or mood within these homilies is at best a subjective judgment, and absence of such a tone can hardly be used to unequivocally declare that the preacher was a mere priest rather than a bishop.

Most recently, Mayer has also chosen to combat those arguments concerning the amount of preaching Chrysostom could have done in any one location, declaring that he probably preached just as regularly in Constantinople while a bishop, as he did in Antioch. One of her key points in support of this stance is that Chrysostom saw preaching as an integral part of his episcopal ministry, and therefore considered it vital to maintain the link between himself and his congregation by means of regularly preached homilies. Indeed, on an occasion in 400 when Chrysostom was absent from his see, he appointed a 'locum' – Severian of Gabala – who also believed in preaching regularly, thus indicating the importance attached by Chrysostom to this duty.[36] It is also worth noting that while at Antioch, Chrysostom steadily grew to take over more and more of the diocesan duties from the bishop Flavian, so that he would have been just as 'busy' there as when actually a bishop himself in the capital city.[37]

While I agree with much of what Allen and Mayer have to say, I would point out that it is possible to detect signs of serial preaching in *some* of Chrysostom's sermons. There are many occasions in which he alludes to the previous day's stopping point and carries on from there, or even warns that certain themes will be covered on the next occasion they meet to discuss the same Scriptural text: 'Today it is necessary for me to pay the debt, which yesterday I deferred in order that I might address it to your minds when they were at full strength.'[38] We have also seen how on occasion he felt called upon to apologise for some offensive remarks made the day before, before continuing with his exegesis of the Pauline epistle. It would seem therefore that on occasion Chrysostom chose to preach a number of consecutive homilies on certain texts, while others of his sermons were simply arranged in series for ease of publication. It might have been possible that the preacher reviewed his transcribed sermons with a view to this organisation and thus added the linking passages at a date later than their initial presentation. However, for the same reasons I presented when arguing above for the case of extempore preaching, I do not find this very likely. The linkage is not consistent, and it is not present in every sermon, and so we must ask why Chrysostom would have chosen to link some sermons and not others if we were to accept this theory. I feel it best therefore simply to keep an open mind on the issue – accepting concrete evidence of provenance or serial preaching where it is offered, but applying it only to the individual sermon where it is found, rather than to an entire, artificially created series.

## The preacher's audience

Who actually came to hear these carefully crafted performances? Once again this is a hotly debated issue. Christianity as a religion prided itself on its universal appeal, claiming that gender, race or social standing count for nothing in the eyes of the Lord and that the Kingdom of Heaven is open to all. In light of this we could perhaps assume that all members of the Christian community would attend their local church to hear the teachings of their minister. It is therefore surprising to find that some scholars feel that only the well-to-do members of late antique society attended the liturgy on a regular basis. Ramsey MacMullen is the most thorough in presenting this case.[39] He chooses Chrysostom as his chief example in support of his argument, focusing on the intensely rhetorical nature of his sermons. We have already shown that Chrysostom received a traditional classical education and was well respected as an orator by his own orthodox congregations as well as by pagans who appreciated fine rhetoric. MacMullen believes that such elevated preaching was best suited to an audience who had access to a similar rhetorical training – therefore well-to-do males. He also looks at Chrysostom's many attempts to curtail the excesses of the rich as evidence that only these wealthy people were present at his sermons. Chrysostom addresses his congregation directly when urging them to curtail their lavish entertaining, their spending on fine clothes and jewels simply to gratify their vanity, and when exhorting them to give alms to the poor. MacMullen speaks of how the poor are described by Chrysostom as *ekeinoi* (those people) in such circumstances, in contrast to the 'you' that are rich there before him. As a result MacMullen does not believe the poor of society would even have been present in the church. Slaves would have attended since they came with their masters and mistresses – indeed the number of slaves accompanying each member of the nobility was a public display of wealth and status – something else Chrysostom was to complain about since it meant that the rich moved throughout the city with huge retinues of slaves causing congestion everywhere they went, all to indulge their vanity.[40] But Chrysostom also warns his rich congregants at one point to take care not to trample on the poor members of society who were huddled at the back of the church, thus indicating a more universal audience.[41]

Only on feast days and special occasions can MacMullen envisage the poor and the ordinary folk of the community attending church services. On such days people would travel in even from the countryside where they did not have such regular access to preachers and the consequent Scriptural education. MacMullen is not so definite on the subject of women, conceding that they were probably present for the preaching of sermons, but attended church in lesser numbers than the men, and were not generally addressed directly. In the ensuing chapters I will show in greater detail the inadequacy of this stance, but for now, suffice it to say that Chrysostom often had occasion to reprimand the female members of his congregation for arriving to worship arrayed in clothes better suited to a dance or court revel than for communion with their Divine Master.[42] I would therefore contend that Chrysostom's failure to speak directly to particular groupings within society does not imply the absence of these groups from the church congregation.

MacMullen believes that other Church preachers had a similarly skewed audience, citing the Cappadocian Fathers as examples of those who address mainly the rich. But Basil on at least one occasion pays direct tribute to those members of the working class who have come to hear his discourses, promising not to keep them long from their jobs since he knows they earn only a subsistence wage according to hours worked.[43] Rousseau disagrees with MacMullen on the specific question of Basil's audience, feeling that a diverse audience would have assembled to hear both this bishop and Ambrose of Milan preach.[44] Liebeschuetz, indeed, speaks almost in direct contradiction to MacMullen, feeling that all social classes would have been represented at the liturgy and that some of the poorer attendees could have spent the previous night sheltering in the church.[45] The idea that the poor too would have attended Chrysostom's preaching is a stance supported by Wendy Mayer in a recent and extremely comprehensive review of the issues surrounding the debate concerning John Chrysostom's audience. She points out that a system of predominantly addressing the male elite of the congregation does not necessarily imply a lack of any other socio-economic groups within the audience, but rather an awareness of the societal status and influence of these particular segments in the community.[46]

Although we have no way of resolving this debate conclusively, I would like to suggest a possible, and closely related, explanation for the focus of Chrysostom's rhetoric on the rich, which would be especially relevant to his ambition to create a specifically Christian urban community. One of his great passions was the abuse of wealth on the part of the upper echelons of society. His sermons constantly return to this theme, often running the risk of offending those rich people present.[47] Chrysostom attempts to persuade them to adopt a new attitude to their material possessions – winning their salvation through a policy of almsgiving. The regularity with which such urgings occur throughout his work cannot be emphasised enough, often surfacing in apparently disconnected sermons, and occupying the preacher's attention until his time ran out. We can safely say that the concern with wealth was the great theme of all Chrysostom's preaching. But in order to effect its redistribution, he must of necessity address those who actually possessed it. Hence the direct appeals to the 'you' who were the wealthily dressed members of the congregation. He urges them to help those less fortunate than themselves – the *ekeinoi*. In fact even in Chrysostom's portrayal of the ideally Christian city, he still presumes that there will be a wealthier class in place who have the material means to assist those less well off than themselves. For this purpose therefore, it is of little use for Chrysostom to address the poor, since they will not be in a position to adopt his advice. Therefore he looks to another target for his appeal, but this does not necessarily prove the absence of the poor from his congregation. Indeed at one point he does suggest that the poor, through their very poverty, have an important role to play in civic life. They provide the opportunity for the wealthier classes to save their souls by donating alms.[48] This is an interesting – if not necessarily original concept – and might well have been presented by Chrysostom as a way of comforting the poor present in the church while he focuses the greater part of his attention on those whose conduct could actually do with some improvement.

Aside from the redistribution of wealth, Chrysostom hoped to effect more wide-ranging changes in the civic environment. The forces for such change lay in the control of those who possessed power and influence within society, and once again these were the well-to-do members of the community. With such an ambitious aim as Chrysostom's it would serve little to speak to the lower echelons since they had little practical power to assist in the remodelling of the city, and time was certainly of the essence in Chrysostom's mind. Thus, for those parts of Chrysostom's sermons in which he speaks of general issues and questions of Christian living, we do indeed find the wealthy addressed more directly than the poor, or even the middle classes. But this, I have argued, was a conscious and practical decision on the part of the preacher, rather than the fact that the poor simply were not there to hear him. On a moral level it may well have been that because not preoccupied with the grim business of simply surviving, Chrysostom's wealthier charges may have had more leisure and opportunity to wander from the straight and narrow path, thus requiring more chivvying and correction than their busier and poorer counterparts. Nor, finally, must it be forgotten that there was an exegetical part to most of Chrysostom's homilies in which the Scripture readings of the day were analysed and expounded.[49] This section of the sermon provided a doctrinal education that was applicable to and essential for all members of the Christian community, regardless of social standing, and it was thus deemed vitally important for all to attend. In such a context few occasions for direct address to specific groups within the congregation would arise, and so once more we cannot interpret a lack of overt notice from the preacher as a definite absence on the part of a group of people.

Returning to the question of Chrysostom's high-flown rhetoric and who in the audience would have understood it, MacMullen firmly believes that the complexities of the prelate's public oratory implied an educated audience, themselves trained in such discourse. Nor is Chrysostom the only Church preacher with a similar training. The Cappadocian Fathers all practised the arts of rhetoric in their early years and made use of them to a greater or lesser extent on taking up their ecclesiastical positions. Basil, we have already seen, argued for the usefulness of a classical education, but then declared that when it came to preaching, priority should be given to the message of the sermon rather than the style with which it was delivered. Gregory of Nazianzus seems to have wholeheartedly imbibed the classical rhetorical tradition, so coloured is his speech and writing with its tropes.[50] Gregory of Nyssa would seem to have been the most restrained of this group in relation to his style, and yet even here we see the clear legacy of his classical training. Augustine's advice to employ pagan traditions in the work of spreading the Christian message has already been dealt with, and so we can see a widespread application of good rhetoric on the part of Church authorities. In this they are showing themselves simply, and at times unconsciously, to be the products of the contemporary education system, rather than deliberately tailoring their style to a particular class of audience. Gleason has spoken of the way in which male citizens of the empire demonstrated the level of their familiarity with culture by exhaling literary references and tropes as naturally as exhaling breath.[51] While our preachers have not quite reached such a position, their rhetorical expertise nevertheless underlines their worth as leaders of a congregation and serves to bolster their authority within Christian society, since rhetoric remained the locus of public power and persuasion. Their elevated style of preaching therefore serves to win the confidence of their communities as well as offering external proof of their masculinity and citizenship. The use of complex preaching styles may therefore have been more to do with the preachers themselves than the nature of their audience.

This is not to say that a usual church congregation would not have been able to follow the oratory of their preaching. It is certainly true that we see Chrysostom on occasion recognising that his audience are struggling with his train of thought, while Basil tries to modify his style to make it accessible to all. We have also seen Augustine acknowledge that a congregation sometimes require repeated explanations of certain points until they are satisfied that they have grasped their meaning. But in all of these cases it is equally possible to argue that it was the content of the sermon that caused the problems rather than the way in which it was delivered. Christianity had many problematic doctrinal issues at its heart, not always easily comprehensible to the faithful. It is such topics that nonplus the congregations, rather than the rhetoric of their preachers, and for which skilled oratory was necessary in order to render them more accessible.[52] Indeed it is suggested by Chrysostom at one stage that it is his congregation's ignorance of the contents of the Scriptures that leaves them confused rather than his style of speaking.[53] To further support this stance it must be pointed out that rhetorical training was so much a part of life in urban society that it would have been well-nigh impossible for any member of this society to escape its influence. If good oratory was the currency of masculinity and citizenship, it would have coloured all areas of life, and thus even the poorer inhabitants of the imperial city would have been accustomed to following arguments delivered in an elevated style. It has also been pointed out that the Christian homily had much in common with the pagan diatribe which was most usually delivered by

Cynic philosophers or other orators on street corners, and therefore very accessible to the ordinary members of the public.[54] Particular techniques are employed by Chrysostom in his exegesis to make his discourse more interesting and accessible to his audience. Most of these methods were inherited from pagan culture, and included devices such as rendering the words of certain Biblical characters in dramatic speech, and expanding on their arguments within these hypothetical inverted commas. The diatribe was also a popular form to employ in this work.[55]

Aside from this, many features of Chrysostom's homilies actually facilitate the listener – regardless of the standard of education. The many repetitions of an idea that lead us today to consider his sermons to be chaotic if not turgid, may instead have been deliberate attempts to ensure that everyone understood what was being spoken of. The language of the homilies was also very much akin to that of the liturgical prayers and Scriptural texts, and so an audience would have been accustomed to hearing such elevated styles presented orally.[56] Chrysostom's sermons are also highly dramatic affairs. He has a great fondness for holding debates with imaginary opponents – be they pagan, Jewish, or one of the perennially inquiring Greeks – for asking rhetorical questions of his audience, and generally adopting a great variety of facial and vocal expressions. This too would have helped to render his preaching comprehensible to even a diverse audience.[57] In this his style of preaching has many similarities with oral literature – repetition, stock phrasing, and even some ring composition – even if the resemblance is not always deliberate.

It would seem that many of the best Christian preachers walked a fine line between elevated rhetoric and abstruseness. While someone such as Chrysostom was obviously polished in the style of his speaking, for the most part he kept his sentence structures simple. His bluntness and outspokenness would also appeal to the listener – what has been called a 'vulgarity' that resembled the Cynic diatribe.[58] Even in the case of Augustine, the gap between his oratorical style and the language of the ordinary rustics he was addressing was probably not as wide or uncomfortable as we might perceive it to be today. Another Latin preacher, Caesarius of Arles of the sixth century, also kept his sentences short and stylistically simple, with plenty of repetition in order to engage with a varied audience.[59] Thus a lack of stylistic simplicity need not imply a barrier to the diverse audience. In the absence of conclusive evidence on one side or the other, however, the debate regarding the preacher's audience is likely to remain wide open.

### Attendance and attention within church congregations

Whatever we decide about the composition of the usual church congregation, we face even greater problems when it comes to assessing the physical numbers who attended church on a regular basis. Numbers of Christians within the ancient city can only be estimated. Chrysostom speaks of about two thirds of the Antiochene population as being Christian – perhaps 150,000 to 200,000 people – but does not present us with any similar guesses for the city of Constantinople.[60] Even then there are a number of reasons for regarding his figures with some wariness. Ancient population figures are notoriously unreliable and so we cannot even arrive at an accurate total population figure for Antioch – regardless of religious persuasion.

In any case, regardless of how many Christians there may have been in Antioch, we have no way of ascertaining how many of them attended church on a regular basis. It has often been remarked that the Christianisation of the empire did not automatically imply complete devotion on the part of the population. Since laws alone do not a Christian make, it may well have been that many people simply changed the title of their faith without doing anything more concrete about it. We also hear directly from Chrysostom himself of the difficulties in maintaining attendance numbers when faced with the rival attractions in the city. Often the preacher had cause to complain that his congregation had been diminished on the occasions when theatrical events or sporting competitions took place elsewhere in the city. Rather than caring for the welfare of their immortal souls, they preferred to rush off to see their favourite actors or bet on a promising horse.[61] Chrysostom bewails the moral damage inherent in such activities, but I think we can also assume that his pride was somewhat injured at being sidelined in this fashion. After all, he was certainly considered a good enough source of entertainment when nothing else was going on. Even when he did preach to a full house on special occasions such as Easter, he worried afresh that people were only there for the social side of the event, hoping to see and be seen as part of the customary interaction of a civic community, rather than tending to their immortal souls. The preacher therefore began to play the ratings game himself. He became adept at preaching exciting or well-polished sermons – especially on the days when he found his congregation diminished by some more secular attraction. He hoped that in this way word would spread to those who had stayed away that they had missed a virtuoso performance, therefore encouraging them to be more diligent in their attendance, if only to appreciate his golden tongue. Presumably he hoped that once he got these lukewarm Christians into his church, something of the divine message would filter through to them and work some lasting good.

Aside from the battle for attendance figures, however, we can explain Chrysostom's many complaints against the secular entertainments of the city as part of his efforts to redraw the appearance of that city. This will be discussed in more detail in the coming chapters, but for now suffice it to say that if Chrysostom could persuade his congregations to avoid patronising institutions so much at the heart of the civic structure, in favour of ecclesiastical activities, he could then have some chance of altering the established organisation of the secular city. There is also probably something of his concern with gendered behaviour in these outbursts. Sporting events and theatrical spectacles were highly emotive occasions, arousing a collective spirit that often overtook its boundaries and dissolved into riots and disorder. Self-discipline, and control over the expression of emotions was, however, a necessary qualification for a claim to masculinity, and so was something Chrysostom was eager to promote. Since all emotions aroused in the church were directed to a higher authority, they were well structured and adequately contained. And they were therefore quite appropriate to male behaviour. Thus, in inveighing against the mass groupings at the hippodrome, Chrysostom might well be attempting to restore the shaky boundaries of gender-appropriate behaviour.

Whatever Chrysostom's reasons for speaking out on the subject of attendance figures, however, and there is probably an element of all of the above in it, his complaints seem to have achieved little on a practical level until the summer of 399. As time went on he grew increasingly impatient – especially when the noise from the races at the hippodrome in Constantinople drowned out even his voice and the hymns in his church, distracting those citizens who had come to hear his teaching of God's Word. His disapproval finally registered with the secular authorities and a law was drawn up prohibiting the staging of theatrical performances or games on Sundays – unless of course the emperor's birthday happened to fall on the Sabbath.[62]

It was thus a constant struggle for ecclesiastical leaders to keep the faithful coming to church in spite of the purported Christianisation of the society. Once there, the problems of wielding some influence over the congregation continued. Even if the shouting from nearby sports arenas did not distract them, a preacher's audience were well capable of growing bored themselves. Chrysostom speaks of his flock allowing their attention to wander at particular points of the liturgy, perhaps when dealing with an intricate question of doctrine, or even if he himself fails to engage their interest sufficiently. Their disenchantment is signalled through yawning, the shuffling of their feet and the bored expressions on their faces. They are on record as complaining vocally if he speaks too lengthily on a subject they have heard dealt with before, wanting always to hear new material, and of gossiping among themselves. 'For in truth there ought always only to be one voice in the church ... but when there are many people conversing about many different subjects, why should we disturb you for no reason?' he demands sarcastically on one occasion.[63]

By the same token, an attempt to substitute another preacher for Chrysostom met with extreme disapproval from one of the bishop's congregations at Constantinople. All of these instances point to a sense of Church preaching as an entertainment medium on the part of the Christian laity. This again informs on the use of polished rhetoric on the part of our preachers, since this was the style of oratory best calculated to interest and entertain the secular audience who were very much products of urban imperial society. They cheered when an argument was nicely phrased, enjoyed the vivid imagery employed by someone such as Chrysostom, and demanded a polished performance every week. Such an outlook does not really point to great devoutness in these urban dwellers in spite of claims by some scholars that there was an unambiguous shift towards Christianisation of late antique society.

## A Christianised discourse and the transformation of the city

What the preaching exercise does indicate, however, is the means by which Church authorities worked to present Christianity as the dominant institution of power within society. The education of the leading preachers of this time meant that their rhetoric was so thoroughly imbued with the conventions of the classical heritage that it was second nature to them. Thus, in spite of their condemnation of over-concentration on style rather than content when spreading God's message, Chrysostom, Basil, Gregory Nazianzus, and to a lesser extent, Gregory of Nyssa, all use considerably more rhetoric in their homilies than they theoretically approved of. The audience's reactions show that this was a good means of reaching them – indeed the only one in such a secular society – and hence for the most practical reasons we have the appropriation of classical traditions by Christianity. The authorities then used this tool to denigrate the rest of the pagan traditions – mocking the literature, philosophies and theatre of the classical heritage.[64] Beyond such condemnations pagan culture is not mentioned by these preachers. Instead the Bible becomes the new literary corpus, and Christ's teachings the new philosophy. The homiletic form then becomes the means by which this new culture is transmitted. It is especially suited to this job because of the frequency with which sermons are preached, the repetitive nature of the themes contained in them, and the broad social and intellectual range of the preacher's audience. By appropriating classical rhetoric to this end, the Christians appropriated an institution of power, refigured it according to their own purposes, and disseminated it through the society. This entire process is described as the Christianisation of the prevailing discourse in the late Roman empire. It is an admirable public relations exercise on the part of the early Christians in which they appropriated the conventions of the classical heritage and remoulded them with a Christian stamp. But it must always be remembered that this was done to further what the church authorities saw as a vital, and spiritually rewarding, aim. Thus Augustine's suggestion that Church preachers should appropriate the existing styles of oratory for their own ends can be seen as an example of this process. Not only does the use of classical tropes attack the unconvinced Christians on familiar territory, lulling them into a false sense of security and subtly working to disseminate the message of the Faith, but it also ensures the maximum audience possible for this message. Citizens of the imperial city were used to rhetorical performances in all areas of their life and held them in high regard. Anything less polished and elevated would not even be considered as worth listening to, and we have already seen the necessity of winning and holding the attention of ordinary churchgoers against more secular attractions. The use of good rhetoric was therefore the only means by which Christian preachers could reach their audiences.

# 4

# A Guide to Chrysostom's Preaching Style

This was a nerve shock even to me, to hear that the villagers thought Christianity was like some old picture show that was way out of date.... Father told Anatole he respected and valued his help ... but was disappointed by the villagers' childlike interpretations of God's plan.... He said he would work on a sermon that would clear up all the misunderstandings. Then he announced that this conversation had come to an end, and Anatole could consider himself excused from the table and this house.

Barbara Kingsolver, The Poisonwood Bible, p. 151

Before beginning the more detailed examination of the themes of gender and wealth in Chrysostom's preaching, it is worth discovering the kind of context these remarks had. This will allow us to decide whether the opinions we will spend time focusing on were representative of Chrysostom's approach, or were rather isolated instances of over-enthusiasm for a particular Scriptural message.

A perusal of even a few of Chrysostom's homilies on the Pauline epistles will show us a remarkable constancy of approach. A detailed breakdown of two sermons, preached on different occasions, will give us a clear idea of this *modus operandi*. I will look first at *Homily IX on the First Letter to the Corinthians*, which will also give us a useful insight into some of Chrysostom's anxieties on the subject of excessive wealth. The second sermon I will focus on in this way will be *Homily XX on Ephesians*, in which the subject is the ideal Christian marriage, thus shedding substantial light on Chrysostom's preoccupation with appropriate gender roles and on his plans for the restructuring of the urban community.

*

In almost all cases the Scriptural text for the day is presented at the outset of Chrysostom's homilies. While we cannot be sure whether this text was drawn from a preceding reading, or was selected independently by the preacher, he began his sermons by quoting the passage he wished to explain and discuss. In the case of *Homily IX on I Corinthians*, the text is ch. 3, verses 12-15 of Paul's first letter to the citizens of this community:

> If any man build upon this foundation gold, silver, costly stones, wood, hay, stubble; each man's work shall be made manifest: for the day shall declare it, because it is revealed in fire; and the fire shall prove each man's work of what sort it is. If any man's work abide which he built thereon, he shall receive a reward. If any man's work shall be burned, he shall suffer loss: but he himself shall be saved; yet so as through fire.

Chrysostom immediately sets the tone for his discourse by announcing that this is 'no small subject of enquiry' but instead about something of concern to all humans; does the punishment of hellfire have any end? He already has an answer for this, drawn from Mark's Gospel, in which Christ himself declared that the fires of hell would not be quenched and the worm of death would never die.

Chrysostom now acknowledges some of the possible reactions of his audience to such a bleak beginning. This is a common approach of his – he describes and empathises with the emotions of his audience, forging a bond with them that will allow him to show them how best to allay their own fears. He knows that they feel a chill on hearing these things, but it is God's command that he should continually instruct his flock in this manner. He can quote the book of Exodus in support of this, while Paul's letter to the Romans is quoted in order to reassure his congregants that if they live good lives they have no reason to fear the hellish torments of which he speaks. Already then, in the first moments of his sermon, Chrysostom has demonstrated the wealth of his own scriptural knowledge, quoting supporting passages for his recommendations at every turn. His next paragraph increases the quotation rate as he draws references from three Pauline epistles and the Gospel of Matthew in order to emphasise the everlasting nature of the punishment for sinners.

Now, however, he changes tactics as he presents a hypothetical argument against such severity, another favourite approach. He verbalises some of the possible objections of his audience in order to present his own position more effectively:

> And do not say to me, 'how can this be the rule of justice, if the punishment has no end?' Instead, when God does anything obey his decisions, and do not subject what he says to mere human reasonings.

This is one of Chrysostom's recurring themes, that mere mortals should not presume to question the rule of God, and he constantly works to encourage unquestioning obedience on their part. In this case he argues that his flock have actually been very blessed in their lives, and have not been treated according to their just deserts. For if the strict rule of justice were to be applied in all cases, we should have been destroyed at the very outset, when Adam committed the first sin. And it is all the more distressing that a human should wrong such a benefactor as God, 'who breathed his soul into him, who gave ten thousand gifts of grace, whose will is to take him up into heaven'. How could such a misdeed be pardoned when Adam was cast out of Eden for a single sin?

When a hypothetical objector theorises that Adam's punishment was so severe because he had the temerity to commit a sin in Paradise itself, where everything imaginable had been granted to him, Chrysostom is quick to disagree. He believes instead that it is far worse to carry out misdeeds against the background of misery and affliction that is the daily lot of his audience. They should have a greater appreciation of 'the evils of this life' and should strive instead to make it better. It is as if they were prisoners who continued to practise the crimes for which they had been jailed in the first place.

Again Chrysostom acknowledges what a serious and weighty discussion this is, and knows that his audience must be finding it hard to bear – he knows from his own experience that it is not exactly a subject to gladden the heart. But he assures them it is necessary in order to save them from the torments in question, reiterating his credentials as their friend and protector before teaching them a lesson that many will find hard. After this brief moment of respite, then, the preacher returns to Adam, presenting the first man as a contrast and a salutary lesson to his descendants 5,000 years on. Adam did not have any advice from the prophets to guide his behaviour, and committed only a single sin. God was not lenient, however, and expelled him from Paradise. Chrysostom's congregants on the other hand have had the benefit of constant instruction from the prophets and from Christ himself, and the priceless promise of the kingdom of heaven as their reward, and yet they still commit not single, but innumerable sins. And just because a sin takes only a short time to commit, this does not mean that the punishment should be of equally short duration. In fact Chrysostom points to those murderers or fornicators who had carried out some wrong in a very short space of time, and yet are serving lengthy prison sentences. Why should errant Christians believe that they are any the more deserving of a truncated punishment?

Chrysostom also goes on to warn his audience of the severity of God's judgement, in spite of the fact that he is a loving deity. This same God caused the deluge that destroyed the ancient world, with Noah and his family as the sole survivors, and who later rained down fire on the earth. Punishments devised by men pale into insignificance beside such as this according to Chrysostom, since God's great mercy is also matched by his great punishments. In this way Chrysostom holds the attention of his audience, even on such an unpleasant topic, by appealing to the macabre sense in most people that allows them to find entertainment even in tales of pain and punishment. It is almost the late antique version of a horror film, terrifying people at the same time as riveting their attention, and in Chrysostom's case, at the same time as educating and saving their immortal souls.

God's leniency is evident from the fact that he did not make unreasonable demands of his people. He did not ask that anyone who was not able
should adopt virginity as their way of life, or even that anyone should give
up all their possessions. Chrysostom maintains that these should have
been easy for the devout Christian, but all that has really been asked is
that they be chaste in their marriages and avoid avarice in their financial
dealings: 'What excuse then have we for not observing precepts so easy
and light? We cannot name any at all. That the punishment then is eternal
is plain from all that has been said.'

Thus far, Chrysostom has been expounding on the general sense of
Paul's words, but now he feels the need to deal with them in more detail:
'But since Paul's declaration seems to say something else to others, let us
take it and examine it thoroughly.' Chrysostom intends to break the
Pauline text in question into its component pieces for the benefit of his
listeners. This is generally a cue for him to begin to introduce themes and
issues that were of particular concern to him as a pastor. A detailed examination of a Scriptural verse allows great scope for tangents, asides and
other biblical references. According to Chrysostom's interpretation, the
'work' referred to by Paul, that is built by men and then either left to
remain or destroyed, is their actions or their deeds. And Christ should be
the foundation of this work. Chrysostom feels sure that Paul means this
passage to allude to the deeds of men, since the apostle will soon have
cause to speak against those who commit fornication. To this end he is
laying down what Chrysostom calls the 'preliminaries', preparing the
ground for a discourse that is yet to come. By alluding to other teachings
of Paul, Chrysostom shows that this is an established approach on the part
of the apostle, and in this way, before ever addressing the issue of fornication directly, Paul is 'beginning to agitate with fears the soul of the man
who has been unchaste'.

The next elements of the Pauline text are the 'gold, silver, costly stones,
wood, hay, stubble', and Chrysostom explains these as representing the
extent of the faith of the various builders. Quoting from three other
Pauline epistles, Chrysostom makes the point that the quality of a
person's faith is evident from their deeds. In theory everyone should have
equal faith, but because life is varied, there are different levels of application of faith:

> ... in life there is room for some to be more diligent, others more
> slothful; some stricter, and others more ordinary; the errors of some
> people are more grievous, but others are less noteworthy.

And as a logical result of these differing standards, different rewards are
granted to each person according to his due. Faith is not sufficient alone
without good works to go with it – something Chrysostom summarises
again to assist his audience in following his train of thought. And the
quality of a person's works is evident from whether they have adorned

their 'building' with gold or with hay. All of these works will pass through fire, and whether this is a punishment or simply a trial will depend on the quality of the adornments. Those whose works are signified by gold will merely have it burnished more brightly by the fire, whereas those deeds that are 'hay' will be consumed by the blaze. And so the fire can be both a punishment and a symbol of salvation, depending on the circumstances. Chrysostom then urges his audience not to be surprised that Paul speaks of burning and destruction in terms of Salvation: 'For it is his custom to use fair expressions for things which are ugly, and to act in the opposite manner for things that are good.' Here Chrysostom can refer to other instances throughout Paul's writings in which this is borne out. 'Captivity' for example would be considered as an evil by most, but when Paul uses it in the context of being a prisoner of obedience to Christ, it becomes a positive concept.

The preacher now begins to dissect the concept that each person is the temple of God. This means that the penalty for destroying the temple of God is all the more severe. Chrysostom even tries to reassure his audience somewhat, lest they be terrified by such a threat. Since no one has yet been singled out, he says, the rebuke can be spread out among the collective, rather than taken to heart by any individual. In this way a reprimand can be administered effectively, but not to the extent that it paralyses the congregation with fear. Chrysostom's approach during this lesson is to present his audience with a short verse of scripture followed by a quick explanation, and so this passage of the homily takes an almost quick-fire tone. But he then expands his thoughts a little more when he reminds his listeners that success or approbation in the temporal world is of little account if they are held captive by sin. So strongly does Chrysostom feel about the possibility that members of his congregation might allow themselves to be enslaved by sin that he spends some time on this concept, using some of his richest metaphors in his efforts to convey the seriousness of the situation to his listeners:

> For if a man was a king and was then enslaved by barbarians, he would be the most wretched of all men. So too with sin, since sin is a barbarian, and it does not know how to spare a soul that it has captured, but instead acts as a tyrant to all who admit sin into their lives, until they are ruined.

It is interesting to note that in this metaphor, and in the one which follows, Chrysostom personifies sin as a female character, thus emphasising how terrible it is to allow oneself to be ruled over by sin:

> If a painter was to draw the picture of sin, he would not be wrong in depicting her as follows: a woman in the form of a beast, savage, breathing flames, hideous and black, just as the heathen poets depict their Scyllas.

Such a grim portrait is carefully calculated to arouse horror in the listeners, and to encourage them to mend their ways. Chrysostom is also deeply concerned that those who allow sin to rule their lives to such an extent are actually forfeiting their humanity in some way, and becoming more like base beasts. In order to convey the seriousness of this situation, another extended metaphor is employed, in which Chrysostom compares those who are covetous or rapacious to greedy, slavering dogs. They feel no pity for others or compunction for their deeds, and as such they are inhuman. Humans would respond in some way to those who are afflicted, but beasts are lacking in basic compassion, and so continue to work to gratify their own needs and desires to the exclusion of all else.

We will examine some of the implications of this approach in greater detail at a later point. Such a passage tells us much about Chrysostom's attitudes to wealth and to appropriate gender roles, but it is also representative of his preaching style. He has been relatively restrained in his exegesis up to this point, explaining each point of the text in question and offering other scriptural references where applicable. This is probably just as much a display of his own education as it is for the edification of his audience. But in the latter stages he has become steadily more fervent in his efforts to encourage his audience in a particular mode of behaviour, using such detailed metaphors as we have seen above and spending quite a bit of time making each point.

He continues to invest all of his rhetorical energies in warning his audience of the threat to their humanity if they continue in their avaricious ways. They will become more like demons even than beasts – thus sinking to another level. The devil himself is engaged in this struggle to drag mankind down, encouraging people to harm even their own families and friends. Chrysostom knows that the unequivocal nature of his words on this subject will make many resentful. But the preacher feels only pity for them, and prays that they will abandon this savage and bestial behaviour, since Scripture is clear in warning against it: 'For not only me, but also the prophet, banishes these people from mankind, saying "Man being in honour has no understanding, but is like unto the senseless beasts." ' The preacher closes by begging his congregation to become men at last, and direct their attention to heaven, so that they might receive their just blessings from Christ. Chrysostom then finishes the sermon in what is his customary manner – invoking Jesus, the Father and the Holy Spirit, and closing with an Amen.

So we have seen Chrysostom move through a detailed exegesis of a passage of Scripture, sometimes briefly and with little digression, at other times with a more extensive level of commentary, and with support drawn from other biblical sources, through to becoming drawn into an extensive discourse on a subject which causes him anxiety, using all his powers of persuasion to encourage his audience towards better behaviour. This approach can be seen in most of his preaching, and it is a rare sermon indeed in which he does not become somewhat carried away on at least one occasion.

*

*Homily XX*, preached on Paul's letter to the Ephesians, is a good example of a sermon in which Chrysostom gives full scope to his rhetorical talents, and lingers at length on issues that are close to his heart. The result is a very long sermon, one that may have taken around two hours to deliver. It is also somewhat different from the homily on the letter to the Corinthians discussed above in that Chrysostom spends less time providing exegesis of individual phrases from the Pauline text, and much more time providing his congregation with advice as to how best to manage their households, with a number of vividly painted pen-portraits to help his case.

This is a homily I will return to a number of times throughout this book, as it does much to illustrate Chrysostom's ambitions for individual Christian households and, by extension, the ideal Christian urban community. This is because it is an exposition of Paul's instructions to women to be obedient to their husbands:

> Wives, be in subjection unto your own husbands, as unto the Lord. For the husband is the head of the wife, as Christ also is the head of the Church: being Himself the Saviour of the body. But as the Church is subject to Christ, so let the wives also be to their husbands in everything.

Chrysostom begins with a reference to Ecclesiastes, Genesis and Paul's letter to the Galatians in order to prove that a woman dwelling in harmony with her husband is chief among all blessings and for this reason God made provision for men and women to marry and be joined together as one. The love between the sexes is described by Chrysostom as surpassing all other kinds of love, and the close bond between man and woman is both demonstrated and underlined by the fact that the woman was created from the man. God is shown to have organised everything most providentially:

> He permitted the man to marry his own sister; or rather not his sister, but his daughter; nay, nor yet his daughter, but something more than his daughter, even his own flesh. And thus the whole He framed from one beginning, gathering all together, like stones in a building into one.

In this way God ensures that the human race is not pulled asunder, encouraging them to forge ties throughout the community and working to prevent isolation by forbidding marriages among close kin.

Chrysostom follows Paul closely in ascribing such importance to this subject, believing that Paul would never have expended so much energy on urging wives to be obedient to their husbands if it were not crucial to the overall health of the community. If the relationship between the spouses is established in this manner, then all other societal relationships will fall into proper order – between parents and children, householders and servants, neighbours and other members of the community. But if husbands and wives do not enjoy a harmonious relationship then chaos rules and the very structures of society suddenly come under threat.

At this point Chrysostom feels it is important to resolve a potential contradiction within the pages of Scripture. The Gospel of Luke quotes Jesus as saying that no one could follow him unless they bade farewell to their spouse. In many ways following Christ could seem to be the antithesis to ordinary human relationships. But Chrysostom is at pains to claim that serving one's spouse is an important and devout way of serving God. The best way of demonstrating this devotion is to accept the structure of marriage whereby the husband is the head and the wife is the body. This is the next line of the Pauline text under examination, and Chrysostom sees it as crucial to his arrangement of society.

From this basic foundation, husbands are then urged to love their wives, just as Christ loved the church. This ensures that the bonds of marriage and therefore the household are strengthened and welded securely. Loving one's wife is the primary means of securing her obedience, and a good husband should be willing to undergo any kind of suffering for the sake of his wife, just as Christ sacrificed himself for the sake of the Church. So even if a wife is haughty or scornful, a loving husband can compel her surrender. A man might be able to rule over his servants through the medium of fear, but he should never treat his wife and the mother of his children in this way:

> For what sort of union is that, where the wife trembles at her husband? And what sort of pleasure will the husband himself enjoy, if he dwells with his wife as with a slave, and not as with a free-woman?

Chrysostom then goes on to explain how blemished the Church was when Christ condescended to take her as his bride, and work to sanctify and cleanse her. He draws from a number of Pauline epistles to emphasise how impure the Church was before the intervention of her saviour. The result was the adornment of the Church beyond all comparison. Similarly husbands should accept their wives – even blemished – since they are 'of God's fashioning'. Chrysostom urges the men in his audience to look beyond the external appearances of their mates to the inner beauty of their souls as a means of avoiding disquiet in the home:

> Outward beauty is full of conceit and great licence, and throws men into jealousy, and it often makes you suspect monstrous things. But

does it give any pleasure? Maybe for the first or second month, or at most for the year: but not for any longer than that; familiarity makes the admiration pass away. And meanwhile the evils that arise from the beauty still survive – the pride, the folly, the contempt.

Chrysostom lingers on this concept of outward beauty and then introduces the many troubles that might actually ruin this beauty – disease, old age, even a lustful and dissipated lifestyle. He does not let this opportunity to decry wealth slip by unnoticed, but reminds his audience that riches give rise to 'foolish and hurtful lusts', and that men must learn to look beyond the superficial in favour of true and lasting beauty. Here Chrysostom hopes to alarm his audience into a more Christian outlook by presenting such a vivid picture of the transience of beauty, and the dangers of excessive riches.

Chrysostom moves to the next stage in laying out how his husbands should love their wives by focusing on Paul's exhortation to husbands to love their wives as they love their own bodies. Thus did Adam acknowledge his wife as his flesh, and so too does Christ acknowledge the Church. And it is for this reason that men leave their parents in order to marry, and they and their spouses become as one flesh. This 'cleaving' of husband to wife is a further reason that he should treat her properly at all times, since she is as his own body. Chrysostom points out what a bond this is when he notes that even if a man is lame or has a diseased part of his body, he does not remove the offending part since it is an aspect of himself. So even if a wife should be less than perfect in some way, since she is the body to the husband's head, he should not be prompted to shun or neglect her, but should love her all the more for her imperfections.

By this stage Chrysostom has moved considerably beyond the original Pauline passage cited at the outset, as he expands on the notion of a Christian marriage being like Christ's relationship with the Church. It is one of the central mysteries of the Church that Christ should have become human and sacrificed himself for the sins of mankind. And it is a similar mystery that a man should leave his own mother in favour of another woman. But as Chrysostom points out, parents are not distressed at this event, but rather welcome it with rejoicing. Paul is therefore shrewd when he compares a marriage to Christ's taking of the Church as a bride, for in this way the closeness of the bond and the reason for joy and gratitude are made clear.

Chrysostom expands on the details of the Christian marriage still further when he announces that it is to the wife's benefit also if she fears her husband. He reminds her that she is not equal to her husband but in second place to him. It is his place therefore to love, and hers to fear. Chrysostom is aware that this might seem odd to his audience – how can there be love in the same place as there is fear? But he maintains that a woman who fears and reverences her husband will also love him, just as the body loves the head that has the authority over it. Here Chrysostom is insistent that a division of authority cannot co-exist with peace, but that harmony depends on a single ruler emerging. And of course this must be the male for power to be wielded appropriately. Chrysostom then goes on to spend more time on Paul's various discourses on the importance of love within marriage, maintaining that the apostle spent more time on love than he did on fear or reverence out of a keen desire to see love as the guiding principle within all marriages. And even if a wife should fail to appreciate how lucky she is to have a husband enjoined to love her, and fails to be properly obedient to him, he should nevertheless continue to love her so that he can clearly feel that he has performed his duty. Similarly a wife should continue to show her husband reverence, even if he has not done his duty in loving her. Under this scheme both men and women can obey God's law and not be negligent in any aspect of their duty.

This is a truly Christian and spiritual marriage according to Chrysostom, and as such will be free from strife and even from the demands of the flesh. The preacher draws on the Old Testament now in order to find a fitting example of such a marriage, and he comes up with that of Abraham and Sarah. Indeed Chrysostom believes wholeheartedly that a good marriage owes nothing to the desires of the body, but is a union of the spirit and the soul. And lest any be tempted to dismiss marriage as something to be condemned, Chrysostom reiterates the comparison of Christ and the Church with a bridegroom and his bride. At this point we see Chrysostom repeating himself to a certain extent as he strives both to present his ideal picture of a marriage and to make a stand against those heretical factions – presumably Gnostic – which felt that marriage had no place in the pursuit of true holiness. Chrysostom is at pains to point out how a properly organised household is in fact a way of worshipping Christ, and must not be denigrated on any account. Given Chrysostom's own ascetic leanings this might be seen as a difficult task for him, but his dedication is clear in his application, as he reiterates his opinion regarding the sanctity of marriage again and again, with quotes from Scripture to support his case.

He also feels the need to speak at greater length on the subject of the fear a wife should have of her husband, and how the husband should comport himself in this relationship. He should not compel her as he would a slave, or indeed desire that she feel a slavish kind of fear of him, but simply that she should learn to keep her appropriate and subordinate place within the relationship. He urges husbands to be restrained in their approach, since the weakness of the female sex demands a greater level of support. Indeed if they love their wives properly as they are commanded, they will have far greater success in ensuring obedience than if they simply rule through fear. This is even the case in second marriages, he says, since these unions are not to be condemned as Paul himself permits them. This sudden introduction of the subject of remarriage seems to reflect an anxiety on the part of Chrysostom. It certainly does not arise directly from the Pauline text; rather he introduces it as a question raised by a hypothetical audience member. And his response to the question is a somewhat grudging acceptance of the concept of remarriage. I think this is an instance in which his biases emerge from his exegesis of a Pauline text, or from his attempts to bring into existence his idealised Christian community.

After this brief intervention, Chrysostom returns to the concept of a close union between husband and wife, maintaining that if a husband cleaves to his wife, harmony in the household will follow. The example of Abraham and Sarah is introduced again here, since they had a harmonious home despite its large number of inhabitants. Indeed the love and reverence Abraham and Sarah felt for each other so influenced the household that even the servants were ready to hazard their lives for their master and his son. A good marriage is therefore seen as the foundation for such lasting harmony. If husbands are properly thoughtful for their wives, their children and their servants, then their own task of governing will be made easier, since the ground for respect and honour will already be laid. And Chrysostom believes that a key part of this is to look beyond money and the superficial concerns of wealth in favour of 'spiritual excellence'.

In this perfect household posited by Chrysostom, therefore, everything will be done as much for the sake of Christ as for the gratification of the individuals within the household. And there will be no teasing, slander or gossip. Wives will not listen to slander against their husbands, nor will husbands believe ill reports of their wives. A good wife will not be suspicious of her husband, and a good husband will not do anything that gives rise to suspicion. Even if a man must be out all day with his business associates or his friends, he should devote his evenings to his wife so that she has no reason to complain or feel suspicious of his activities. And even if she does complain about his absences he should not be annoyed but should see that her suspicions and anxieties arise out of her affection for him and her fear that anyone might have come between her and her husband.

Next Chrysostom moves on to paint a picture of other jealousies that can arise in a marriage; namely one or other of the spouses making too many demands of the servants. Once again Sarah and Abraham are the exemplary couple here, especially given their approach to Abraham's relationship with the servant Hagar. Sarah prompted this relationship so Abraham might have a son, but Abraham always took care not to alienate Sarah on this account, and was quick to put Hagar aside once he felt Sarah might be grieved by it.

And if men should put their wives first in all things, so should a wife be respectful in all her dealings with her husband, and she should refrain from berating him or nagging him. Here Chrysostom presents a paraphrase of some wifely nagging which would probably have struck a chord with most of his audience, at the same time as being quite entertaining. But the entertainment value of this passage only serves to emphasise the seriousness of Chrysostom's point – that a wife should remember that she is in the place of the body to the husband's head. And he, by the same token, should remember his authority, and should use it to mould his wife's character from the very first day of the marriage. This passage of the homily will be returned to at a later stage in this book, but it is a lengthy section in which Chrysostom gives detailed instructions as to how a husband should manage his wife, and by extension his household. As part of his strategy, Chrysostom lingers on the minutiae of such a household – its furnishings and décor, the demeanour of the wife, even her appearance. Naturally Chrysostom includes a number of references to wealth throughout this discussion, since he sees it, and its management, as an intrinsic part of any domestic relationship. His focus on the perfect household therefore highlights the appropriate place of wealth, and points the way for his congregation to follow. Portraits of excessive riches show all the more clearly what behaviour they should avoid, but at the same time they hold the audience's attention, functioning almost as a late antique version of a gossip magazine. The congregation can enjoy a sneak preview of the lives of those richer than themselves, at the same time as feeling superior in virtue as they are encouraged to avoid emulating them.

In the perfect marriage husbands will spend more time with their wives and children than they will in the market place. They will pray with their household, guiding them in the spiritual behaviour required of a Christian. And in this setting the entertainments of the wealthy and famous, such as lavish dinners, will be of ever-decreasing importance. So many of Chrysostom's recommendations regarding the Christian marriage have some connection with wealth and learning to shun it. Men are even advised to choose poor wives over rich ones, since a rich woman will tend to be extravagant and insolent and less respectful of her husband. Riches can in fact get in the way of a true partnership in the marriage as each partner struggles to retain ownership of the portion they brought to the marriage – an attitude Chrysostom finds both abhorrent and destructive.

Chrysostom brings the homily to a close by reminding his male congregants that they should behave with restraint and graciousness throughout all their dealings with their wives, even when 'training' them to be appropriately modest and respectful. A moderate approach will actually be more effective than a harsh one, as can be learnt from the raising of children. Here Chrysostom's comparison of wives with children is carefully calculated to underline the inferior position of the woman in relation to her husband. And so Chrysostom suggests ways in which the men can flatter their wives into better behaviour, coaxing them like recalcitrant children. His logic also seems to suggest that the less wealthy the woman is to begin with, the more open she will be to this kind of persuasion.

Throughout this homily we have seen how closely wealth and a good relationship between the sexes are linked in Chrysostom's mind. He believes that all the instructions for a good marriage are to be found in the Scriptures, something we have seen borne out by the substantial numbers of quotations from both Old and New Testaments which he has employed to support his various points. It is also a sermon with a large degree of repetition as Chrysostom labours over his pictures of husbands cleaving to their wives in the sanctity of marriage, and of the comparison of such a union with Christ's authority over the Church. Chrysostom evidently feels strongly enough about the issue to spend a great deal of time on it, expanding on almost every point with Scriptural references but also with detailed pen-portraits designed both to retain the interest of his audience and to encourage them towards their preacher's idea of a Christian community. It is a homily that provides us with examples of almost all of the rhetorical tricks employed by Chrysostom in the course of his preaching, and as such is an excellent example of both his style and his overall philosophy of Christian living.

# 5

# Role Models for the Christian City

Few things are harder to put up with than the annoyance of a good example.

Mark Twain, *Pudd'nhead Wilson*, ch. 19

### Rhetoric and reality

Throughout his sermons, when Chrysostom wishes to furnish his audience with an example of behaviour to emulate or shun, or even when he wants to inject a note of interest into his exegesis, he refers either to members of society present in front of him or to more generic characters, easily recognisable by all, in order to make his point. But in order to see the yardsticks against which he judges these characters, it is worth spending some time on those men and women Chrysostom presents to his audience as role models – both negative and positive.

It is always difficult to decide the extent to which Church oratory is representative of actual events occurring within the later Roman empire. Some scholars feel that most ecclesiastical performances were carefully crafted public relations exercises, designed to further the Christianisation of the discourses of power in this society. The Christianisation of discourse has come to be understood as the means by which the language and symbols of power and of common understanding within Roman society became Christianised over time. To discuss it in those terms, however, can make the growth and consolidation of the Christian church within the Roman empire seem like a purely self-conscious bid for secular power. Those who interpret the process in this light would be apt to read confrontations between Church and state authorities as entirely stage managed affairs designed to publicly demonstrate where the balance of power lay. So, for example, Ambrose of Milan's facing down of Theodosius I, and his insistence on the emperor's public penance for the massacre at Thessalonica could be seen as Ambrose's bid for dominance in the secular power structure at the same time as allowing the emperor to admit culpability without loss of face.[1] Those who view Ambrose's strictness in this light would also be likely to see the conflicts between John Chrysostom and the empress Eudoxia as similarly choreographed events in which Christianity can be seen to triumph over secular authority.[2] However this more cynical interpretation glosses over the fact that most, if not all, of the

Christian authorities did in fact hold genuine personal beliefs in God and in the structure of their religion, which went deeper than simple exercises in power, Ambrose and Chrysostom among them. In fact Ambrose's clash with Theodosius could just as likely have been motivated by a sincere wish to bring the emperor back to the path of righteousness after straying, just as Chrysostom's public disapproval of the empress probably had more to do with his frustration regarding the abuses of wealth among his flock than with a conscious effort to belittle his secular leaders in public. In fact the two positions could co-exist quite effectively among ecclesiastical leaders, and a desire for secular power and spiritual fulfilment need not be mutually exclusive.

Efforts to dictate public religious observances can indeed be viewed as a desire to dominate within the community, but must also be considered as a sincere attempt to guide as many people as possible towards eternal salvation. The public oratory employed in this effort can therefore be read, or heard, on different levels, and it is impossible to state with any degree of certainty which ambition was espoused by the rhetorician – the wish to establish a Christian power-base within the community, or the desire to bring Christian salvation within the reach of the faithful. I have interpreted Chrysostom's rhetoric as illustrating a passionate belief in a Christianised society and in his own ability to begin its incarnation in the later Roman world. A natural consequence of such a fervent belief would indeed be a desire to see his church established as the leading social structure within the community, but I do not believe that this was his consciously primary aim, but rather a means to his ideal end of seeing a Christian city manifested on earth.

As we move on, we will see that much of Chrysostom's preaching is inspired by those members of his congregation who fail to follow his recommendations to achieve this end. The spontaneity of such outbursts leads me to believe that they were indeed prompted by situations that actually faced him on a daily basis, rather than being representative of purely rhetorical exercises with a political agenda. The urgency with which Chrysostom speaks indicates that he was thoroughly engaged in trying to rewrite the everyday behaviour of ordinary people within the urban community. He is rarely specific in his references to members of his congregation, preferring instead to use readily recognisable generic characters. Occasionally, however, he is prompted to be a little more precise in his references, employing various *exempla*, either from the pages of Scripture or from society around him. Many men and women alike exercised a strong influence on Chrysostom in the course of his life and career, while others from the pages of history impressed him strongly in other respects. It is worth discussing some of the passages where these characters feature at this point since they create a context in which his other addresses or comments on gender can be read. In seeing what Chrysostom has to say about readily identifiable examples – both negative and positive – we come to a fuller understanding of the standards he applied to the rest of his congregation. This is especially interesting when we consider the way in which these portraits were drawn. Chrysostom's use of Biblical characters is a useful insight into his attitude to his congregation, since these characters are already presented as stereotypes within the pages of Scripture for the purposes of spiritual edification. His approach is to consolidate and expand on these stereotypes as standard-bearers for his congregation. This means that his extremely stringent standards quickly become apparent, also opening up substantial opportunities for his flock to disappoint him.

## Female role models

### Exemplary widows

While fewer on the ground, personalities from Chrysostom's own life and career are also pressed into service as *exampla* in the course of his ministry, whether negative or positive. First among these in terms of chronological importance was his mother, Anthousa. Widowed at an early age, Anthousa wins praise from her son for not having desired to remarry, despite the trials of running a household without male help. He paraphrases her despair at her widowed state:

> For no words are adequate to describe the storm-tossed condition of a young woman who, having only recently left her paternal home, and being inexperienced in business, is suddenly tortured with an overwhelming sorrow, and compelled to carry a load of care too great for her age and sex. For she has to correct the laziness of servants and to be on the watch for their trickeries, to repel the designs of relations, to bear bravely the threats of those who collect the public taxes, and harshness in the imposition of rates. And if the deceased should have left a child, even if it is a girl, great anxiety will be caused to the mother, although she is saved from much expense and fear: but a boy fills her with ten thousand alarms and many anxieties every day, to say nothing of the great expense which one is compelled to incur if she wishes to bring him up in a liberal way. None of these things, however, induced me to enter into a second marriage, or introduce a second husband into your father's house: but I held on as I was, in the midst of the storm and uproar, and did not shun the iron furnace of widowhood.[3]

Elsewhere, when speaking of a widow's ability to raise children, Chrysostom points triumphantly to the numbers of illustrious men who were reared without overt influence from any father figure, and one cannot help but wonder if he had himself and his own mother in mind here.[4] At any rate it was Anthousa's determination to do the right thing that led to Chrysostom being educated to the standard he was, and her devout Christianity was no doubt a strong influence on him also. Anthousa is therefore the ideal role model for widowhood – the standard-bearer for all others who may find themselves coping with the loss of a husband at a relatively early age. This said, Chrysostom is not above attributing feminine weakness even to his mother, as he paints her pleading with him not to go to the desert while still young, thus widowing her a second time. This request led to Chrysostom's postponement of his ascetic dream for some years. Even his own mother, therefore, can be depicted as being a hindrance to the male pursuit of virtue, regardless of what her motives might have been. This quickly and effectively demonstrates the extent to which the female character was viewed as flawed by Chrysostom and many of his contemporaries. Even a woman he is prepared to allude to as a positive role model, his own flesh and blood, can be painted as weak and self-centred on another occasion.

The prioritising of widowhood over remarriage which is so clear in Chrysostom's depiction of his mother, common in Christian thought, is not something he spoke of only in relation to his mother. He is consistent in this attitude in his sermons, just as he was in his earlier written treatises. The preacher is even inclined to outstrip Paul's severity in this respect, longing to categorically forbid second marriages, but unable to, since Paul declared them to be legitimate. He wishes he could forbid second marriages or at least denounce them as wanton behaviour, but since Paul has declared that a woman did not sin through being married he is unable to do so.[5] Here it is clear that Chrysostom is very much against remarriage, in spite of claiming to accept it. Thus, although in his homilies we will see the manner in which he offers instruction to women within conventional female roles as wives and mothers in order to assist their chances of salvation, and also to further his conversion plans for the ancient city, his preferences still seem to lie with those women who choose the path of celibacy, since this is as yet the truest form of devotion to God. The cares of family and husband, even the second time round, take up too much of the woman's time to allow her to belong to the admired group of widows within society who rank second only to the virgins.

The best known 'real' female influence in Chrysostom's life is of course the deaconess Olympias, about whom much has been written in recent years, in no small part due to the fact that there seems to have been some spark of attraction between the two, in spite of their respective ascetic leanings.[6] Kelly remarks in an aside that those scholars who have applied a Freudian interpretation to Chrysostom's interaction with Olympias 'are entirely correct in so doing'.[7] Olympias was another celebrated widow in Constantinopolitan society, with a huge inheritance to support her status. So wealthy was she that the emperor Theodosius, a cousin, was intent upon remarrying her in order to safeguard the family riches.[8] But Olympias was determined to devote the rest of her life in a celibate state to God. Her determination in this respect won Chrysostom's admiration, and familiar words of praise in which he speaks of her overcoming her female limitations and becoming like a man in her courage and her resolve. We will see elsewhere how women who transcend their normal gender boundaries to the extent of becoming like men are a source of grave anxiety to Chrysostom. Here, though, it occurs only within a spiritual sense. It may also have been that he felt this instance was acceptable, since Olympias very obviously played a female role when interacting with the bishop. Leader of an order of nuns in a convent established next door to the episcopal palace, Olympias visited Chrysostom's establishment every day in order to prepare meals easily digestible by his ravaged system. Sometimes it is said that she shared those meals with him. In this respect she acts out the domestic and the submissive role in their relationship, creating a virtual household between convent and episcopal palace. Chrysostom plays the dominant role – both by being the waited upon in domestic terms, and also by adopting the role of advisor to her in political, spiritual and financial situations. He took this role sufficiently seriously to even suggest that she be more careful in the distribution of her money, donating only to worthy causes and not everyone who came begging.[9] This will appear all the more interesting when we see later how Chrysostom urged his audience to be generous in their almsgiving, regardless of the recipient, since it was not for mere mortals to judge who might be worthy of receiving their charity. No doubt the uses the Church might have for Olympias' money made Chrysostom more jealous of how it was disposed. There is much to suggest that Olympias went her own way in this respect, and was considerably more independent than Chrysostom would have liked to think. But it would seem that she was happy to at least play the role of submissive female, enabling his more authoritative stance.[10] He was therefore able to confirm his own masculine superiority by considering his greater ability in such financial matters.

This same kind of relationship can be traced in many of the letters written to Olympias by the exiled Chrysostom. Although her side of the correspondence no longer survives, we can determine from his replies that she was concerned for his health and physical comfort, thus carrying on the feminine role of nurturer, even from afar. Likewise he maintained the stance of spiritual guide and comforter, as he urged her not to lose heart while waiting for his recall. Once again, therefore, he was able to retain the position of superiority, even though he was the one in exile.

Chrysostom had similar relationships with a number of wealthy ascetic women within Constantinople, although none is documented or discussed to the same extent as that with Olympias.[11] What is most interesting about these examples drawn from his circle of family and friends, and what will become apparent as we progress throughout the body of this work, is that Chrysostom's attitude to, and respect for, these individual examples of female virtue are in marked contrast to his more customary remarks about women in the course of his preaching. It is a clear instance of his private position being quite separate from his public stance when dealing with a wayward congregation. In his preaching he is consistent in his affirmation of female inferiority, and yet in his personal relationships, especially with Olympias, he accords women with far higher levels of ability, often entrusting them with important diplomatic or missionary tasks. It is this duality in his approach that makes the homilies of Chrysostom all the more interesting, and we can only wonder to what extent a contemporary audience would have been aware of his double standards.

## The empress Eudoxia

It might be asked whether Chrysostom was so complimentary about these women because they were genuinely impressively virtuous, or because their wealth and social standing purchased them an automatic right to respect.[12] One strong argument against such duplicity on his part lies in his relations with the empress Eudoxia. His turbulent dealings with this particular woman have been well documented by those examining his friends and enemies and his dramatic fall from grace in the last years of his career, such as Kelly and Liebeschuetz. At the outset of their dealings with one another, Chrysostom's attitude to Eudoxia was one of approval, as he described her piety and fervour in accompanying a procession with a martyr's relics to the city. He speaks of her in the same terms as those ascetic women who were the focus of so much of his admiration, telling of her adoption of a stance akin to that of a handmaid while walking in the procession, clinging tightly to the relics and not allowing her physical weariness to turn her aside from her devotion.[13] Like the ascetics, Eudoxia has cast aside her worldly status and is, temporarily at least, careless of physical discomfort or royal dignity.

With the Affair of the Tall Brothers, however, Chrysostom's relationship with the empress deteriorated rapidly. The entire business extended over a period of two years, during which Chrysostom frequently alternated between being in and out of royal favour. Kelly suggests that Eudoxia was herself a hot-tempered and impetuous woman, and she was by no means constantly opposed to Chrysostom during this period. However, sources indicate that he grew steadily more outspoken on the topic of imperial wrongs, even going so far as to compare the empress to the Old Testament character Jezebel.[14] A new dispute between Chrysostom and the visiting Syrian bishop Severian arose, and there was much bickering and tension in ecclesiastical circles in Constantinople. Eudoxia had become fond of the Syrian and his preaching, and so stood against Chrysostom in this instance. However, as the arguments wore on and mob violence between opposing factions increased, it was she herself who made the first move in appeasing Chrysostom. With a great flair for dramatic spectacle, she visited him in his church and set her infant son on his lap, pleading with him to find some solution to the problem. Eventually she persuaded him to give way, and there was a publicly staged reconciliation between all parties.[15] Kelly speaks of this incident as marking a turning point in Chrysostom's career, in which he lost his superior standing with the empress. Certainly she seems to have been responsible for orchestrating the resolution of the crisis, and she created the theatrical atmosphere of the plea to Chrysostom and his subsequent return to his congregation. This was something much more usually the role of Chrysostom himself, and it must have struck him hard to be the actor in one of his dramas rather than the director and producer. However, Eudoxia cleverly adopted the role of suppliant in this play, and outwardly deferred to his greater knowledge and ability – leaving it to him to find a solution. She thus allowed him to emerge as the dominant player, even as she got what she wanted. In this way even the empress showed herself to be somewhat constrained by societal expectations of what was appropriate for her sex.

This truce between Chrysostom and the royal household was obviously an uneasy one, however, and unfortunately short-lived. The controversy surrounding the Tall Brothers deepened, and Eudoxia was embroiled in its very centre by her public support for them. During this time (403) Chrysostom preached a sermon attacking female vices and weaknesses. We do not have an exact note of which homily this was, and as we shall see, many of Chrysostom's sermons contained violent anti-female remarks which could be seen as directed at people actually present in the church just as easily as generic chauvinist rhetoric. Regardless of his intentions, however, as a result of the prevailing climate of distrust and suspicion, this particular outburst was represented to the empress as a deliberate attack specifically on her person. Kelly thinks it may well have been a thinly veiled rebuke, with the bishop under the impression that she had been conspiring with his enemies against him.[16] But an affront, however oblique, to Eudoxia, was an insult to the emperor, and the incensed royal couple must naturally have felt less inclined to support Chrysostom in his contest with Theophilus. Condemned to exile after the Synod of the Oak, Chrysostom is said to have preached a number of angry sermons, railing against Eudoxia in terms that compared her again to Jezebel, and also to Herodias, the queen who had conspired to bring about the beheading of John the Baptist. He was exiled from the city only to be recalled a day later on account of Eudoxia's suffering a miscarriage, which some sources say coincided with an earth tremor also striking the city. Evidently the empress still felt a strong degree of innate respect for God's representative on earth, in spite of the tension between them.[17]

Once Chrysostom agreed to return to the city, things seem to have proceeded calmly for a number of months, until the day on which a silver statue of Eudoxia was dedicated amid much celebration in the city. The triumphant procession unhappily coincided with Chrysostom's liturgy, and the customary singing and dancing drowned out his own preaching. Never slow to attack offenders, Chrysostom again lashed out, calling such rituals insults to the church. Naturally reports of this quickly reached Eudoxia's ears, and she was understandably furious. A new set of charges was brought against the tactless bishop and he was exiled completely in June 404.

As mentioned earlier, it is important to remember that Chrysostom had accumulated a number of very powerful enemies without the empress, and so his many public clashes with her should not be seen as the sole reason for the demise of his career. Indeed Eudoxia's death in October 404 did nothing to lead to his recall or the decrease in hostility against him, since he remained in harsh exile until his own death in 407. However, his lack of caution in his dealings with her shows not only Chrysostom's perhaps deliberate lack of political adroitness, but also the lengths to which he was willing to go in prioritising his version of the Christian community above secular concerns. Eudoxia's position of immense power, influence and wealth in no way protected her from the bishop's acerbic tongue, which would seem to clear him from any charges of hypocrisy in his dealings with the female members of his community. What we do see is a man so intent on Christianising the society around him that he threw caution to the winds when it came to speaking of the female sex and its flaws. Even within his sermons on the Pauline epistles there are some passages sufficiently virulent, and aimed sufficiently high, for us to speculate that Eudoxia may have been the intended target. In *Homily XI on Ephesians*, Chrysostom speaks angrily to a woman, not specified, whom he accuses of spitting on him and aiming blows at him in her disgust for him, and thus of buffeting the church itself.[18] This outburst could well relate to Eudoxia's continued clashes with Chrysostom and what he perceived as her disrespect for church institutions. Alternatively it could simply be an attack on female lack of respect in general. *Homily III on Colossians* shows the preacher complaining of a similar lack of respect for his person and his position of authority.[19] He forcibly reminds his detractors that as long as he sits on the episcopal throne he holds dignity and power, regardless of his personal foibles. Once more this could be directed at the empress or other high-ranking officials who sought to depose him, and it may be representative of what Holum calls the struggle between bishop and empress over her *basileia*.[20]

### Biblical females

There is one final group of women in Chrysostom's homilies who need to be discussed at this point, and these are the examples, good and bad, he draws from the pages of the Bible. Much like the contemporary ascetics we will see Chrysostom allude to at a later stage, these women established standards for the congregation to live up to, or to avoid sinking as low as.[21] The positive examples come largely from the acquaintances of Chrysostom's hero, Paul, those women who offered him hospitality and financial support throughout the course of his missionary work. Chrysostom examines Paul's greetings to these women, and concludes that they are singled out by the apostle on account of their superior virtue, their austerity, and their ascetic leanings.[22] The female followers of Paul in Rome are similarly praised, admired for their virtue which rises above all the conventional trappings of femaleness, 'the gorgeousness of this day, the adornments of dress, the costly jewellery, the anointing with perfumes'.[23] It would seem, however, that in the case of these disciples of Paul, Chrysostom really only has cause to mention them as part of his exegesis. Paul's greetings to them occur within the passages Chrysostom intends to expound for his audience, and so it is necessary for him to discuss them and the reason for their mention. He does not dwell on any of these characters in great detail, but he is quick to exploit their appearance within the epistles in order to shame the rest of his audience into better behaviour – a process that will become very clear as we discuss it in greater depth in the following chapters. In addition to Paul's female helpers, however, the example of Mary, mother of Christ, is held up as a shining light for all Christians, but also as a means of shaming men into greater attempts at virtue, lest they be outstripped by mere women:

> For we are honoured, in that there are women of this sort among us, but we are put to shame, because we men are left so far behind them. But if we recognise how they come to be so greatly adorned, we too shall speedily overtake them. Where does their adornment come from? Let both men and women listen. It is not from bracelets, or from necklaces, nor from their eunuchs either, or their maid-servants, or gold embroidered dress, but from their labours on behalf of the truth.[24]

What is interesting about this and other remarks like it is the way in which historical women are employed by Chrysostom in his use of a guilt-shame complex on his audience. We will see him do this with those members of the audience who are present in front of him, pointing out their sins in order to shame them in front of their peers, or alluding to virtuous characters to embarrass the less exceptional inhabitants of the community into better behaviour. But here he is also willing to work the same process on those women from the pages of Scripture, shaming his audience by comparing them to people who are not even accessible to them on a daily basis. These exemplary women are also described largely in terms of their forsaking of riches. The truest evidence of their holiness is their unadorned appearance, while, by extension, the wearing of jewels and fancy clothes is seen as a great barrier to communion with God.

Even Old Testament characters are employed in this process, with figures such as Rebecca and Sarah coming in for frequent praise from Chrysostom on account of their humility and obedience to God's will. In the case of these women he mentions them spontaneously, without prompting from Paul. This could simply be because he was particularly fond of these well-drawn characters from the Old Testament as examples for his congregation to follow.[25] It could also be, however, that Chrysostom hopes to appeal to his audience for their cooperation by demonstrating that 'even' the Jewish community had exemplary women among their number, while those who are members of the true Faith are shamefully idle in their pursuit of virtue. This is something that has been recently discussed by Elizabeth Clark in her *Reading Renunciation*. Here she suggests that Chrysostom employed Old Testament *exempla* both for the purposes of shaming his audience, and for demonstrating that the gap between Old Testament and contemporary *mores* was not as large as some people wished to believe. Even the seemingly dubious actions of Sarah, in sending her servant girl to Abraham's bed, can be rehabilitated if one considers that she was undertaking to perform her wifely duties as best she could. In this way Chrysostom can demonstrate a steady tradition of continent behaviour from the earliest Jewish societies to his own time.[26]

Within the pages of the Bible, however, there are also examples of evil or ensnaring women, who are once more described with the conventional language of censure for women. One character Chrysostom returns to on a number of occasions is the queen of Egypt, wife of Potiphar, who tried to seduce the great leader Joseph. She is vilified by Chrysostom for her abandonment of an appropriately female role. It was she who played the aggressive part in trying to win over Joseph, and as such she behaved more like a man than a woman. At the same time, however, she is also described as being unable to control or discipline her emotions, a characteristic female failing. In speaking of her thus, Chrysostom makes this woman the object of the audience's gaze, just as he does with more contemporary examples of misbehaving women:

> For you know that for the woman who is in love to such extent, nothing is so lowly but she can bring herself to say it, taking upon herself the attitude of a supplicant. For this woman was so debased, even though she was wearing gold, and was of royal dignity, that she threw herself perhaps at the knees of the captive boy, and perhaps even entreated him weeping and clasping his knees, and resorted to this not only once, or twice, but many times. Then he might have seen her eye shining very brilliantly. For it is probable that she would set off her beauty, not in a simple manner, but with excessive care, as if hoping by many nets to catch the lamb of Christ.[27]

This picture of Potiphar's wife is painted so vividly for two main reasons; she is an interesting character in herself and is behaving in a scandalous and therefore fascinating manner. But she is also an example of how not to behave, and the more scandalous and debased Chrysostom can make her appear, the greater his chance of making this apparent to his eagerly watching and listening audience.

One other Old Testament character attacked for inappropriate behaviour is Job's wife, on account of her questioning of God's will in sending so many sufferings to Job, and of her husband's own inexplicable patience in bearing them: 'For when indeed the wife of Job speaks, a Devil is at work.'[28] Thus again the female is perceived as instrumental in the temptation of the male through her innate curiosity, and her lack of patience and self-discipline. As we progress, however, it will become apparent that Chrysostom's approach to these female *exempla*, either from his own acquaintance, or from the pages of Scripture, were merely variations on his approach to those faceless women who formed part of his parish. We will see the same cycle of shame and guilt enacted on rich women sitting in front of him, using examples drawn from among their number rather than from the Bible, while both men and women alike are expected to respond to Chrysostom's tactics in order to achieve his hoped-for restructuring of the city.

## Male role models

### Friends, ascetics and teachers

Interestingly enough, in light of his prioritising of the truly masculine character, which will become apparent as we progress, Chrysostom throughout his work pays little tribute to actual male figures who may have had any form of influence on him. Understandably, his teacher of rhetoric, Libanius, is not alluded to, as an exponent of the very creed and way of life that Chrysostom hoped to see completely replaced. The preacher's audience cannot have failed to notice that Chrysostom was himself very much a product of this culture, but it is an issue which is deliberately laid to one side throughout his career. This is a clear example of the Christianisation of discourse process, whereby the shared cultural language of the inhabitants of the late antique city was overlaid with a Christian set of references. As such, Libanius, his pagan contemporaries and his predecessors, along with their ideas, are put to one side, while the Church orators and thinkers merely reiterated their familiar concepts in different terms.

The death of his father while Chrysostom was still a child meant that the preacher had no masculine authority figure to refer to in the same way as we saw him mention his mother with affection. Indeed the only living male characters we hear Chrysostom refer to in his preaching are the male ascetics in the wilderness who match his idea of true Christianity. We have seen him detail the lifestyles of such men, and the rigours they embraced for love of God. Their successful pursuit of this life was a vindication of their masculinity, yet even here, it is the group of ascetics as a whole who meet with his approval, and whom he employs as an example to spur on his more worldly audience, rather than any particular individuals:

Can you not see those who are in the mountains? They leave their houses, and wives, and children, and all distinction, and shut themselves away from the world, and clothe themselves in sackcloth, and strew ashes beneath them; they wear collars hung about their necks, and have shut themselves up in a narrow cell. And they do not stop here, but torture themselves with fasting and continual hunger.[29]

In his text *De Sacerdotio* Chrysostom introduces us to the character of Basil, the close friend of his youth. This young man is described as exceptionally disciplined in his pursuit of the philosophic life, he being the one who turned Chrysostom aside from the secular path he had begun to tread, introducing him instead to the joys of the ascetic lifestyle.[30] At this point Chrysostom speaks of his friend with respect and admiration. Indeed out of all Chrysostom's boyhood friends, Basil is the one who truly merited the title of friend in terms of the equality of their standing, and the great love they felt for one another. Yet, when news arrived of their imminent involuntary ordination, it was Chrysostom who took the lead in their deliberations as to how to avoid this calamity. He was also responsible for the deception practised on poor Basil, by means of which he managed to dodge the draft, as it were, while his duped companion was elevated to the office of the priesthood. From this point onwards in the text, we get a very sparse picture of Basil's personality, since he becomes merely an interviewer of Chrysostom, facilitating the author's revelation of his thoughts on matters such as the priesthood, asceticism and public preaching. We see Basil simply as the distraught and betrayed friend seeking some kind of explanation from Chrysostom of his recent trickery, bemusedly wondering what has gone wrong. From this portrait we can certainly see the qualities Chrysostom esteemed in a holy man – gravity, modesty, and diligence with regard to one's studies – but it sheds little light on his opinions of the more ordinary masculine character. Basil is mentioned nowhere else in Chrysostom's work, somewhat surprisingly for one who was once Chrysostom's best friend, leading some commentators to believe that he may in fact have been a rhetorical invention on the part of our author.[31] In addition to this we have already seen the ambiguous nature of *De Sacerdotio* as a text, and so characters portrayed in its pages should be regarded with a degree of caution, since they may well serve as rhetorical devices rather than realistic representations of actual persons Chrysostom knew.

### Secular and religious leaders

We saw from the previous section the extent to which the empress Eudoxia influenced the latter stages of Chrysostom's career, and how some passages within his preaching could be interpreted as poorly veiled attacks on her. In contrast to this situation, Chrysostom is remarkably restrained when it comes to the person of the emperor. It would seem that Arcadius either did nothing to overly irritate Chrysostom, or that the preacher drew the line at conflict with the supreme head of secular authority within the empire. It has also been suggested by one author that Arcadius was no more than emperor in name, with Eudoxia wielding enormous power and influence over her husband.[32] If this was the case, then Chrysostom would not have had much reason to find fault with Arcadius or any of his measures. But I cannot help but feel that if Arcadius had been so dominated by his wife, Chrysostom would have been deeply disturbed at such an overturning of appropriate gender roles, and in such a public and obvious manner. We have seen him to be unrestrained in his condemnation of Eudoxia when he felt that she had stepped out of line in her other activities, and it is unlikely that he would have curbed his tongue at the sight of an even graver offence if it existed. I would therefore hold to the opinion that Arcadius did not antagonise the bishop in any noticeable manner, and so avoided being targeted in his preaching or writing. At one stage Chrysostom alludes to the preceding emperor – Theodosius I – as the leader who threatened the city of Antioch with annihilation following the Riot of the Statues, speaking of the incident as an example of the way in which power could transform kings into tyrants.[33] In his preaching on the Pauline epistles it is, however, the only direct reference he makes to the source of secular power, and it actually says more about Chrysostom's opinions of political power than his concept of behaviour appropriate to the masculine character. Nor is there any mention of the great enemy of the bishop – Theophilus – in these sermons, indicating that the homilies on the Pauline epistles were most likely preached at an earlier date than his great clash with the Alexandrian bishop which dominated the last two years of his ministry in Constantinople.

### Biblical masculinity

Although Chrysostom has little to say about contemporary male figures, biblical examples feature very strongly in his preaching. Among his favourites from the Old Testament is Joseph, on account of his modesty and his disciplined approach to the trials he encountered. Chrysostom is particularly proud of the way Joseph fended off the sly attack of the Egyptian queen, safeguarding his chastity in spite of all her threats and promises. In doing so, his firmness and restraint stood in marked contrast to her feminine weakness and excess of emotion.[34] Joseph stands as a disciplined and restrained ruler when granted power, and an appropriate superior to the depraved desires of the queen. Chrysostom also approves of Joseph's humility, which he maintained in spite of his great sanctity, forbearing from being puffed up with pride at all the attention he receives from those in authority.[35]

The character of Job also meets with Chrysostom's approval, since his endurance of all God's tests is the ultimate sign of his masculinity, as is his restrained attitude and his resolution not to be guided by his more fickle and less enduring wife.[36] When discussing the harmony appropriate to the Christian household it is Abraham who becomes Chrysostom's role model, since he admires the respect with which Abraham always treated Sarah, even when she was unable to provide him with an heir. He would not grieve her by divorcing her or seeking his carnal pleasures elsewhere until she began to urge him to do so, sending her maidservant, Hagar, to Abraham's bed.[37] Elsewhere Abraham is praised again for being a good householder – since he enjoys the respect and loyalty of his servants, and he is able to entrust them even with seeking a spouse for his son.[38] His hospitality and generosity to travellers and strangers also shows him to be a good antecedent of the Christian *paterfamilias* Chrysostom hopes to have presiding over all the households in his community.[39]

In many ways Chrysostom's use of these *exempla* is intended to shame his audience into better behaviour so that they may not be outstripped by Old Testament characters who were, after all, Jews. This is something Ambrose of Milan also used to do in the course of his preaching. Ambrose used Old Testament characters to spur his congregation on to greater lengths so that they could live up to the 'giants of old' and so confirm a social identity for the Christian church. As such, his comparison of contemporary figures with those of the Old Testament is not quite as negative as that of Chrysostom, who intends his audience to be ashamed of their inability to measure up to characters from Jewish history.

It is when we come to the New Testament, however, that we see Chrysostom's full enthusiasm let loose. First and foremost among his heroes is of course, Paul, but he was not the only apostle who was admired by Chrysostom. Peter was also popular with him, as were the other disciples of Christ. Peter wins particular praise for the strength of his faith, and his absolute honesty in his missionary work in the early Church. Chrysostom speaks with admiration of his openness and the scorn he had for danger, such that he would not be tempted to dissimulate even in order to avoid punishment or torture.[40] It was on this account that the resurrected Christ first showed himself to Peter, being well aware of that man's honesty and great loyalty, the same qualities which made him fitting to be the founder of the Church.[41] Chrysostom's approval of these characters stems largely from their simplicity and their adherence to their standards in spite of secular distractions and political pressures. This endurance would have been seen by him as particularly masculine in nature.

However, in spite of this admiration for these characters, Chrysostom announces on many occasions that there is no one quite like the Blessed Paul, and that Paul's virtue surpasses that of all others.[42] Chrysostom is particularly approving of Paul's manner of speaking. Although lacking in a conventional rhetorical training, Paul was nevertheless very sophisticated in the way he addressed the communities under his patronage, knowing instinctively when to harangue them, when to be gentle, when to threaten and when to persuade. Although such an approach might seem inconsistent or even fickle on the part of Paul, Chrysostom understands such seeming inconstancy as part of Paul's rational plan for conversion of the Gentiles. One of Chrysostom's favourite metaphors was that of the physician, who used different approaches and cures for each patient and ailment. So too does Paul employ different methods of persuasion for each congregation at each time of his writing. Much of Chrysostom's exegesis in these homilies was devoted to an explanation for his own congregation of Paul's motives and methods, and so it became a firm policy of his to celebrate Pauline inconsistency rather than to find it inconvenient or embarrassing.[43] In general terms, such skilful speaking or writing was deemed highly important within Roman society,[44] and so by admiring Paul's abilities Chrysostom here acknowledges the traditional perceptions of gender qualifications. It is not unfair to say that Chrysostom also saw himself as having similar rhetorical gifts, thus ensuring that his own masculinity was confirmed in the eyes of his secular audience. This may have seemed additionally necessary given what we are told was Chrysostom's own unprepossessing appearance. He was of short stature, even puny, with a balding head and a face that was by no means noteworthy.[45] It may have been for this reason that Chrysostom chose to stand when delivering his sermons rather than sitting as was customary. Perhaps he was anxious to consolidate his own superiority over his audience, and by means of his often virulent and bombastic preaching he further confirmed this position in a public setting. Thus his own performance of gender fits the requirements of contemporary society.

To fully analyse his frequent references to Paul would be a full work in itself, but Chrysostom's opinion of the apostle as the epitome of the male character seems clear. As a disciplined ascetic, a brave Christian, a valiant speaker, and of course extremely virtuous, Paul fulfilled all the requirements of masculinity, within both the secular and the religious cultures of the day. He also showed the quality of endurance of hardship which Chrysostom saw as particularly necessary to be confirmed as truly male. Paul is constantly depicted as being caught up in a manly struggle or competition, and not for merely worldly reasons of rivalry, but in a quest to achieve heavenly glory.[46] And this is one of the reasons Chrysostom is so irritated by the failure of his congregation to follow the apostle's words as closely as he himself does. He urges them to read Paul's letters, and to apply themselves to his teachings, as the best possible guide to Christian living.[47] Their refusal to do so implies a distressing lack of commitment to their faith, but also a weakness in their own masculine bearing, since Chrysostom would have hoped that the proper Christian male would demonstrate his gender by his disciplined study of the Scriptures. The ignorance of his flock on this front – Old Testament as well as New – shows that they do not see things in the same light, thus forfeiting Chrysostom's Christian version of masculinity.

One area in which Chrysostom is particularly proud of Paul's achievements is the manner in which this simple man contrived to outstrip all the previous philosophers and sages who had gone before him. There is a degree, however, to which such discussions of Christian 'simplicity' were themselves rhetorical tools. Thus Chrysostom's praise of Paul and Peter as simple and untutored men, who nevertheless won a huge following, extends beyond simple admiration, and serves as part of the ongoing 'Christianisation' of discourse, whereby traditional heroes of pagan culture are replaced by their simpler, and by extension more sincere, Christian counterparts.[48] A detailed examination of

Chrysostom's treatment of Greek philosophers has in fact been carried out, from which it emerges clearly that the preacher is for the most part derogatory in these references and comments, allowing only that Plato was the most skilled and best known of the group. The author of this study fails, however, to engage in any analysis of Chrysostom's approach, and ignores the many passages in which the prelate actually appears to echo the philosophic sentiments of the Greeks with a Christianised bias. It is interesting to note from his survey, however, that within the homilies on the Pauline epistles, it is Plato who appears most often as a figure of comparison, with Aristotle being the next most popular reference.[49] It is not exactly clear as to why this may be so, but it could be that Chrysostom felt that his audience's familiarity with Plato was a direct threat to the status of his beloved Paul. If he could consistently attack the one philosopher who was immediately known to his congregation, even through allusion, then the great achievements of Paul in his missionary work could be thrown into sharper relief. Incidentally, in Chrysostom's work as a whole, Josephus is the Greek writer who ranks next to Plato in terms of frequency of reference.[50]

Throughout his preaching Chrysostom frequently alludes to Paul's uneducated status, calling him a simple tent-maker, and yet for a formerly devout and well informed Jewish male this depicted lack of tutoring cannot have been strictly accurate. Nevertheless, Chrysostom can often be heard to boast that a man with no official training, and without lofty rhetoric, attracted many more followers than Plato or Aristotle, and also had the advantage of seeing the true meaning of life more than these misguided Greeks ever had. Thus Paul confirms Chrysostom's views of strength of character being necessary for the preaching of God's word, and for any claims to masculinity:

> So that there is a need, not for grandiose words, but for strong minds, for skill in the Scriptures and for powerful thoughts. Do you not see that Paul put to flight the whole world, that he was more powerful than Plato and all the rest?[51]

Such views also contribute to Chrysostom's related project of Christianising the prevailing discourse of the day, since if he can demonstrate Plato's intellectual achievements as insignificant, and even as somehow failures, he can establish Paul's message in their place, thus rewriting the cultural heritage of his new Christian citizens.

\*

These then are the personalities Chrysostom uses as his measures for the rest of his congregation. Devout Christians can aspire to the virtuous heights of a Paul, a Joseph or a Virgin Mary. Less diligent members of the faith can be reminded of the task ahead of them. And for all involved, the dangers of straying from the path of righteousness are presented clearly. It is now time to see how ordinary members of the congregation fared in relation to such lofty role models.

# 6

# Construction of Gender: Two
# Compelling Models

If we compare the picture of Orlando as a man with that of Orlando
as a woman we shall see that though both are undoubtedly one and
the same person, there are certain changes. The man has his hand
free to seize his sword, the woman must use hers to keep the satins
from her shoulders. The man looks the world full in the face, as if it
were made for his uses and fashioned to his liking. The woman takes
a sidelong glance at it, full of subtlety, even of suspicion. Had they
both worn the same clothes, it is possible that their outlook might
have been the same.

Virginia Woolf, Orlando, ch. 4

## Introduction

The past number of years have shown an increase in scholarship on the
place of the female sex in antiquity, and this is often the first place people
look when considering the broader concept of gender. Much of the work
that has been done in the area of gender studies and ancient history has
involved the rediscovery or reclamation of the female experience from the
past. This has been highly worthwhile work, but after its initial importance it may perhaps seem a little one-sided. In the rush to acknowledge
the importance of women's lives and behaviour as providers of information on the society of antiquity, the more holistic question of gender can
often be lost. While we have become familiar with the ways in which the
writers and thinkers of antiquity spoke of and treated women, less
thought has been given to how the male sex was actually constructed by
these same commentators.

While much has already been written and said about John
Chrysostom's attitudes to the female sex therefore, his overall, and more
complex, attitude to gender has been somewhat neglected. Studies of
women in Chrysostom's work have also largely concentrated on the opinions presented in his ascetic texts, thus ignoring the majority of ordinary
women he would have encountered on a daily basis in the course of his
ministry.[1] It is only very recently that some discussion of his attitudes to
these ordinary women and to the male sex has been introduced, particu-

larly by Blake Leyerle, but as yet almost nothing has been said about how his attitudes to gender matters might have influenced his Christian ministry.

This will be the subject of the following chapters as I demonstrate the way in which Chrysostom's spoken directions to each of the sexes can inform the gender debate on a number of levels. On a most basic level, his sermons show how he himself thought of both women and men in his congregation. They also demonstrate the way in which gender was generally constructed within the society of the day – what were the norms, what was considered aberrant, and how these norms were enforced. And finally Chrysostom's preaching shows the way in which he used an appeal to gender as a means of bringing his aspirational Christian city into being.

## Constructing gender

Studies in feminist issues over the past number of decades have left us familiar with the concept of gender being a cultural construct far more than a simple fact of biology. Over time and through constant reinforcement, a society comes to an agreement as to what the embodiment of a particular sex should mean in terms of appearance, behaviour and place within that society. Deviation from these established 'norms' is presented as shameful and dangerous, and as somehow undermining the organisation of that very society. This 'policing' of gender roles was both a warning to potential transgressors, but also a means by which these roles could be continuously bolstered and defined for subsequent generations. In Graeco-Roman society this reinforcement was done through the literature, the religion, the politics and even the art of the community. Myths and stories familiar to even the youngest members of the community showed the stark consequences of ignoring one's allotted place within the cosmos. Publicly displayed sculptures or even the paintings adorning pottery for everyday use performed a similar function. In many cases the message was conveyed by means of a negative *exemplum*. So stories of wild women – the Amazons or the character of Medea – or effeminate men were illustrations of how not to behave at the same time as providing entertainment for the senses. At the same time there was a constant stream of images of the ideal to act as a counterpoint to the examples of aberrant behaviour. Dutiful wives and daughters were displayed on household vessels and were praised on grave markers. They were singled out for praise by politicians and philosophers, along with the characteristics which had qualified them for such notice. Men worthy of praise were spoken of effusively, or displayed in public art performing manly duties, leaving the observer in no doubt as to the divide between the behaviour appropriate to each of the sexes.

This is a process which Christian writers and leaders continued within their own sphere of influence. In addition to existing constructs of gender we now have Christianised versions of the same. The process is almost identical, and the chief difference lies in the fact that now the *exempla* are drawn from Scripture or the growing body of hagiography that comes into existence during this period. Chrysostom is only one of many Church leaders who continued to construct gender roles as he wished to see them by means of his public preaching as well as his less widely available written work. However this aspect of his work has not yet been examined to its full extent, particularly the crucial role played in this process by his sermons.

What will quickly become apparent as we begin to explore this area is the way in which it is negative comments about either of the sexes that come to the fore. We may be forgiven for dismissing some of Chrysostom's tirades – particularly those directed at women – as the rants of a misogynist on this basis. But just as Greek stories of wilful women coming to tragic ends show what the ideal should have been as well as the consequences of misdemeanours in this respect, so too the Christian outspokenness on such issues of gender demonstrates the Christian ideal that was being deviated from.

### On the *subintroductae* – a study in gender roles

A pair of treatises penned by Chrysostom in his early career provide us with an immediate introduction both to his own conceptions of appropriate gender roles, and to some of the processes by which these roles were constructed. Two tracts on the *subintroductae* were intended as a warning to ascetics whose righteous way of living had fallen into disrepute. The *subintroductae* were virgins who cohabited with male ascetics, and they seem to have been a growing cause for concern among church leaders of the third and fourth centuries AD. There were many reasons offered by the ascetics involved as to why they should have such living arrangements. Some women claimed to need the physical and financial protection of the male. Some men felt they needed the housekeeping skills of the female. And still others argued that living in such close proximity actually allowed them to improve their chances of salvation as they triumphed over these greater levels of temptation.

What is most likely, however, is that practical reasons compelled many women to approach asceticism in this manner, due to the structure of society and the ascetic culture of the day. Asceticism was intended as a withdrawal from the trappings of daily life, and a conscious effort to deny the body of worldly pleasures. The easiest way to achieve this was to move as far away from normal society as possible. Out in the desert, or in high mountain caves, ascetics could be sure that they would not be distracted by the noise, activities or expectations of a conventional community. They would have the space and the silence necessary to concentrate on their spiritual devotions. But this was a way of life that was easier for men than for women. It was not necessarily safe or practicable for a woman to venture out in desert areas alone, and there were very few monastic groupings of women at this time. Needless to say, females were not welcomed to those male monastic communities which did exist, although stories do survive of intrepid virgins managing to conceal their sex until after their death, being accepted into such communities as devout eunuchs instead.

Women who were intent on living such an austere life were therefore forced to take a slightly different approach. Many of them remained within the confines of the city, and so practised asceticism in an urban context. Of course this meant that the distractions of a more traditional life could not be fully ignored, and indeed ascetic women may have stood out quite prominently among their more conventional peers. It also meant that they had to conceive of new living arrangements. Some women were lucky enough to possess independent wealth, or to have tolerant families. These women could keep their own establishments, or at least practise their self-denial in the safe surroundings of the family home. But others were actively defying their families and friends through this lifestyle choice, and so could not count on their hospitality to the same extent. Formalised female ascetic communities, or 'convents', were thin on the ground, and the response of some women was therefore to create their own ascetic community wherever possible. At times this could be with an ascetic of the opposite sex, and hence the problem of cohabiting virgins, or *syneisaktism* as the practice was sometimes called.

Chrysostom and other Church leaders like him were dismissive of such reasons for these living arrangements, concerned instead about the overwhelming danger to the souls of those involved. In Chrysostom's treatises we can see his great unease at the scope for abuse of Christian asceticism that has been exposed by these wayward celibates. Suddenly Christian ascetics are in danger of becoming a laughing stock, as outsiders can point to these irregular households and raise eyebrows at the levels of celibacy and self-denial being practised by those involved. It is a threat that requires immediate action from Church leaders, and while some worked to create Church laws outlawing *syneisaktism*, Chrysostom's response is to focus on the gender roles and interaction in question, appealing to people through the most basic relationship of their society. He devotes his energies to demonstrating how *syneisaktism* encourages women to become more forceful in their dealings with members of the opposite sex, while men become passive and accepting of a lowlier role in the household. This is against all the normal rules and expectations of the society of the day with regard to gender relations. Chrysostom hopes to appeal to his readers' sense of what is right and proper, and he will work towards this by painting as many negative effects of the behaviour of the *subintroductae* as he possibly can. And so his portrayals of the women concerned focus on weaknesses and foibles that are seen as intrinsically female, and do much to compound this image. Men are portrayed as emasculated and pathetic, depictions that speak for themselves since everyone reading would have had the same conventional ideas as to what it meant to be male. These treatises show clearly the models of gender which were in operation in late antiquity, and they show this through a discussion of a possible breakdown of these models – it is both an economical and an effective approach.[2]

But opinions of the possible audience of *Adversus Eos qui apud se habent subintroductas virgines* and its fellow tract, *Quod Regulares Feminae Viris Cohabitare non Debeant*, are divided. Some scholars believe that the joint treatises were written and circulated in the course of Chrysostom's Antiochene career, while he was still enthused by the ascetic lifestyle.[3] Others feel that they were written in response to the corruptions Chrysostom found in Constantinople when he took over the bishopric of the capital city.[4] And still others feel that perhaps the treatises had two airings, the first in Antioch, and the second in Constantinople in answer to a perceived need.

We must next consider the range of the audience for such written discourses. Since the problems addressed are those pertaining to the ascetic lifestyle, it would seem likely that the treatises were first circulated among the celibate community, which was not necessarily as large as we might be led to think from the enthusiastic tone of contemporary writings. Even if Chrysostom's treatises were released for more general circulation, we would have to ask questions regarding the literacy rates in late Roman society. It would seem probable that such works would be chiefly accessible to the upper, educated classes, rather than to a broader social audience.[5] Blake Leyerle, however, has recently discussed the entertainment value in these texts, and their similarities in structure to the dramatic plots of Aristophanes among others.[6] This could mean that Chrysostom constructed his treatises so as to be comprehensible and interesting to as wide a range of people as possible, hoping that their message would filter down through the various strata of society. Hence an extra interpretive layer is added, which would colour our understanding of gender representations within these discourses. It may not have been solely the ascetic community who came to hear of the views on *syneisaktism* expressed by Chrysostom, and indeed such a limited audience may have been entirely contrary to his intentions. He may have hoped that a wide audience would have access to his warnings regarding the threat to societal order if gender roles in the ascetic framework were not properly monitored. This view would also be supported by the suggestion of two publication dates for the treatises, broadening the audience base still further. Certainly *syneisaktism* does seem to have been a widespread phenomenon in the ancient world, since no less than six church councils in the fourth century alone found it necessary to issue legislation on the subject, while it was even a practice which spread as far as the Celtic society in Ireland and Britain.[7]

Chrysostom's rhetoric in these tracts shows him to be resolute in his opinion of women as naturally sinful and weak. What is more interesting is the seeming paradox that this inherent weakness is held fully responsible for the downfall of the men involved. Chrysostom describes them as having been 'enticed' into the women's houses under ascetic pretences; 'That man's madness is your work,' declares Chrysostom,[8] while elsewhere he claims that these women:

> ... make all the men they capture easy for the Devil to overcome. They render them softer, more hot-headed, shameful, mindless, irascible, insolent, importunate, ignoble, crude, servile, niggardly, reckless, nonsensical, and, to sum it up, the women take all their corrupting feminine customs and stamp them into the souls of these men.[9]

This blunt statement clearly embodies the contemporary perceptions of female nature as something weak, vice-ridden, and dangerous.

Regardless of the ultimate audience of these texts, therefore, what emerges most clearly throughout is the way in which Chrysostom automatically speaks of these dubious virgins in terms more normally applied to prostitutes. He depicts them as actively seducing the male ascetics in a manner similar to the commercial activity of harlots. This 'active' approach implies a transgression of the gender boundaries in place in society, leading women to engage in commerce and trade, and to hold prominent, if not reputable, places in the public gaze. A true ascetic, however, like Pericles' model wife, should shun such publicity, and prefer instead to hold fast to her anonymity as a symbol of her modesty and virtue. The flaunting air of the *subintroductae* is anathema to Chrysostom, since it represents a flagrant breach of the rules of behaviour laid down for each of the sexes if society is to function effectively.

Disgusted as Chrysostom is at the behaviour of these women, he does have an existing opinion of women as inherently sinful, which leaves him at least unsurprised at the depths to which they could sink. He has different expectations of the male sex, however, based on conventional perceptions of the sex as having the monopoly on attributes such as virtue, courage and intelligence. This different starting point means that Chrysostom has a different plan of attack when it comes to reprimanding those male ascetics caught up in dubious living arrangements. When he wishes to rebuke men for their transgressions he bases his arguments on the platform of how they are expected to behave. He appeals to the male sense of superiority and rational thought so as to employ his favoured cycle of public shame and guilt. When attacking those men who had introduced virgins into their ascetic homes, or had agreed to enter into the domicile of a female celibate, his chief concern is that in acting thus, these men have forsaken their natural superiority over the female sex. The prelate is by no means convinced that such a lifestyle in fact demonstrates any greater degree of self-mastery, as has been claimed in some instances, since he cannot quite believe that the men involved manage to maintain an aloof bearing when faced with such obvious temptation. Instead they succumb to the temptations of these young and attractive virgins, thus abdicating their rightful position of eminence in any male-female interaction. Such a confounding of the divinely ordained hierarchy within society is deeply distressing to Chrysostom, and it surfaces very regularly indeed in his homilies. It is a position that illustrates both his deep personal distrust of the female sex, but also his increasing fear that the appropriate behaviour of the devout Christian male is quickly being forgotten in the pursuit of transitory and temporal indulgences. So enmeshed are such men in the affairs of secular living, and in gratifying the desires of their flesh, that they no longer stand out within the urban community as being obviously Christian, a matter of grave concern to anyone in a position of leadership of the faith.

In the treatise directed against those cohabiting male ascetics, Chrysostom begins with an amazed questioning of those men who would voluntarily introduce such temptations into their lives, sympathising with what can only be a diseased mind to remain thus oblivious of the danger of such a situation. He argues against hypothetical justifications brought to him by imaginary male ascetics, and consistently reminds them of the dangers facing their immortal souls. Proof that they are in such peril arises from the fact that they find themselves in thrall to their *subintroductae*, unable to tear themselves away, but instead fanning the flames of their illicit desire by constantly looking without being permitted to touch.[10] When laying out his position in this methodical manner, Chrysostom remains true to the opinion we are familiar with from other Christian authors – namely that women are responsible for arousing desire in men. In line with this, Job refused even to look at a virgin, let alone live with her, while Christ declared that any man who looked at a woman lustfully had already committed adultery with her in his heart. Here we see the concept of the eyes as a gateway to the soul through which temptation can enter, but also the female as the object of the male gaze. The problem is not laid entirely at the woman's door, however, for in this treatise, although the distinction is sometimes almost too subtle for notice, Chrysostom is most worried about the consequences of a man allowing himself to be enslaved to such an extent. When speaking to females, Chrysostom speaks of them as the causers of male sin. But now, when addressing the men directly, he targets them for their willingness to be so easily ensnared, using this appeal to their sense of autonomy as a means of encouraging them to take some responsibility for their own morality. To fall prey to feminine wiles in this manner shows an abdication of male superiority and strength, which calls into question their very worthiness to be classed as men at all. Such foolish male ascetics demonstrate their new slavery by their fantastic excuses for their living arrangements; the woman is poor and needs financial assistance, the woman needs male protection from the attacks of society, her natural inferiority requires his support and aid. The men concerned are in fact claiming to enact traditional male roles within society; protecting the females, engaging in commercial activities, and generally interacting with the civic world on behalf of the women. Chrysostom however, scorns these excuses, pointing out that there are many ugly, disabled or aged women who can be thus helped if they wish to proclaim their masculinity through action, and yet these men have a predilection for assisting only the young, rich and pretty females. By acting in this way, they have called into question the integrity of the church body as a whole, but also their own gender status:

> This is why we have won the reputation everywhere for ourselves of being gluttons, flatterers, and above all slaves of women, because we have dashed to the ground all the nobility given us from above and exchanged it for earthly servility and shabbiness.[11]

We can see already the preliminary qualifications for being considered truly male, foremost among which is a maintaining of a position of superiority over the female. Indeed servility of any kind is inappropriate for the masculine character, whether it be to foolish women or worldly concerns, something which will become more and more apparent as we turn to the sermons. Closely linked with this adoption of a slave position is the sin of excess, which is also deeply worrying to Chrysostom. It is women who are generally deemed most guilty of the sins of over-indulgence and lack of control; ' ... for a man is by nature stronger than a woman, more like us in his needs, and not so extravagant',[12] thus reiterating the concept of female giddiness and excess which is familiar to us from the preceding treatise. This is even seen as the way the sexes were created by nature, smoothly overlaying the traditional Aristotelian model with a new Christian bias. For a man to confound this ordered structure through a failure to moderate his desires or his actions is for him to call into grave doubt his own fitness to be called a man. Indeed such ascetics now run the risk of becoming more like women than men, as they immerse themselves in the domestic and material concerns of the females, running backwards and forwards on trifling errands, collecting mirrors from silversmiths, discussing aromatherapy with perfume makers, concerning themselves with linen and umbrella makers, weavers and embroiderers, instead of with the prayers and devotions which are more properly their work as celibates.[13] Once more Chrysostom conceives of this behaviour as 'ignoble slavery' and even compares these men to eunuchs, making very clear the extent of their emasculation:

> Even in this holy and formidable spot [the church], they proclaim their lack of self-restraint to everyone and what is still worse, they show off about things which ought to make them blush. The men receive the women at the door, strutting as if they had been transformed into eunuchs (*kai anti tôn eunoukhôn ginomenoi sobousi*) and when everyone is looking, they guide them in with enormous pride. Nor do they slink away, but go so far as to glory in their performance.[14]

The inability of these men to control their slavish behaviour, or to exercise any kind of restraint on their desires, is what appals Chrysostom in this scenario. And the consequences of this adopted servility are suitably dire; the men are described as eunuchs, the ultimate insult for any self-regarding male. But what is also apparent here is the extreme importance attached by Chrysostom to the concept of the public gaze. Indeed within this treatise he announces that although it will seem shocking to many people, it is nevertheless worse to commit a small sin in full public view, than a larger transgression behind closed doors.[15] It is what is perceived to be done that is of consequence under this scheme of things, and this is a philosophy that will have a considerable bearing on Chrysostom's public preaching. The fact that these men are not the least bit ashamed of their behaviour and that they go so far as to make a performance of their wrong-doing, merely serves to compound the offence in Chrysostom's eyes.

The images of emasculation continue, even drawing from classical precedents. The Christian lifestyle is seen as a contest, in which the devout male is a well-armed warrior. But if such a warrior were suddenly to forsake his duties and retire from the battlefield to sit among mere women, he could justifiably be run through with a sword in disgust. The episode in the *Iliad* in which Paris does indeed sit in the apartment of Helen rather than fight in the war of his making, springs instantly to mind here, and Hector's response to such behaviour was indeed to consider his brother as something less than a man.[16] Further on these cohabiting ascetics are compared to lions shorn of their manes – the symbol of their sex and their superiority together – while Chrysostom believes that men who behave in this manner cannot but be vagabonds or the rabble of society. With this list of comparisons, he works again to arouse the compelling cycle of public shame and guilt. A shorn lion is very obviously shamed, just as a man who appears as a eunuch, or effeminate, or even as fallen in social rank, is also shamed in the eyes of the public. A fear of similarly obvious indignity and degradation should therefore frighten the readers into better behaviour. Chrysostom's choice of eunuch imagery not only shows the severity of his own disapproval therefore, but may also have been calculated to most quickly arouse the disgust of the audience of this treatise. Eunuchs as a societal group were increasingly reviled in the late empire, especially as their influence within aristocratic and imperial circles grew. Thus they were regarded with suspicion and distrust, both because of this influence, but also on account of their failure to conform to any of the established gender categories. They were in fact, something of a 'third sex'.[17] Yet they operated in the full glare of the public eye, opening the way for a prurient interest on the part of the rest of society which Chrysostom seems to have been very aware of, and chooses here to make the most of. The eunuchs who wielded such power and influence in high circles of the civic community became social pariahs. By appealing to the importance attached to public opinion within this community, and by employing the imagery of eunuchs with all the attendant pejorative overtones in his rhetoric, Chrysostom works to alter the direction of these errant ascetics' behaviour. He urges them to regain control of their own affairs, and to avoid the indignity of their current slavish behaviour.

Within both of these treatises therefore, we can see the establishment of parameters for masculine and feminine behaviour deemed appropriate to the devout Christian by Chrysostom. They are not indeed new or unique to his thinking, or Christian thought in general, but Chrysostom makes extensive use of this inherited culture in his public preaching as well as in his written texts, and this approach has not yet received much attention in recent scholarship. I have given these treatises so much attention in these pages in order to highlight the fact that Chrysostom's opinions on these matters were fixed at a very early stage in his ministry (if we accept the earlier publication date for these treatises on the *subintroductae*) and that he was by no means slow to proclaim them. Indeed this method seems to become his favourite angle of attack whenever he is concerned as to the behaviour of the members of his flock, and sadly there was much to worry him in the cities of the late Roman empire. The opinions contained in these tracts therefore show us a model of gender relations which Chrysostom held dear, and which he applied to all his dealings with the community in his efforts to guide their behaviour in such a way as to bring his uniquely Christian city into being.

This leads us naturally to regularly preached sermons, in which a similar pattern of gender construction becomes apparent. An ideal model or example of behaviour is juxtaposed with an aberrant version. Each side of the offering is presented as vividly and with as much colour as possible. The usual expectations of 'decent' society leave the audience in no doubt as to which side they should privilege, but Chrysostom's tones of disgust and scorn compound the issue. And so the traditional construct of virgin and whore is invoked in a Christian context, with admirable women being entirely virginal, and transgressors painted unequivocally as prostitutes. Similarly, admirable men are righteous, reasonable and masculine, while those who err become somehow effeminate, emotional and weak. But as well as those who embrace the ascetic lifestyle, Chrysostom must also address the middle ground, as it is here that most of his congregation would seem to dwell. And so a number of other dichotomous pairs are invoked for the benefit of his listeners: rich and poor, passive and aggressive, sinful and virtuous. We will now see how these different extremes are employed in the course of his preaching.

### Virgins and whores

The best established of these artificially constructed dichotomies, and one of the most frequently employed in Chrysostom's preaching, is that of the virgin and the whore. But for all its advanced age, it is a pairing that Chrysostom uses to brilliant effect in his preaching and in his written texts. Indeed so strict is his division between virtuous and wayward women that we hear of very few people indeed who meet his high standards, and so the vast majority of women he alludes to or even addresses during the course of his preaching would seem to fall into his 'whore' category. While Chrysostom is quick to allude to contemporary women, either present or absent, who have irritated him through their wayward behaviour, he is more reticent when it comes to mentioning women who have impressed him through their practice of virtue. There are a number of possible reasons for this muted approach, one of which could be a straightforward lack of 'good' women for the preacher to notice in the course of his sermons. Or perhaps he felt himself constrained by current rules of etiquette which demanded that he did not speak too directly about or to virtuous members of the female sex, lest he impinge on their modesty and on the honour of their families. Or maybe Chrysostom was engaged in an effort to retain the attention of his audience, and recognised the fact that good people were not necessarily the most interesting topics of discussion, especially when so many less wholesome distractions were competing for notice!

Determined not to bore his audience, therefore, Chrysostom restricted his comments on those women who met with his approval to one specific context; namely that of shaming or encouraging the rest of his congregation into greater efforts in their quest for redemption. To this end, his admiration for those women who had embraced the ascetic lifestyle beyond all the perceived limitations of their sex, was boldly declared for all to hear and take notice of. Such women are presented to his congregations as examples of the truest form of philosophic living, which should spur more lethargic members of the audience on to greater lengths in their pursuit of virtue. In speaking of them in such terms, however, Chrysostom makes no effort to avoid expressing the same kind of surprise evident in the words of other Church Fathers, that the female sex should be capable of such impressive deeds:

> Girls who are not yet twenty years old, who have spent their whole lives in private quarters, and in a delicate and effeminate style of life (*en thalamois kai en skiatrophia*) in inner rooms full of sweet ointments and perfumes, reclining on soft couches, themselves soft by nature, and made still more tender through their over indulgence, who all day long have had no other business other than to adorn themselves, to wear jewels, and to enjoy every luxury, who never waited on themselves, but had numerous handmaids standing beside them, who wore soft material softer than their own skin, fine and delicate linen, who revelled continually in roses and similarly sweet odours – yes these very women, all of a sudden, seized with Christ's flame, have put aside all that indolence and even their very nature, have forgotten their delicateness and youth, and like so many noble wrestlers, have stripped themselves of that soft clothing, and rushed into the midst of the contest. Perhaps I seem to be reporting incred-

ible things, nevertheless they are true. These then, these very tender maidens, as I myself have heard, have brought themselves to such a level of severe training, that they will wrap the coarsest horsehair about their own naked bodies, and leave their tender feet unshod, and will lie upon a bed of leaves: and what is more, that they keep vigil for the greater part of the night, and that they take no heed of perfumes or of any of their old delights, but will even let their heads, once so carefully dressed, go without special care, with the hair just plainly and simply bound up, so it does not fall into impropriety.[18]

Chrysostom here embarks on a very detailed description of the appearance of these virgins, making them the object of both his gaze and that of those males in his audience. This was a process whereby, through the words and rhetoric of the speaker, women were made into objects to be 'looked at'. It is an approach we will see Chrysostom enact on many occasions as we progress through our analysis of his preaching on both of the sexes and on wealth. By using his verbal skill in this way, Chrysostom quickly focuses the attention of his audience on those individuals he wishes to employ as good or bad examples, bringing them to life within the confines of his discourse.[19] Here his audience are encouraged to view these admirable virgins, and share their preacher's surprise that such virtue could be displayed by members of the female sex. This surprise, in turn, should contribute to the sense of shame felt by these listeners that they have been outstripped in moral rectitude by mere females.

Chrysostom had presumably conceived his technique carefully, but to us today it may seem to be a somewhat dangerous approach to take in his discussions of ascetic females. These women are supposed to be inviolate, separate from all male influence, and divorced from their sexuality, something which Chrysostom himself insists upon. And yet by speaking of them in this way, the preacher paradoxically maintains the perception of them as sexualised beings and objects of desire. He deliberately draws the attention of his audience to their bodies and physical appearance, while he carefully conjures up the ambivalent image of these women wrestling in the athletic arena – again highlighting the physical form and its movements. It is as if Chrysostom presumes that the danger inherent in such a description can be adequately contained within the confines of his sermon, and the physical boundaries of the church building itself. His congregation, he hopes, will not linger on these images outside of the religious ritual being enacted, but will rather internalise the moral recommendations attendant on these descriptions, leaving the vivid pen-pictures behind them. Otherwise, the lustful thoughts aroused in the male members of his audience by such descriptions would in fact serve to further corrupt their souls, rather than redeem them.

Ironically, Chrysostom is deeply concerned regarding similar images when they are conjured up in the secular arena of the theatre, and he worries about the long-term effects such displays of the female body can have on his male flock. He fears that the men will continue to mull over the physical forms presented to them on the stage, thus allowing sinful thoughts and even actions to follow. His apparent confidence that similar dangers could not possibly arise from his verbal displaying of the female form is interesting to note, perhaps signalling an uncharacteristic naivety on the part of the preacher. Alternatively, this may have been a carefully conceived strategy on his part, in which he employs language as a legitimate outlet for the desires that are innate in all humans. Rather than trying to ignore the existence of such lusts, Chrysostom may have decided to furnish them with a 'safe' means of indulging their desires – within the linguistic boundaries of his sermon. His vivid and lingering portraits of exemplary women might therefore serve another function other than simply holding the flagging attention of his audience. They might also have a cathartic role to play, allowing the audience to indulge their senses in a legitimate form. This particular approach seems to presume that the closure of a church homily would be more effective in containing 'negative' thoughts and emotions than the more open forum of the theatre. We can only assume that Chrysostom was taking a calculated risk. Potential problems however arise in the fact that the method of reception on the part of the audience cannot be predicted or controlled, hence our sometimes surprised reactions on reading these texts in today's context. Similar reactions to Jerome's writings have already been noted by scholars, as his letter of advice to a young virgin paradoxically contains passages lingering on all the fleshy delights and lustful behaviours he wishes her to shun.[20]

Aside from this objectifying of the female figure in examples such as the above passage, Chrysostom's rhetoric also displays the extent to which his views of the female sex are traditional and conventional. The ascetic labours of these young women now mean that they merit comparison with the male sex in his eyes – they are like wrestlers, and they have embarked on a training course as severe as any male athlete. They have also forsworn all the conventional trappings of femininity which the preacher spends so much time detailing at various points in his work. Thus they have put aside their very nature. Here his description of the clothes and accessories which had been the trappings of their former lifestyles is such that these adornments become tantamount to a signal of gender. Under this scheme therefore, it becomes clear that abandoning fine clothes, perfumes and an idle lifestyle is equivalent to abandoning one's very sex. In this context gender becomes very apparent in the public mind of late antique society as a system of behaviour and appearance, rather than simply a biological given, and it is this perception of sexual boundaries as modes of behaviour which Chrysostom operates on when trying to monitor the behaviour of his flock.[21]

It is interesting to note that even here, while dealing with those who live as austerely as they possibly can, wealth figures strongly in Chrysostom's rhetoric as he judges the achievement of such women by the lavishness of the lifestyle they have given up. The more refined and aristocratic they were to begin with, the more surprising and the more inspiring their new commitment. Melania the Younger was also extolled in these terms by her biographer, who detailed the delicacy of her nature in an anecdote regarding a skin irritation she suffered from in her youth on account of the fine embroidery on her gown being too coarse for her standards of physical refinement. And yet when she embraced the ascetic lifestyle, she clothed herself in horsehair for all the hours of the day and was granted the strength by God to endure it. The greatness of this event was directly proportional to the greatness of the wealth left aside by Melania in her zeal to experience the philosophic life, while the changes in her clothing marked her progress in its practice.[22] Jerome's close friend Paula is also extolled in similar terms, since her ascetic contribution could be measured by the extent of the poverty she embraced for herself and her descendants in her eagerness to spend the considerable wealth of her family on works of charity. This poverty could be measured outwardly by the shabby dress and unkempt appearance of the saint. Even her lack of hygiene could be interpreted in a positive light.[23]

In this way suffering and poverty become indices of sanctity in Christian literature. By lingering on the details of the privations ascetic women underwent, and on their altered appearance and health, Chrysostom and authors like him actually conspire to make such women objects of envy. So the untidy and unwashed Paula, or Melania with her skin irritation, can actually become figures to emulate. Their virtue is emphasised through the lingering descriptions, while the more pedestrian members of the congregation are shown models for their own behaviour, with pain and poverty becoming the signals of their relative success.

Elsewhere in his sermons, Chrysostom spends time instructing ascetic women in the modesty appropriate to them and their chosen style of living. In *Homily XII on Colossians* he declares that they have no place at a wedding, especially since marriage ceremonies in late antique society have become mere excuses for debauchery and pagan excesses. The traditional custom whereby virgins attend to the bride along with respectable matrons does not meet with any disapproval on the part of the preacher, since both parties represent the life-stages the bride is moving between. But it has become rare, he laments, that weddings are as subdued and tasteful as a simple celebration of this rite of passage would warrant.[24] It has become common for harlots to be present at the nuptial celebrations, such is the extent to which they have been integrated in society, and their attendance at a ritual that is to do with chastity and self-discipline is a mockery, hence the need for true virgins to keep to their chambers rather than mixing with such undesirable company. Despite the fact that virginity and the chaste lifestyle is worthy of all praise and admiration, Chrysostom is intent on ensuring that the virgins themselves should not become public talking points, and hence should keep out of the public view as far as is possible – a call that is somewhat ironic considering his own transformation of them into objects of the male gaze within his discourse.

In this and similar passages we see Chrysostom employ the conventional dialectic between whore and virgin which played such a large part in many discussions of the female sex in the ancient world. The purity and virtue of the ascetic women is highlighted all the more through juxtaposition with the lewd and unrestrained behaviour of the prostitutes present at the wedding ceremony, or the hustle and bustle of daily life in the civic arena. It is a comparison worked through vivid descriptions of the appearance of both extremes, and of their respective actions. Gender is once again shown to be a matter of behaviour, but it is the unfeminine behaviour of the harlots that calls *their* sexual status into question. They are forward, abrasive, and brash in manner, and above all, they have intruded on the male territory of commerce and financial activity. This collapse of order in gender matters is deeply worrying to Chrysostom, hence his insistence on guarding the moral standing of the ascetic women in his care. The behaviour of the prostitutes at weddings is described in terms of a contagious disease by Chrysostom, and it is this spread which he wishes to prevent by means of separating the virgins from the source of danger, and by holding it up to his audience as an example of something to be avoided at all costs.

A further cause of anxiety for the preacher is the way in which ascetics themselves might feel prompted to mix too freely with the outside world in general – not just with the morally bankrupt harlots at a wedding feast. This becomes apparent when he insists that poverty is no excuse for their mingling with crowds. Presumably some virgins would have pleaded that their straitened circumstances made it necessary for them to attend these wedding feasts, and other public gatherings. It is possible that their attendance guaranteed them a nominal payment. Chrysostom, however, is reluctant to sanction such behaviour, believing that a good character is more priceless than any amount of wealth. Even slaves who possess no property have modesty which they should safeguard.[25] In this respect, Chrysostom may seem to have become caught up in his idealised version of ascetic living to the extent that he is blind to the realities of life for single women within Roman society. It does much to illustrate his high standards, however, and what his aspirational Christian city might look like.

Aside from remaining secluded from the public gaze and refraining from social intercourse with those whose gender status is questionable, the next most obvious way for the virgin to prove her worth is in her modest and sober dress. We will later see Chrysostom speak about the way in which false virgins can do much with their dress to enhance their appearance and render themselves more alluring. This, however, constitutes an act of adultery against their Bridegroom, who is the Lord himself. Again therefore, harlots and virgins are set in close proximity to each other within the sermon, thus underlining one of Chrysostom's major fears; namely that conventional societal boundaries, by which one might instantly recognise a person's character and occupation, have been utterly broken down. It is no longer possible to tell which are the courtesans and which are the ascetic women, he says, since both take such pains with their appearance as to seem preoccupied with attracting male notice. This is not in the true spirit of the ascetic contest, which is again compared to male athletic competitions such as wrestling:

> Observe the contestants and wrestlers in the games. Do they worry about their style of walk or their dress? No, but despising these things, and simply throwing about them a garment dripping with oil, they care only for one thing, to wound, and not be wounded. The devil stands grinding his teeth, waiting to destroy you in every way, and yet you remain unconcerned, or concerned only about this satanic ornament (*su de meneis apêskholêmenê peri ton kosmon touton ton satanikon*).[26]

Here, those female ascetics who are sufficiently modest in their dress and behaviour win the accolade of being compared to male athletes – well known and admired within secular society. Virginity for females automatically entails a rising above their femininity. Those women who have only the appearance of modesty overlying a corrupt soul actually embody what Chrysostom considers to be customary female vices; vanity, frivolity, falsity and seductiveness. In doing so, they discredit the very category of virgins, and become the laughing stock of those who should rightly be their inferiors. In considering marriage as only second best to a life of celibacy, Chrysostom was in agreement with many of his contemporaries and predecessors.[27] But now he paints a picture of married women and housewives ridiculing and despising those ascetics who are in fact more concerned about worldly matters than they, whose whole business it is to reside in the world, themselves are.[28]

Despite the fact that true virginity ought to be a greater state than marriage, or even widowhood, Chrysostom is elsewhere adamant that its practitioners should not be given to pride or arrogance on that account. He refers to the foolish virgins in the New Testament who had not sufficient oil for their lamps, interpreting the oil as representative of charity and humility. On this account they were barred from the wedding feast by the Bridegroom. Contemporary ascetics should therefore remember this, and always conduct themselves with due humility in the face of God.[29]

This is just a brief survey of some of the occasions throughout his preaching on the Pauline epistles in which Chrysostom focuses on virgins and holds them up as examples to his audience. It might seem from this that he spends a large portion of his preaching time on the subject, but throughout the homilies preached on the Pauline epistles, there are in fact very few passages relating specifically to virgins. This is perhaps surprising if we recall Chrysostom's own interest in the philosophic life, but might indicate a firmer grasp of reality than we might sometimes expect of him. Given the proportion of his congregation who seem to have been wealthy, it is unlikely that many of them felt tempted to abandon everything and retire to the mountains or the desert to commune with God. Thus there would have been very few females within Chrysostom's flock inspired to follow the examples of the holy women described above in any practical sense. He was also speaking mainly to city dwellers who had established their own households and family units, and so had very obviously chosen a different path to those who were committed ascetics. His main reason for mentioning celibate women, therefore, is to establish a standard of behaviour that everyone in his congregation, male and female, can aspire to within their existing lifestyles. The comparison of virgins with harlots is especially effective and necessary in this regard, since the pictures of prostitutes painted by the preacher function as warnings and deterrents to his audience. Such courtesans are the lowest elements within society, despised by all. No one would therefore wish to be accused of behaving or appearing like them. The more graphic Chrysostom's descriptions of prostitutes, the more disgust for their behaviour he can hope to stir up in his audience, therefore dissuading them from consorting with, or behaving like, such whores. To his male listeners he says:

> You would never choose to wear a piece of clothing which your slave wears, being disgusted because of its filth, and you would rather go naked than use it. But will you abuse a body that is unclean and filthy, and which is used not only by your slave, but by numberless others, and not be disgusted? ... Tell me, what if you and your servant should go to the same woman? And I would hope it was only your servant, and not, let's say, the executioner! You could not bear to take the executioner by the hand; but you kiss and embrace her who has become one body with him and you do not shudder, nor feel fear![30]

Chrysostom knows very well that this is a skin-crawling picture, but by speaking so bluntly to his congregation, and employing a rhetorical device so skilfully, he hopes that he can influence them for good. On those occasions when descriptions of virgins and their lifestyle are juxtaposed with such graphic accounts, as in the wedding description above, Chrysostom works to present an ideal for his flock to strive for immediately after they have been persuaded to despise the contrasting alternative.

From such passages in Chrysostom's homilies, we can see the extent to which his opinions of the female sex were conventional, and acquired from a traditional cultural heritage. The juxtaposition of virgin and whore in his sermons indicates the manner in which he sees women as inherently sinful, while meriting approbation only when they succeed in transcending their assigned gender limitations. This rise above their 'nature' could only be accomplished in Chrysostom's mind by embracing the ascetic lifestyle. Fresh from his own experiences of self-denial and physical mortification, Chrysostom held resolutely to his belief that such an existence was the only way to achieve true closeness with God. When practised by men, such asceticism was both a demonstration and an improvement of their innate capacity for virtue. When women followed suit they achieved a transcendence of their natural weakness and sinfulness.[31] But these assumptions regarding the apportioning of virtue and the capacity for improvement among the sexes were of course not original Christian concepts. Aristotle, many centuries previously, felt that the female soul was an incomplete version of the male's, lacking the authority and full deliberative powers possessed by the free-born male.[32] Judaism also based its religious instructions on the premise that virtue was a distinctly male property; its practice both proved one's masculinity and helped to maintain it at an appropriate level. The Jewish female, on the other hand, was deemed incapable of practising the self-restraint that was a necessary component of virtuous living.[33] Such opinions were founded on the assumption that gender was more a matter of behaviour than biological appearance.[34] Within a Christian context, therefore, the ascetic lifestyle marked a change in visible behaviour on the part of those females who embarked on it, and thus presumably a shift in how their gender was perceived. Hence the many plaudits we find in patristic literature for those females who had become more like men than the women they were created, by means of their great virtue and bravery in accepting the trials of virginity.

# 7

# Gendered Sins

At one time his wife had been mad about him. Her love had expressed itself in an attitude of servility the only effect of which was to estrange him still more. Once gay, generous and fond, she became, as she grew older (like flat wine which turns to vinegar) a woman of difficult moods, shrill-voiced and nerve-ridden. In the early days of their marriage she had suffered much but complained little; had seen him run after all the village drabs, hang about all the places of ill-fame, and come home to her at night physically exhausted and stinking of liquor.

Gustav Flaubert, *Madame Bovary*, ch. 1

## Feminine sins and transgressions

What should have begun to emerge from our study so far of Chrysostom's attitudes to the sexes is the way in which he sees certain sins or misdemeanours as being the natural preserve of women. The corresponding assumption is that there are other wrongdoings that are more likely to be committed by men. As Chrysostom dwells on the instances in which members of his congregation fall from grace, his intention is not only to persuade them into better patterns of behaviour, but also to continue his bolstering of the gender models appropriate to his ideal society. Strange though it may seem, therefore, even immoral activities can be used as indices of gender status.

In this respect it quickly becomes apparent that love of ostentatious display and pride in one's appearance is a rebuke most often directed at females in Chrysostom's audience. He has a strong sense of the vanity and fickleness of that sex, which leads him to lay the blame for many of the abuses of wealth in society at their door. It is very telling that it is women who are accused of the heinous crime of having silver chamber-pots commissioned for them, while men are merely criticised for making the funds available for such pettiness:

Do you pay such honour to your excrements, as to receive them in silver? I know that you are shocked at hearing this; but those women who make these things ought to be shocked, and the husbands that minister to such distempers.[1]

He then returns to his attack on the women who have sparked off this extraordinary tirade, warning them that if he should have occasion to speak to them again on such an issue he will bar them from his church; 'For what need have I of a crowd of distempered people?'[2] Within this particular sermon, Chrysostom has indeed spent some time reprimanding his male audience for having excessive pride in their intellectual abilities and in their social standing, but he does not accuse them of anything so foolish as he here targets the females with. It is a frequently occurring contrast that highlights the different expectations Chrysostom, and most of his peers, had of the different sexes.

Similar attitudes come to light when Chrysostom discourses on the appearance of women, and the pains they take to enhance their God-given beauty. They are accused of vanity, frivolity, of insulting God, and of working to seduce male admirers. But these are all relatively passive sins, and sins founded on a base of deceit, or at least an attempt to obscure the true nature of things. Why should a woman care so much about her appearance that she paints it red and white, against the design of God, unless it is to ensnare some man into adultery or fornication?[3] Here Chrysostom both views and depicts women as temptresses and the causers of male sin. It is a largely passive form of wrongdoing, since the women are deliberately working to become the objects of the male gaze. They want to be looked at, so that their planned seduction can proceed. But in spite of this passivity of approach, Chrysostom is clear in his belief that they are responsible for the wrongdoing of any man they might thus attract. It is a somewhat paradoxical position in which a passive seduction can lead to active guilt. Prostitutes, as we have seen, were more active in their bids to seduce men, and hence were all the more vilified by the preacher. They were seen as having completely transgressed the normal bounds of activity for their sex.[4] Ordinary married women who strive to ensnare men through their external appearance are at least being conventionally feminine in their transgressions. Their sins are passive in nature – and even sly. Women are described as using their looks to ensnare others, enhancing these looks through vanity and self-obsession, and of being generally selfish and over-emotional. We will see that male sins discussed by Chrysostom are in an entirely different league.

One interesting development occurs when Chrysostom has occasion to personify sin itself as a female character in an effort to bring home to his audience how abhorrent it is. Since the construction of the female sex has been so far directed towards emphasising its inferiority to the male sex, this simile has two distinct results. In the first place, the personification of sin as female does much to confirm existing negative impressions of the sex as a whole. But for those who have allowed themselves to fall into a sinful life, it is doubly ignominious since not only have they transgressed against God, they have also allowed themselves to be dominated by a force that is characterised as female:

For it is absurd for those who are being conducted to the kingdom of heaven to have sin as an empress over them, and for those who are called to reign with Christ to choose to be the captives of sin, as though one should hurl the diadem off his head, and choose to be the slave of a frantic woman, who came begging, and was clothed in rags (*daimonôsêi gunaiki kai prosaitousêi kai rhakia peribeblêmenêi doulouein etheloi*).[5]

On occasions when Chrysostom has cause to refer to members of other religious groups, it is interesting to note the way in which the sins attributed to Jews and heathens are also markedly similar to those deemed particularly feminine. The Jews especially are accused of avarice, ostentatious display and sly practices.[6] Thus once again, the lowest standard of behaviour is that of the female, or the non-Christian. The subliminal equation of the two sends clear messages to the remainder of the congregation as to what is acceptable from them.

## Masculine sins and transgressions

Just as with women, when we come to look at Chrysostom's references to men in his homilies, we see a range of transgressions that the preacher sees as particularly troubling when displayed within the male character. Such sins can be regarded in two different, but related lights. The sins are generally active in nature, which implies that they are associated with masculinity. But at the same time, the very fact of sinning implies a loss of control, and specifically a loss of masculine control. At its very worst this loss of control can lead to a degree of effeminacy that is almost classified as a third sex.

To begin with there are transgressions that mark a lack of control that calls into question the very masculinity of the transgressor. Lust, avarice and pride are all sins that result from a lack of self-discipline and diligence in the pursuit of virtue. Chrysostom speaks derisively of those who have too haughty a bearing when they perceive themselves to be in full public view:

For why, I ask, do you stiffen your neck? Or why do you walk on tiptoe? Why furrow your brows? Why stick your chest out? You cannot turn one hair white or black, and yet you go around with as lofty a bearing as if you could command everything. No doubt you would like to have wings, and not walk upon the earth at all![7]

Here, as elsewhere, Chrysostom makes an appeal to reason. Man cannot change his divinely ordained state or nature, and so it serves little for him to strive to rise above himself in this manner. It is a similar approach to that used by Chrysostom when he tried to persuade his congregation that decorating their transport animals would merely serve to detract attention from themselves – a kind of polemical appeal to logic.

But the pride that is rebuked here is regarded by the preacher as a male transgression. There is a passage in the homilies on Thessalonians in which Chrysostom paints the picture of the wealthy woman entering church, shaking out her gown behind her and being entirely preoccupied with thoughts of who might be watching her, and in examining this passage the contrast in Chrysostom's conceptions of gendered sins becomes apparent.[8] Close on the heels of this rebuke directed at such women, Chrysostom turns his attention to men who behave in a similar manner. However, instead of accusing them of mere fickle vanity, Chrysostom levels the greater charge of pride against them. These men are not so much concerned as to how the folds of their robes fall, or whether their jewels shine particularly brightly, although these of course are important issues, but more whether they are noticed and esteemed as wielding power and influence within society. Their priority is to establish a crowd of admirers and followers about them, and to carefully regulate this group so that no one detrimental to the public image of the man might be seen to be close to him. And so the poor, those begging for alms, and other lowly petitioners are kept well back from this personage by his loyal servants:

> Then when he is seated, the cares of his house immediately intrude themselves, distracting him completely. The pride that overwhelms his soul overflows. He thinks that he does a favour both to us, and to the people and perhaps even to God, because he has come into the house of God. But how shall the man who is so inflamed, how can he ever be cured?[9]

In this regard we can even see the way in which undue attention to appearance can have different ramifications depending on the gender concerned. Women are reprimanded for caring too much for their actual dress and accessories, while these men are more zealous with regard to their body language as an indication of status and power. In the case of women, their frivolous concerns are purely superficial, extending no further than the desire to be noticed on account of one's appearance. In the case of the male members of Chrysostom's congregation, however, outward appearance is seen as an index of social standing and so to be cultivated on that basis.

Adultery and fornication are two other sins that particularly concern Chrysostom when speaking of the spiritual welfare of his male flock. Adultery was the one area in which Christian teaching had made most difference to Roman secular approaches. Whereas pre-Christian opinion had considered it natural for any male to enjoy romantic affairs, whether he was married or no, Christians considered fornication to be a sin of equal magnitude for both sexes, regardless of marital status. It had always been considered unlawful for a female to be unfaithful to her husband, but this condemning of what had been deemed 'normal' male activities was a new departure within late antique society. This is not, of course, to ignore various philosophical schools such as Stoicism, or even generally held opinions of ideal behaviour, which had often urged restraint on the Roman male. Christianity, however, due to its higher profile and its effective manipulation of public discourse, succeeded in drawing much more public attention to this new doctrine than had previously been accorded. As a result it was only natural for Chrysostom to address most of his remarks on adultery and associated sins to the male members of his congregation, whose behaviour in this regard most needed changing. As part of his arguments against the sin, Chrysostom continues to urge discipline and control over the physical body, much as he does when speaking out against pride or avarice:

> Therefore, I beg you, let us guard against this sin. For just as we punish those women who, although married to us, give themselves to other men, so we too are punished, not by Roman laws, but by God.... The man who has not learned to fornicate will not know how to commit adultery either. But he who wallows with harlots will also arrive quickly at adultery, and will pervert himself, if not with a married woman, then with those who are single.[10]

This equality of approach to the issue of chastity is what leads Chrysostom to speak of the Christian marriage in terms of mutual respect in *Homily XIX on I Corinthians*:

> But in this place we hear no more of greater and less, but it is one and the same right. Now why is this? Because his speech was about chastity. 'In all other things,' says he 'let the husband have the prerogative; but not so where the question is about chastity.'[11]

In other sermons it is made clear that marriage is an unequal partnership, where the woman functions as the deputy to the male, and where her duty is to respect and obey, while it remains his prerogative alone to love, something we will see played out in the coming chapters. In this particular sermon, however, Chrysostom is concerned with the disciplining of sexuality, and so has no qualms about speaking of chastity as something equally required of both men and women. But men who insist on behaving in an unchaste manner, and who consort with harlots, allow themselves to be overcome with dishonourable passions, thus making themselves vulnerable to public mockery:

> For what can be more debased than a man keeping watch at the doors of the prostitutes' rooms and being beaten by a lecherous woman, weeping and lamenting, and turning his superiority into shame? (*ti gar an genoito aiskhroteron tou thuraulountos pro tôn pornikôn oikêmatôn, kai rhapizomenou para pornês gunaikos, kai*

*klaiontos kai oduromenou, kei tên heautou kataiskhuntos doxan;)*
And if you also wish to consider the loss, recollect, I say, the expenditure of money, the extreme risks, the contests of rival lovers, the wounds, and the scars received in such skirmishes.[12]

The transgression here is doubled in its enormity by the fact that not only have such men allowed themselves to be enslaved by their baser passions, but that they have allowed themselves to be lorded over by mere women, thus offending against the natural order of things as well as against their own masculinity.

These few examples indicate that Chrysostom saw one fundamental difference in wrongdoing between the sexes. Women, we will remember, were accused of largely passive and deceptive sins, of working slyly to seduce the male and thus destroy his soul. Men, on the other hand, are generally accused of active transgressions – fornication, adultery, theft, robbery, avarice, covetousness. In each of these instances the male actively performs his sin, rather than adopting more passive means. Even those transgressions which lead Chrysostom to describe them as unmanned, or bestial, are active sins performed without any restraint whatsoever, with the added insult that such behaviour is carried out in public. We saw female wrongdoing contained, for the most part, within the walls of the home. Responsibility for preventing these misdeeds becoming more public rests with the husband or the father, and the discipline he exerts within the household. For a man with this kind of power and responsibility to himself err in full view of the public gaze compounds the nature of his sin, hence the anxiety expressed by Chrysostom on these issues.

The crucial exception to this division of wrongdoing into passive female transgressions and active male ones is the sin of homosexuality, in which men are very definitely seen as behaving in a passive manner – the point which makes it such a heinous crime to begin with. Chrysostom, therefore, maintained his concept of gender boundaries even in the area of immorality and wrongdoing, with sins carefully apportioned to each sex depending on the nature of the transgression. And in the case of the male sex, moderation is the virtue he urges them to cleave to for the welfare of their souls, and to live in an appropriately Christian manner within the community:

He who does not commit adultery or fornication, who avoids gluttony and drunkenness, who does not adopt a showy appearance, and who takes enough care of himself as is sufficient for health reasons only, glorifies Christ through his physical body.[13]

Aside from this gendering of sin, however, the one misdemeanour that particularly upsets Chrysostom is one that threatens to overturn all divisions between the sexes, and this is the abandonment of the natural order of things. This becomes especially apparent when we hear him preach on the danger of allowing women to hold an instructor's role within the church administration, or even within the home. We will see his opinion on this issue in the following chapters, and his anxiety that such forward-ness on the part of women is an attack on established gender boundaries. But he also sees it as paving the way for other sins on the part of the male if he permits this initial step to be taken. Once a woman is granted pre-eminence in such matters, there follows a relentless slide into degeneracy. There is an overturning of God's established order, and it implies that the man has permitted this to happen on account of more base desires. We see women urged to remain within their proper place, with appropriate submission to their husbands, on account of the first transgression of Eve in this respect. Here, however, we see Chrysostom make it very clear to his male listeners that it is their responsibility to ensure that the women find no opportunity to rise above their ordained station. His appeal to God's divine plan is frequent in this respect, by means of which he hopes to appeal to the devoutness of his listeners, but also to their natural pride in being marked out as superior to all others from the beginning. Indeed God is described as having a fourfold plan of man's position as leader of the human hierarchy:

> There is a second scale of superiority, indeed, also a third, and a fourth. The first is that Christ is our head, and we are the head of the woman; the second is that we are the splendour of God, but the woman is of us; the third is that we do not come from the woman, but she comes from us; the fourth scale is that we are not made for her, but she for us.[14]

This illustration of the paradigm for the Christian hierarchy between the sexes follows on from Chrysostom's instructions to women to keep their heads covered in church on account of their inferiority, joined with a similar injunction to men to remember the head covering appropriate to them lest they forfeit their privileged situation. When dealing with the female, whether it is in the domestic and private sphere, or in more public circumstances, the male is urged by Chrysostom to at all times remember his innate superiority, both of intellect and strength. He must therefore take on his role of guide and mentor as befits this superior standing, rather than allow the weaker and more talkative sex to take over in such a crucial area. The same holds true when Chrysostom counsels the husband to treat his wife with respect, and to refrain from beating her, even if she provokes him. The male should endeavour not to be angry, since she is after all less fortunate than he in matters of intellect and self-restraint. Even in the face of insolence the husband is advised:

> 'But the woman is insolent', he says. Remember, however, that she is a woman, the weaker vessel, whereas you are a man. For this reason you were ordained to be a ruler; and you were assigned to fulfil the

role of a head for her, so that you might put up with the weakness of her who is put under you.[15]

While this teaching ensures that the female stays in her subordinate role within the household, it has the added effect of persuading men to control their anger as better befits Christians, and truly masculine, disciplined characters. By exaggerating the insolence of the nagging wife, Chrysostom increases the nobility of those men who manage to respond with rational arguments instead of blows, as well as flattering them by such an appeal to their logic and their superior intellect.

It is this superior intellect that permits the man to fill the role of instructor to the woman in matters of doctrine. Her weaker mind needs to be guided by a stronger, and when she seems to be going astray, the responsibility is her husband's to restore her to the right path. Chrysostom in fact argues that this is a mutually beneficial scheme since if the woman must be submissive to the man to the extent of being taught, she will behave in an orderly manner, and thus harmony will reign in the household. But if the onus is on the husband to instruct his wife in this manner, he must be constantly attentive himself while in church and when learning of Christian matters, since if she were to err through his failure to inform her of her duties, the fault would be his.[16] On another occasion the preacher appeals to male superiority as he envisages the husband guarding his wife from excessive grieving or distress if some calamity should befall the family. Her natural weakness might lead to her being traumatised by the loss of riches or jewels, but the appropriately virtuous man will counsel her to make light of her loss and bear it with a calm fortitude.[17] Again we see Chrysostom both flatter and persuade his male congregation to take responsibility for their own moral welfare, and to bolster their own masculine attributes.

### Manly men and the third sex

We have seen ample evidence so far of Chrysostom's perception of gender as a public performance. There is a certain type of behaviour that characterises a man, and misuse of riches, or some of the other transgressions we have seen listed, are certainly not fitting examples of this behaviour. Indeed excess in this respect casts doubt on even the humanity of those who are guilty. What emerges is a further slant on the way in which gender is constructed within the society of the day. Men who fail to live up to Chrysostom's high standards are deemed to have failed their gender and their humanity in some way. This is an idea returned to in *Homily XIII on Timothy*, in which Chrysostom muses upon what it is that actually defines a man. The term he uses is *anthrôpos*, and so not necessarily gender specific. But the definitions Chrysostom uses are all drawn from male examples in Scripture, and from traditional concepts of male activities rather than female ones. He cites the 'heathen' definition of a man as one who is rational and capable of intelligence and acquiring knowledge, and as we have seen already, this was deemed a particularly male preserve. But Chrysostom is reluctant to be guided only by a pagan cultural heritage and so turns for support to the Old Testament.

There he alludes to Job as one who can particularly be defined as a man, since he was upright, respectful and fearful of God, and disciplined in his avoidance of evil. Chrysostom would no doubt also have approved of Job's exceptional powers of endurance in the face of the many hardships God chose to send him. Quoting Proverbs, he also decrees that the quality of mercy gives added value to the already great figure of man. The emphasis then is placed on the necessity of constantly working to maintain one's gender status, lest one forfeit the right to be regarded so favourably:

> The Scripture refuses to acknowledge those who do not answer to this description [of a man as someone merciful and God-fearing], even if they have intelligence, and are more than capable of acquiring knowledge, but it calls them dogs, and horses, and serpents, and foxes, and wolves, and animals more contemptible, if there were any such. If a man is of such a kind then, he who lives in pleasure is not a man; for how can he be, who never thinks of anything that he ought? Luxury and sobriety cannot exist together: they are mutually destructive.[18]

Chrysostom makes it quite clear that Scripture has chosen particularly lowly animals for purposes of comparison, and that he agrees with this choice. The animals are either servile and enslaved, or deceitful and destructive, thus demonstrating the dangers of a selfish lifestyle to one's dignity and standing as a male. In Chrysostom's scheme of things there is no room for fornicators, effeminate men, or murderers, thus ranking these offenders with, or below, dumb beasts, thereby indicating that through sin they have forfeited their masculinity. It is most distressing to the preacher that a person who has been given an advanced position in the world should in fact sink lower than mere animals in their failure to practise the virtue that would confirm their superiority. A hierarchy in his perceptions of the world quickly becomes apparent; man is defined by the attribute of reason, while woman possesses reason to a lesser extent. Animals do not possess any degree of reason, and yet those men who practise adultery, murder or fornication are even worse than dumb beasts, since they have allowed their sovereign reason to be overcome by base lust. Instead we see the truly manly man as one who has intelligence and reason coupled with the Christian values of mercy and humility before God.[19] It is the Christian soul that makes one into a man, according to Chrysostom. Otherwise we have merely walking and talking animals. Elsewhere he accuses some of his congregation of kicking like asses, bearing malice like camels and being shameless like dogs in their failure to maintain the health of their precious souls.[20] Thus the traditional concepts of masculinity are here Christianised in Chrysostom's preaching.

Wealth and its misappropriation are by no means, however, the only area in which Chrysostom has cause to rebuke the male members of his audience and feel concern as to their masculinity. Men are chastised for abandoning their natural control and superiority in a number of instances. However, money and luxurious living seem closely connected to most of these misdemeanours, indicating how crucial Chrysostom deemed the even distribution of wealth in his Christian community. One of the most striking examples of this is in Chrysostom's preaching on the Pauline Epistle to the Romans. This of course was the letter in which Paul spoke out against 'unnatural' practices in the Roman community – namely same-sex love.[21] Paul saw this as evidence of the depravities in secular society that the early Christians had to contend with. Chrysostom upholds this opinion and speaks at considerable length as to what exactly makes homosexuality such a heinous crime. What strikes him as particularly bizarre is that there is no restriction on heterosexual marriage in this society that would make such desperation more understandable. Since this was not the case, the turning of men to other men for carnal pleasures indicates a mere perverseness of spirit. He is at loss to even think what pleasure could be derived from it, since, to employ a philosophic trope, 'genuine pleasure is in that which is according to nature'.[22] But what is of particular concern to the preacher is the ensuing confusion of gender boundaries in such circumstances. Here, as elsewhere, sexual misdemeanours function in Chrysostom's thinking as an index of societal corruption:

> When both gender roles are abandoned it is clear proof of the utmost degree of corruption, when he that was ordained to be the instructor of the woman, and she who was told to be a helpmate to the man, in fact perform the actions of enemies towards one another.[23]

Chrysostom in fact believes that it is living in too great a degree of luxury that has allowed such depravities to develop, thus connecting wealth and sexual boundaries very explicitly. He accuses these men of actually having lost their manhood, and of straddling the two sexes. This is particularly disturbing to him, since such men have lost the superiority which was naturally theirs, but have not actually changed their nature, and so they stand as traitors to both sexes at once. Thus we have a 'third sex' emerging from these criticisms, something Chrysostom sees as monstrous. As we have already seen the way in which eunuchs were reviled for being neither men nor women, but merely anomalous, we can therefore speculate that Chrysostom's audience could be expected to be similarly disturbed by this situation. The image of the prostitute is also employed to good effect once more, with such male offenders accused of selling their bodies:

> But there is nothing more worthless than a man who has prostituted himself (*anthrôpou de peporneumenou ouden akhrêstoteron genoit' an*).

For not only the soul, but also the body of someone who has been treated in this way, is disgraced and deserves to be driven out from every place.[24]

Even in ancient Greek society men who had behaved so shamefully were designated *atimos* and lost all right to be considered legitimate citizens of the *polis*.

Accusations of becoming bestial also fly as Chrysostom becomes steadily more irate at these transgressions. In fact he is so emotive on this topic, that it has been suggested that he felt the sin to be rampant in his current congregation. Alternatively it could simply be that one shocking case of such behaviour had come to the recent attention of his congregation, and that once more Chrysostom is depending on prurient interest and public disgust to make his case for him. Regardless of the extent of such practices, however, it remains true that such confounding of gender boundaries is a deep preoccupation with the preacher. Again he lays the blame at the door of excessive luxury, since he believes that those who become accustomed to living in finery allow themselves to grow soft and unconcerned with their spiritual welfare, and thus sinful. Chrysostom feels that luxurious living on the part of the male leads to an abdication of masculine characteristics such as vigour and endurance, thus paving the way to even more destructive behaviour.[25] The insistence of Chrysostom that homoerotic relationships were unnatural as well as illegal, confounding the natural order of things and thus being a very public concern within the community, is the focus of B. Brooten's analysis of this homily in her *Love Between Women*. She interprets Chrysostom's virulence and intensity as evidence that same-sex love between men and women were equally well known and prevalent in the society of the day. R. Tanner comes to a similar conclusion, as he argues that Chrysostom's exegetical approach to Paul's letter shows clearly the preoccupations of his ministry. Chrysostom's persistent dwelling on the issue of same-sex love, and of deviant male sexuality in general must therefore indicate that these were concerns uppermost in his mind.[26] I do not necessarily agree, though, that Chrysostom was as concerned with contemporary deviant sexuality as Tanner would suggest. Certainly he returns to the issue without any lead from Paul in these sermons, but nowhere else in his preaching on the Pauline epistles does he pay similar attention to the actual sexual practices of his congregation, preferring instead to discuss less physical delineations of gender and its transgression. It was rather that this was a useful way of encouraging his audience to appreciate his view of the importance of appropriately gendered behaviour. The sensational nature of this subject allowed him to speak so fervently on the topic, thus making his point about masculinity very effectively, while perhaps pandering to his audience's love of gossip or scandal at the same time.

Thus far, Chrysostom has followed Paul's lead in speaking on the question of homosexuality, since it forms part of his exegesis of Romans 1:26.

However, in *Homily IX* on the series on Romans he returns to the subject and this time without any prompting from Paul. Bestiality too makes a re-appearance here, as Chrysostom discusses the depravities some men have sunk to. Cohabiting either with members of the same sex or with animals shows a lack of reason, and an abandonment of the natural order of things, as well as an excess of physical lust. Chrysostom here speaks of men having relations with mules and so compromising their masculinity and even their humanity by cohabiting with creatures devoid of reason or intellect. Gillian Clark has also suggested to me that Chrysostom's use of the mule in this tirade might stem from the fact that mules were sterile animals – themselves caught between two sexes, and so especially suited to the topic in hand.

The theory of luxurious living being the catalyst for such a decline into immorality is also returned to here, as Chrysostom advocates the disci-pline of hard work as a guard against sinfulness. Such regulation of one's life would also serve as a means to demonstrate and maintain one's masculinity, since it required the self-control and endurance seen as intrinsic to the male character. This is a new angle on Chrysostom's approach to the linkage of gender and wealth. Generally, as we will see, he speaks of the disciplined use of wealth as what renders it good or bad, whereas now the wealthy are required to actually work to safeguard their moral standards as well as their gender status.

This concept of a third, anomalous, sex is by no means particularly reserved for those men guilty of homosexuality. Heterosexual lust too is categorised in by now familiar ways, since it represents men as unable to control their thoughts and their desires, and therefore in breach of their masculinity. As we have seen, one element that did much to exacerbate this problem was that of the secular theatre. Chrysostom regularly alludes to the dangers of temptation arising from the phenomenon of public spec-tacle – sometimes more explicitly than others. We have observed the way in which the female figure was made into the object of the male gaze by means of his vivid and descriptive preaching. Elsewhere, however, he speaks directly to men as to how they themselves can take control of this situation and avoid such dangerous temptations:

> Are you lustful and squandering? Make it your resolution to not even look at a woman again, or to go to the theatre, or to concern yourself with the beauty of other people that you see around. For it is far easier not to even look at a woman with a good figure, than once you have looked and allowed the lust in, to banish the disturbance that comes from this. The struggle is easiest at the outset.[27]

Here, although the female figure is still the arouser of lust in the male, the emphasis is placed on the masculine ability to exercise his intellect in order to overcome mere physical desires. He ought to be sufficiently disci-plined to control his wandering gaze, keeping his sight carefully restricted.

Failure to do so can lead to emasculation and effeminacy. But the theatre and gazing at women is not the only way in which men can lose control and compromise their masculinity. In fact most of the conventional male activities within the civic sphere are deemed dangerous by Chrysostom, if not approached with a sufficiently Christian spirit:

> What can be more wasteful than this [vainglory and caring about the opinions of others]? What is more disgraceful or offensive? The fact that this condition is a wasteful one is obvious from the people who spend without any purpose whatsoever on theatres, horse-races, and other such irrelevant expenditures: from those who build fine and expensive houses, and fit out everything with an excessive style of extravagance, which I must not begin discussing in this discourse.[28]

Even a comparatively minor sin such as the use of bad language is considered dangerous to the state of one's gender, since again it marks an inability to control one's actions in a sufficiently disciplined manner. Chrysostom describes such 'filthy talking' as thrusting the speakers into the ranks of buffoons and prostituted women, with all the attendant doubts cast upon their masculinity which we are by now familiar with from the regular use of the prostitute as a negative *exemplum*.[29]

Chrysostom laments that such activities as listed above have taken the place of spiritual care in the priorities of his congregation. Is it any wonder, he cries, that the truly devout are flocking to the desert from the city, since this is the only place they can hope to live truly Christian lives? Previously we have seen him paint vivid pictures of the benefits of the ascetic life in order to encourage his flock to strive harder in their quest for true Christianity, or to shame those men who have suddenly been outstripped in their virtue by mere women. Here, however, he acknowledges that not many of his congregation will ever be likely to embrace such a lifestyle. The fact that so many people have decided to try nevertheless is a sad indictment on the city and its lifestyle. If each man can return to the appropriate state of disciplined life, however, the cities can become truly Christian communities.[30] Here Chrysostom seems to believe that a truly Christian city can exist, in which all members of the faithful would feel at home. The current 'pagan' state of affairs, however, has left the urban community as an alien landscape, and a place that devout Christians should feel inclined to shun. Through his preaching, Chrysostom hopes to reclaim the civic arena for the use of his flock, but his anxious sermons here indicate the distance that still needs to be travelled on this road.

In *Homily XXIII on II Corinthians* we see Chrysostom particularly worried about another instance in which the men in his congregation are rendering their gender status ambiguous. In this case it is their willingness to be deceived by those preaching heretical doctrines. Chrysostom reminds them of how Eve was deceived by the serpent in the Garden of

Eden, thus causing the great Fall. Now, if these men turn away from the truth on account of having allowed themselves to be similarly deceived by those preaching a different gospel to the one they know, and who attempt to corrupt the simplicity of Christ's teaching through unnecessary complications and complexities, they render themselves no better than women, and are unworthy of forgiveness on this account, just as Eve was. Here Chrysostom operates according to the received notion that the female sex was easily deceived and led astray by new ideas and fashions, something which had led even the Christian faith to be criticised in its early days since it seemed mainly to attract such credulous women and others of a weak intellect. If the male members of Chrysostom's audience act in a similar manner, therefore, they are in fact acting like fickle and weak-minded women.[31]

In this, and all the above mentioned transgressions, the men Chrysostom addresses have sunk from their natural position of authority on account of being unable to exercise an appropriately masculine discipline over their desires and their lifestyles. And so they stand accused of effeminacy or of becoming worse than women. But they have not actually become women in Chrysostom's eyes, and instead occupy an ambiguous space as being less than men, but not as yet becoming entirely female or bestial. This then is a kind of 'third sex', even though it is not always explicitly referred to as such. It is a third sex which can arise from any multitude of sins and misdeeds, and not simply from a lack of male genitalia as in the case of eunuchs, which would be the conventional interpretation in the secular sphere. Such is the price for reneging on the advantages and privileges bestowed on man by God. He does not simply fall into sin, but rather is stripped of his superiority in the world, and reduced to the level of those he is supposed to rule over and guide. It is a punishment far more severe than any visited on errant women, since these females are merely chastised for their sins, and lectured on their natural inferiority. The only way a woman can alter her gender status is to rise above her limitations and become more like a man in her pursuit of virtue. For a man the slide is in the other direction, and more to be feared and avoided on that account.

# Natural and Social Order in the
# *Oikos* and *Polis*

Mrs Tyrold now yielded; she never resisted a remonstrance of her husband; and as her sense of duty impelled her also never to murmur, she retired to her own room, to conceal with how ill a grace she complied. Had this lady been united to a man whom she despised, she would yet have obeyed him, and as scrupulously, though not as happily, as she obeyed her honoured partner. She considered the vow taken at the altar to her husband, as a voluntary vestal would have held one taken to her Maker; and no dissent in opinion exculpated, in her mind, the least deviation from his will.

Fanny Burney, *Camilla*, ch. 1

### The Christian housewife

In the previous chapters we concentrated on the way in which perceived norms for each of the sexes were constructed over time and reinforced by a variety of means. The art, literature, philosophy and rhetoric of the day were all employed in this process, and we have seen Chrysostom make particular use of rhetoric to this end. And in the case of Chrysostom, deviations from the established norms were punished by means of some stern and publicly delivered rebukes. It is now time to see how Chrysostom and his contemporaries would have seen society progressing if everyone adhered to the correct models of behaviour. Just as individually appropriate gender roles can be constructed through rhetoric, so too can an ideal society. And as we saw negative examples employed to act as warnings to members of both sexes as to what would happen if they strayed beyond their constructed boundaries, so too disturbing pictures of an order-less society or home are presented to warn listeners of large-scale danger of ignoring their preacher's advice.

We are by now familiar with Chrysostom's opinion of women as naturally frivolous and vain, with an inordinate love of gold and public admiration. Only those women who rise above their femininity by denying it in the practice of asceticism can avoid being categorised as such. We have also seen his expectations of the male sex with regard to maintaining their intellectual superiority in all their activities and attitudes. It is this assumption of female inferiority and male superiority that allows Chrysostom to follow Paul's lead when it comes to discussing the structure of the family unit. Adhering to the account given in the book of Genesis of the creation of woman, Chrysostom understands that God meant the female to be the helpmate of the male in the institution of marriage. Throughout his sermons he in fact shows an interesting interpretation of God's motives at this point in time. On one occasion he describes God as creating the female as equally worthy of honour as the male, only making her subject following her transgression and her leading of the man into sin:

> For with us indeed the woman is reasonably subjected to the man: since equality of honour causes contention. And not for this cause only, but by reason also of the deceit which happened in the beginning. Thus you see, she was not subjected as soon as she was made.... But when she made an ill use of her privilege and she who had been made a helper was found to be an ensnarer and ruined all, then she is justly told for the future, 'thy turning shall be to thy husband'.[1]

Yet elsewhere he is heard to say that the gender hierarchy was the one system of superiority and inferiority that God had always intended to exist:

> And from the beginning he made one sovereignty only, setting the man over the woman. But after that, since our race ran headlong into extreme disorder, He appointed other sovereignties also.[2]

The difference in approach between these two passages can be explained to a certain extent by a difference in context. In the first instance, Chrysostom is discussing the appropriate ordering of a Christian household, with the emphasis laid on harmonious spousal relations. In the second example, however, he is discussing hierarchies in the broader secular society of the ancient city, and so needs to present his audience with an unequivocal paradigm with divine sanction. Even when he does speak of the woman as being created with equal standing to the male, Chrysostom still refers to her as a helpmate or assistant to the man, thus simultaneously undermining her position and making clear the connotations of inferiority which he will continue to build on. Such inconsistency between descriptions of the origins of community living show Chrysostom's desire to perpetuate the traditional domestic structure, according as it did with his ideas of a properly run society, but also to bestow on this system a Christian set of origins. He is thus to be seen using the Genesis account to suit his intentions, finding an age-old subordination of the female, whether it was described as such by God or not.

But the similarity of Chrysostom's methodology to that of previous philosophers and societal commentators is also constantly clear. Just as

Aristotle once argued in his discussions of the organisation of society, Chrysostom too declares that the superior reason of the male enabled him to act in the public arena in matters of civic necessity. Woman – lacking this ability – was therefore suited by God for more domestic concerns. This is something reiterated a number of times in Chrysostom's work, as he tries to convince women of their importance within society at the same time as ensuring that they will not entertain ideas above their station. The key to a successful marriage is the acceptance by the wife of her submissive role, since any struggle for equality can only lead to strife and dissension. The importance of everyone behaving in a manner appropriate to their sex is made very clear here. Everything will be turned upside down if a wife fails to be submissive, and if a husband fails to be the leader in his own household. This threat of chaos is what Chrysostom employs in an effort to jolt his congregation into a new awareness of their Christian duties:

> And Paul would never without a reason and without an object have spent so much effort on this subject, as when he says to her, 'Wives, be in subjection unto your own husbands, as unto the Lord.' And why so? Because when they are in harmony, the children are well brought up, and the servants are in good order, and neighbours, and friends, and relations enjoy the atmosphere. But if it is otherwise, all is turned upside down, and thrown into confusion. And just as when the generals of an army are at peace one with one another, all things are in due subordination, whereas on the other hand, if they differ, everything is turned upside down.[3]

This theory leads to an extended passage in which Chrysostom dwells on Paul's comparison of a wife to the church, subject to her head who is the husband, or Christ. Here the equation of the woman with the body serves not only to underline her inferior status to her husband, but also re-emphasises the fact that a female was not believed to possess sufficient capacity for reason to merit equal authority in a marriage, or to instruct her husband in intellectual or doctrinal matters. As part of this extended metaphor, the Church in her relations to Christ is described in very female terms as being blemished, fickle, gossiping, and unappreciative of her Saviour. But since Christ was prepared to take the flawed church as his bride, so a husband should resolve to be patient with his wife, however imperfect he may have found her. A good wife is then described as being gentle, modest, and affectionate. Chrysostom here too warns against putting a premium on physical beauty, arguing that it gives rise to jealousy and pride rather than harmony. He urges his male congregation to love their wives as they would themselves, looking to the inner beauty and nobility of their souls rather than external appearances.

Chrysostom next explains what he sees as Paul's reasons for directing his discourse on love to men rather than women, further consolidating the divide between the sexes. The elevated emotion of love is not something he deems women to be capable of within a marriage. Theirs is rather the duty of reverence and respect for their husbands. They are to be governed by their male superiors, and to refrain from questioning the motives or actions of the men. But to feel love in its purest form is seen as beyond their reach. Here again, Chrysostom follows the conventional view of women, as he does on the occasion when he paints a picture of the nagging wife, concerned more with the social advancement and wealth of her husband than her own marital duties:

> Neither let a wife say to her husband, 'Unmanly coward that you are, sluggish and dull, and fast asleep! Here is such a person, a low man, and of low parentage, who takes his risks, and makes his journeys, and he has made a good fortune; and his wife wears her jewels, and goes out with her pair of milk-white mules; she rides about every-where, she has troops of slaves, and a swarm of eunuchs, but you have cowered down and you do not live for any purpose.' A wife must not say these things, or anything like them. For she is the body, not to dictate to the head, but must submit herself and obey.[4]

Such a woman should compare herself instead to those poorer than her in society in order to appreciate the good fortune of her own position, and to realise that wealth is only of superficial value in the Christian household. But in Chrysostom's ideal scheme she is to be gently guided in coming to this reasoned position by her husband. The early days of the marriage are what Chrysostom describes as a moulding process, comparing it even to the breaking of a horse! He speaks of the young bride as being a frivolous chatterbox, filled with headstrong pride, and an eagerness to prove herself mistress of her new household. She will be comparatively timid in the early days, however, and it is then that the husband must lay down his law if he is to have any hope of being master in the marriage. Chrysostom considers such women to be like children in their impetuosity and interest in the superficial things of life. It is the husband's role to aid her in the growing up and maturing process, beginning as he means to go on by instructing the young woman to return all her wedding presents unopened, so that she will realise that marriage is a union of two people in the sight of God rather than an opportunity for material advancement.

Once these parameters have been properly established, the way is opened for a recognisably Christian household to be run. With the educa-tion of his wife complete, the husband is free to pursue his civic and spiritual duties, knowing that a harmonious home awaits his return each day. The preservation of this order is seen as the primary duty of a devout Christian wife, and fits perfectly into Chrysostom's own dream of a specif-ically Christian *polis*:

> For a woman undertakes no small share of the whole administration, being the keeper of the house. And without her not even political

affairs could be properly conducted. For if their domestic concerns were in a state of confusion and disorder, those who are engaged in public affairs would be kept at home, and political business would be badly managed. So that neither in those matters, as neither in spiritual, is she inferior.[5]

Elsewhere Chrysostom urges women to remain in their proper place, performing only those duties allotted to them, and not presuming to undertake any of the tasks normally assigned to men.[6] The domestic duties of more ordinary women are deemed vitally important from the point of view of allowing their husbands to go about their daily business unfettered by lesser concerns.

Once the husband has guided his wife in the behaviour appropriate to her, it becomes her task to pass on this knowledge to the next generation. Mothers are called on to bring their daughters up in a carefully ordered way, instructing them in the domestic duties that will be theirs upon their marriage. As in the debate regarding women's dress, the female members of the household are here made responsible for the good behaviour of the males, since a well-reared daughter will save the soul of her future husband, and any offspring resulting from the marriage. Although it is not explicitly mentioned here, I believe that Chrysostom probably had the same situations in mind when addressing wives about their own dress, and about rearing their daughters, referring to similar questions of modesty in both instances. A humble and decorous wife will ensure harmony in the household and will accustom her husband to appreciating the kind of moral beauty which she represents rather than the artificial appearance of other women. He will therefore be disinclined to practise adultery, and so not endanger his immortal soul.

Even those women who are blatantly mistreated by their husbands should continue to be obedient within the marriage. They should of course avoid all likelihood of provoking their husbands, but should also remember that their reward for patience and loyalty, even while being battered, will be rich in heaven. This follows the popular Christian message that it is of no great note if one is good to those who treat us well, while real virtue lies in loving one's enemies, and it marks a new departure from the legal position which allowed Roman wives to leave overly abusive husbands.[7] Chrysostom does criticise violent husbands, but largely because they have forsaken their natural superiority and their innate self-control in becoming so passionate and impetuous. Once again it is his preservation of the marital hierarchy that is his concern throughout his instructions to battered wives.[8]

As has been frequently pointed out in discussions of the impact of Christianity on ancient society, the one area in the Christian household in which the notion of equality was strictly upheld was that of sexual fidelity. Both husbands and wives alike are required to observe their marriage vows and refrain from adultery or fornication. In *Homily V on I Thessalonians* Chrysostom makes this position abundantly clear:

Attend carefully to what I say. For although what is said is offensive to many, it is necessary to say it, to set the matter straight for the future. Not only is it adultery when we defile a woman who is married to a man; but if we ourselves while married to a woman defile one who is free and single, the matter is still adultery.[9]

In a homily delivered on the first letter to the Corinthians Chrysostom reiterates this philosophy, announcing that this is the only reason he has been discoursing about a mutual relationship within the Christian household. Normally the husband has full pre-eminence, but when it comes to chaste behaviour, male and female enjoy complete equality and must support one another.[10]

An automatic part of being the model wife we have seen, therefore, is remaining chaste, obedient and secluded within the domestic sphere. This becomes increasingly apparent when we examine Chrysostom's advice to women concerning more public activities, particularly secular entertainment. Although Chrysostom urges all of his flock to stay away from the theatre, he is especially worried about the influence such pagan activities might have on young newly-married women. One of the perceived hallmarks of the corruption of Greek society in Chrysostom's eyes was that it allowed even virgins to attend theatrical events, thus exposing them to all manner of immoral ideas. Unsanctioned love affairs, and even homosexuality, were often depicted in this forum, as were deeds such as murder, vengeance, suicide and adultery.[11] Even wedding ceremonies have become more like theatrical spectacles in recent years, with all the attendant dangers to the character of any woman present:

For how can it not be worthy of severest condemnation that a girl who has spent her entire life at home and has been trained in modesty from her earliest childhood, should be compelled to suddenly put aside all shame, and from the very outset of her marriage be instructed in imprudence; and find herself put forward in the midst of wanton, unchaste, effeminate, and rude men (*kai aselgesi kai asemnois andrasi kai pornois kai malakois eis meson autên protithenai*)?[12]

Chrysostom makes it clear that safeguarding women from such behaviour is an exercise in self-preservation; 'Tell me then, do you still enquire, "From where come adulteries? From where fornications? from where violations of marriage?" '[13]

The submissive role good Christian women should play in their marriages is further underlined by Chrysostom's instructions regarding female silence in church and in matters of doctrine. Once again he adheres rigidly to Paul's previous teachings, commanding the women in his congregation to maintain silence while attending services, and to seek guidance on doctrinal matters from their husbands when they return home. And of course the reason for this is the inferiority of reason on the part of the female. This insistence on the subordinate and weaker role of the woman is somewhat ironic given what we saw earlier with regard to the female safeguarding the eternal soul of her husband. Then she *was* supposed to educate him in being satisfied with the simple pleasures she represented, rather than the superficial advantages he might find in the material world. It would seem, however, that her influence is consigned solely to the level of the subliminal or unconscious. The only avenue of instruction open to the Christian wife is that of good example, hoping to influence her husband through her own exemplary behaviour. Chrysostom bases this stance on the story of the Fall, brought about by Eve. Her arrogance in presuming to guide and instruct Adam resulted in the exile of humanity from the Garden of Eden, and so the female is commanded to keep silence in the future:

> For the woman taught the man once, and made him guilty of disobedience, and caused our ruin. Therefore, because she made a bad use of her power over the man, or rather her equality with him, God made her subject to her husband. 'Thy desire shall be to thy husband.' This had not been said to her before.[14]

Interestingly enough, Chrysostom here seems to allude to some form of pre-lapsarian equality between the sexes, also claiming that sexual attraction was introduced by God to mend the rift between man and woman before it grew too wide. Now, however, Chrysostom is quick to rebuke women for their current weaknesses – including their gossiping in church. He complains of those female members of his congregation who are clamouring and chattering in front of him, as if they had come to church for social reasons rather than to worship God.[15] Here again, frivolity is seen as a particularly feminine quality, while the more sober and virtuous men are the ones who come to church and understand and learn from what they hear there.

Under this scheme of things, the Christian housewife becomes a very real force for change in Chrysostom's city, in spite of her seemingly restricted role. Her decorous living, and her thrifty management of the household will ensure that the small unit that is the individual *oikos* will become a fitting component of the broader civic structure. The maintaining of order within the basic relationships of a household – male and female – will enable a more ambitious city to be built on such firm foundations. It is when the woman threatens to disrupt this carefully negotiated arrangement, through provocative dress or lack of respect for her husband, that Chrysostom becomes anxious, hence his trenchant remarks on the failings of the female sex, as he struggles to ensure that his dream city does not literally collapse about his ears.

### The Christian householder

As in the case of women, Chrysostom offers a great deal of advice to men as to how to conduct themselves within a Christian marriage in order to further the development of the orthodox *polis*. In this way he upholds the traditional perceptions of the family unit as a means by which social status can be underwritten, or even improved. It is therefore vital that each man can show that his household is harmonious and well run, and there is even a form of competition among peers as to who would have the best-regulated home.[16] Perhaps it is this sentiment that Chrysostom taps into when he details what is, to his mind, the best example of Christian domesticity. He hopes that he will inspire his male listeners to take greater lengths to ensure that their household is run in a more Christian and serene manner than that of their neighbours, thus confirming their masculinity in this newly Christianised sense.

Throughout his instructions to this end, Chrysostom's emphasis is placed on the intellectual superiority of the male, and his role as spiritual mentor of his wife. Chrysostom also believes that it is the husband within any marriage who is capable of the emotion of love, and indeed he advocates that a man should feel love for his wife. This understanding of love is closely allied to the concepts of masculinity that included reason, discipline, and the ability to practise virtue. It is the woman's part to be obedient and submissive to her husband, again proceeding from the assumption that only very few females are capable of the virtue necessary to feel true love for a partner.[17] As in the case of women, *Homily XX on Ephesians* gives most insight into Chrysostom's idea of the truly Christian household. It is indeed a sermon addressed particularly to husbands, as to how they might best regulate the micro-community that is their home. The *paterfamilias* is the head of this unit, as Christ is the head of the church, and as such it is his responsibility to ensure that the body of the family is correctly guided and monitored by his superior intellect. His masculine virtue is what qualifies him for this task, and it will also be the example that the rest of his *oikos* should strive to follow.

The first person whom he must guide is, of course, the wife, who will ultimately be his second in command in this small army for God. Even picking this candidate is an opportunity for the male to demonstrate his self-discipline and his advanced powers of reason. He should not be attracted purely by looks, and should even shun the superficially beautiful woman. Instead, he should look into the soul of the woman and see the true beauty that lies within, and this should be the basis of his decision to marry her. Chrysostom even argues that a husband who picks his spouse solely on the basis of her looks will grow bored with her after a time, much as the rich man does with his gilded ceiling or ornate surroundings, and that therefore the marriage is doomed to failure. Nor should he be influenced by her family connections or the size of the dowry she might bring.[18] Indeed wealth should be the last possible consideration either before or during the marriage, since the truly Christian husband should in fact promote economy in all areas of his household. It is to this end that the wedding presents should be sent back unopened, so that the bride can see from the outset the restraint that is required of her, and the superior virtue of the man she has married and whom she must now obey in all things. It must be wondered what the guests would have thought of such abrupt treatment, but this action paves the way for an entire programme of economic reform within the household. From the start, by putting a 'bridle' on the soul of the woman, and by teaching her the behaviour appropriate to her role, the husband will encourage her to budget carefully in her management of the household affairs, allowing the money thus saved to be offered to the poor. His own disregard for personal ornamentation or finery will show to the wife by example what is expected of her.

Chrysostom feels that some of his congregation will find him ridiculous in trying to regulate such matters, but he foresees that soon the present fashions will pass away, and then people will appreciate his sentiments, and recognise that love of finery is the practice only of 'silly children and drunken men'.[19] Once more an excess of vanity is seen as a transgression unsuited to the masculine character. This regulation of the wife's household spending therefore becomes an obviously moral as well as an obviously economic activity. Here again we see the public interpretations of many of the most private activities in the ancient world. The wife served as the guardian of the household, but in doing so she acted on behalf of the family as a whole, including the *paterfamilias*.[20] It was therefore in his own best interests to ensure that this woman acted in a manner best suited to the image of the home he wished to portray to the outside world. Thus the exercise of control and discipline in all areas of the domestic sphere, and the moral restraint practised by all its inhabitants were the responsibility of the husband, and should therefore direct his choice of wife and his subsequent education of her.

Chrysostom's ideal husband will maintain a similarly controlled economic and moral regime in his dealings outside the home, particularly when he goes to the city forum to conduct his daily business. Rather than spending long hours conversing with his peers and vying to outdo them in their accumulation of wealth or influence, he should instead conduct his affairs as quickly and as quietly as possible, returning home early in the day to continue the guidance of his family. This will have the advantage of forestalling jealousy or envy on the part of the wife, since she will feel she is particularly valued, but even if the husband acts from a desire simply to secure domestic harmony, the net result will be a shift in the civic pattern which cannot but meet with Chrysostom's approval:

> Show her too, that you value her company highly, and that you prefer to be at home for her sake, than in the marketplace. And respect her before all your friends ... [21]

Chrysostom also offers advice on home entertaining, saying to his congregation that if they must give dinners and have parties (and we sense a note of grudging permission here), they must take care that there is nothing immodest or disorderly about these gatherings. A disciplined approach to one's interaction with the rest of the city is what is advocated at all times, and, by means of this outlook, the household can in truth become like a little church, or a mini-monastic unit in its own right. The traditional sense of honour so dear to the Roman male is also catered for, since now his home will be seen as morally and economically superior to those of his peers, and therefore more harmonious – the outward signal of superiority and status.

In a later chapter I will discuss at greater length the ramifications of this proposal for the form and function of the ancient city, but for now it will suffice to point out that such behaviour is the ideal manifestation of Christian masculinity as Chrysostom would see it, while standing out as markedly different from what was customary in late Roman society. Secular considerations regarded the active pursuit of business, the making of contacts, the upholding of the patron-client system, and the circulation of money throughout the society as the definitive activities of the male within this community. While Chrysostom upholds certain of the traditional and internal masculine characteristics such as the practice of virtue and the use of reason, in other respects he works to modify the public perceptions of the male gender. In this way, the Christian householder can appear to be very similar to the monks who lived apart from conventional society. The harmonious atmosphere of his home and the economic lifestyle which he encourages are strongly reminiscent of the monastic communities we saw Chrysostom speak of with such admiration on other occasions. Thus, under the precepts of his preaching, Chrysostom can hope to bring a version of the holy life inside the very walls of the traditional urban unit. This is a point E. Clark makes in relation to the appropriate gender hierarchy to be found in the Christian household. She suggests that Chrysostom's use of Scriptural exegesis works to consolidate the divisions of labour and behaviour between the sexes, rather than simply to promote asceticism. What he actually does is blur the distinction between asceticism and married life, between the Old Testament and contemporary society, so that the same standards of behaviour will be seen as desirable and applicable to all, regardless of their individual career paths.[22]

One of the key duties of the Roman *paterfamilias* was to ensure that his inheritance was transmitted safely down to his descendants. To this end, he must select carefully the woman who will be his son's wife. Again, Chrysostom has plenty of advice to offer in this respect, since as we saw in a previous chapter he disapproves of the increasingly secular attitude to marriage and its celebration. As in the treatise *De Inani Gloria*, Chrysostom feels it is imperative for a young male to be married earlier in his life rather than later. It is his father's duty to safeguard the moral well-being of his son, and with this in mind he must be on the watch for signs of lustfulness and dissipation. A younger man will presumably have less experience of these evils than one older, and so should enter into a chaste and devout marriage before he can be led astray. But, Chrysostom laments, Roman fathers have become more concerned with the financial advantages resulting from a good marriage than with the chastity of their sons, and so they postpone the ceremony for as long as possible in order to find the best dowry on offer:

> But alas! The root of these evils is also the love of money. For since no one cares that his son should be sober and modest, but instead they all are mad about gold, for this reason no one makes this [a good marriage] a matter of concern.[23]

The bad habits that such a tardy bridegroom might fall into are sources of deep worry to Chrysostom, and for the most part they centre on the public activities of the secular community, the theatre being foremost among them. The preacher complains that far from seeking to avoid such temptations, the city's youth actively thrust themselves into harm's way by attending dramatic spectacles with no thought for the damage that might be done to their souls, concentrating instead on how best to amuse themselves and dissipate their wealth. He wonders how they can possibly hope to remain chaste and restrained if they are accustomed to seeing flagrant abuses of morality on the stage on such a regular basis. Again we see the link Chrysostom draws between the male gaze and the growth of illicit desires, and he addresses his rebuke directly to men, thus forcing them to consider and take responsibility for their own actions. For once the temptations arising from the female body and its public display are not blamed solely on the woman. A man who is behaving in an appropriately masculine way would not be so foolhardy in his management of his immortal soul.[24]

Since the uses and abuses of wealth are of great concern to Chrysostom, his suggestions as to how the problem can be addressed are of particular interest with regard to his approach to male gender representations. His response to greed and ostentatious spending is to advocate almsgiving in order to redress the balance prevailing within his community. Such altruistic behaviour is in fact the preserve of the male within this society. Whereas the female can be encouraged to conserve wealth, and to practise fiscal economy, it is the male who has active control over the transfer of funds throughout society. But once he makes the decision to exercise this control in the positive way of almsgiving, he both confirms his masculinity and ensures the safety of his morality:

> The man who gives alms is instructed not to admire riches or gold. And once this lesson is in his mind he has taken a great step in rising towards Heaven, and he has eliminated ten thousand occasions of strife, contention, envy and dejection.[25]

Within this scheme of things, however, Chrysostom advocates a reasoned and cautious approach. Alms should be donated only to the genuinely needy, and with a joyful attitude. Money should no longer be donated to retired clergy or straitened aristocrats, but to those members of the population who truly have not enough to eat or adequate shelter. When addressing men, however, Chrysostom despises those who offer feeble excuses or try to evade this Christian duty by making it the responsibility of the church administration:

> In fact the Church, because of your meanness, is compelled to have as much property as it has now. For, if men always acted according to the apostolic laws, the Church would have its revenue out of your good will, which is a secure coffer and an inexhaustible treasury. But now what is there to be done, when you store up for yourselves treasures upon the earth and lock up everything in your own stores, while the Church is forced to take care of bands of widows, choirs of virgins, the accommodation of strangers, the problems of foreigners, the misfortunes of prisoners, the needs of the sick and the maimed, and other similar causes?[26]

In fact some men refuse to give alms out of the foolish fear that they themselves may be poverty stricken and then be forced into the role of beggar, an excuse Chrysostom characterises as feeble and laughable. No one person can claim never to need another, so to worry about it to this ridiculous extent is to be childish and self-absorbed.[27]

## The natural order of things

Throughout these varying instructions to men and women regarding their role in ascetic life, in marriage, or in their interaction in society, we have seen Chrysostom particularly concerned with the correct order of things, an order set in place through divine instruction and further bolstered by the teachings of Paul. Any transgression of this order is a matter for great concern on the part of the preacher, and can explain many of his remarks. It was the presumption of Eve which caused the Fall, a presumption that led her to move beyond her allotted role of helper and to try to guide Adam rather than remain in submission to him. This precedent shows clearly the great disorder and calamity that can arise from such breaking of divinely established boundaries. But this concept of gender relations serving as an index of the health of society as a whole is also familiar from Aristotle:

> The freedom in regard to women is detrimental both in regard to the purpose of the *politeia* and in regard to the happiness of the state. For just as man and wife are part of a household, it is clear that the state also is divided nearly in half into its male and female popula-

tion, so that in all *politeia* in which the position of women is badly regulated one half of the state must be deemed neglected in framing the law.[28]

Chrysostom is intent on ensuring that none of his congregation should fall into similar error, and that his female flock should remain firmly within their assigned categories. The only time it is permissible for a woman to move beyond her femaleness is in the practice of asceticism, where her bravery, her self-discipline and her virtue bring her to the level of a male. But even here Chrysostom seems anxious about such mobility between gender categories. In one sermon, where he details the rigours adopted by female celibates within their cells all for love of their Spiritual Bridegroom, the preacher makes it quite plain to his male listeners that he is worried that they might be outstripped in virtue by mere women:

> How contemptible! What a shame is this! We hold the place of the head, and are surpassed by the body. We are ordained to rule over them; not merely that we may rule, but that we may rule in goodness also; for he who rules, ought especially to rule in this area, by excelling in virtue; whereas if he is surpassed, he is no longer ruler.[29]

Even as he compliments virtuous women therefore, Chrysostom has ulterior motives. By appealing to the masculinity of his male audience, he can rouse them to greater efforts in their own devotions. If they follow his lead, they will again become superior in the practice of virtue, and will therefore restore the appropriate boundaries between the sexes. As part of this process, we will note if we examine Chrysostom's praise of women that they are not admired for exceeding the goodness of men through their own abilities, but rather as having attained such excellence through the decline in the standards of the men. It is a similar process to that enacted in the juxtaposed descriptions of whores and virgins. The lowest end of the scale of behaviour is presented, along with the ideal. The psychology would seem to be that if the lower end begins to outstrip the ideal in goodness, a grave upset of the natural order of things has occurred, and that society should be roused to resolve the crisis. This method of persuasion applies equally to the standards of behaviour between different classes of females, and to the behaviour appropriate between the sexes.

This is a process also used when speaking of Jews or heretics within Paul's or Chrysostom's own society. Those who question too curiously into the tenets of their faith are rebuked and compared to the pernicious Greeks and their sophistry. Jews are also consistently denigrated for their obstinacy in adhering to what were seen as misguided beliefs and their prioritising of the 'Law' over the moral spirit of obedience to God. So unequivocal is Chrysostom's disapproval of these two groups that his congregation could be in no doubt whatsoever that to engage in unnecessary argument about the nature of God or his teachings would be to sink to the level of the uncivilised and immoral Greeks or stubborn Jews. In this manner, Christianity is presented as unquestionably superior among all other philosophies or beliefs, and its behavioural norms established as the standard for all devout members of the empire:

> For all the Greeks are children ... . Now children cannot bear to take thought for any thing useful; so also the Greeks would be forever at play; and they lie on the ground, grovelling in their posture and in their affections ... . And as children expose their limbs unconsciously, and do not blush for shame; so the Greeks, wallowing among whores and in adulteries, and laying aside the laws of nature, and introducing unlawful intercourses are also unabashed.[30]

As a follow-on from this, the combination of Greek habits and female nature is seen as particularly dangerous, since the heathen predilection for immoral and uncontrolled behaviour is seen as doing much to foster the transgression of gender boundaries. This becomes very clear in *Homily V on Titus*, in which Chrysostom complains of the chaos to be found at ancient dramatic festivals. Women were portrayed on stage performing all manner of immoral deeds; loving their step-sons, killing their husbands, committing suicide, while elsewhere a lawgiver – Lycurgus – advocated that women should take physical exercise such as wrestling, naked in the presence of men:

> Woman was not made for this, man, to be prostituted as common, O you subverters of decency, who use men as if they were women, and lead out women to war, as if to mix up all things, to overleap the boundaries that have been appointed from the beginning, and remove those which God has set to nature. For God assigned to woman the care of the house only, to man the conduct of public affairs. But you reduce the head to the feet, and raise the feet to the head. You allow women to bear arms, and are not ashamed.[31]

Here Chrysostom's worry is that theatrical spectacles and dubious Greek laws will not only arouse immoral thoughts in the audience, leading therefore to sin, but that they will also encourage women to move beyond their appropriate station in life by portraying such wild and unfeminine characters on the stage. Thus the Greek treatment of the female is the worst possible form of feminine behaviour in Chrysostom's mind and he is careful to present this lowest end of the scale to his audience for their future reference.

By contrast we are presented with Chrysostom's own conception of the ideal Christian woman, although she is often displayed through inference rather than by explicit description. She is chaste, modest, neatly and soberly dressed, and she maintains her place in the household with due obedience. This in turn helps to safeguard the structure of that household, which will further contribute to the growth of the Christian city. Thus Chrysostom's pejorative comments about the female sex can be seen to serve a larger purpose than simple disapproval. They illustrate various codes of behaviour which will have no place in the new community, and they serve to shame audiences into more obviously Christian styles of living.

*

From what we have already seen, there is little or nothing which marks Chrysostom out as different from his Christian or pagan predecessors in his philosophy of the division of virtue, reason and self-control among the sexes. I believe his combined aims in propounding these opinions, however, are uniquely his. By spending so much of his time attacking specifically female vices he initiates the cycle of public shame and guilt which he hopes will act on his entire congregation, encouraging them towards better behaviour. But he also hopes to reset the boundaries of behaviour appropriate to the female sex so that they will be enabled to carry out his dream of remodelling the ancient city. The woman who has been re-educated in the roles expected of her by her faith will, he hopes, turn away from those pagan practices which distress the bishop so much. And since her greatest sphere of influence is in the domestic arena, the devout female can execute change in the household, which, as we will see, can negotiate change on a wider scale in the city itself.

But it is also the case that many of Chrysostom's addresses to women served to warn men as to what behavioural boundaries they must not overstep. This did indeed become apparent in those sections of his sermons addressed particularly to or about women. But we have also seen in this chapter a whole range of techniques employed by Chrysostom to persuade his male listeners into a more obviously Christian lifestyle, of which negative comparisons with the female sex formed only a part. Certainly to become effeminate or to behave like a woman was a grievous error indeed in Chrysostom's eyes, not least because it was a wilful and disrespectful treatment of the privileges granted to the male sex by God. But in fact for the most part we see Chrysostom speak of effeminacy in terms of even greater horror, since it led to a kind of 'third sex' rather than a simple shift between the two gender boundaries. Rather than being transgressed, these boundaries are in fact actually blurred and converged, as are those between the world of humans and brute beasts. Therefore, while Chrysostom's negative opinion of women seemed particularly disturbing to us in previous chapters, we have also seen the greater pressures and expectations placed on men, and the proportionately greater punishments and rebukes incurred by those erring in this way on that account.

One aspect that particularly struck us when discussing gendered sins in the previous chapter was the manner in which Chrysostom made the female sex responsible for arousing sinful feelings of lust and desire in the male. From what we have learned in this chapter, however, it would seem that this was one of the only sins in which this process was enacted. Rather, it becomes the male role and function to safeguard the weaker female from falling into wrongdoing, by guiding her through his superior intellect and self-control. Thus we saw the male instruct the female as to how to restrain her excessive emotions, to remain submissive within the household, and to guide her in her reading and obeying of the Scriptures. In fact we have now seen the man made responsible for the female sin of frivolous expenditure. Within late antique society it was the man who had primary control over the accumulation and distribution of wealth, so that if he pandered to his wife's vain love of luxury and ornamentation he was facilitating the damage to her soul and to the rest of society, since it was his part to regulate his wealth in a more effective manner and to guard her moral welfare, since she was naturally less well endowed in this respect than he. Nor do we see Chrysostom in any way reluctant to employ polemic or tirades when rebuking his male audience for their misdemeanours, demonstrating no real difference in his approach to the two sexes on the question of morality and Christian living.

What does emerge, therefore, from our study in these chapters is that Chrysostom sees each sex as responsible for an area of moral well-being in the other. Aside from that he maintains traditional gender roles, although working to Christianise the public perceptions of the qualities involved. What does bother the preacher most in either respect, however, is the wilful conflation of the boundaries between the sexes as a result of carelessness or immorality in the pursuit of worldly pleasures. And overall he works to regulate the behaviour of both sexes in his quest to achieve a Christian version of the household, often making it a mutual task to be worked out between the two partners within the Christian marriage. For the male, however, there is perhaps a greater responsibility in this respect, since he has a wider sphere of influence in the city itself. How Chrysostom sees this aim as being taken beyond the walls of the *oikos* and into the *polis* itself will be the subject of the remaining chapters.

# 9

# The Sins of the Wealthy

'I've got a man in England who buys me clothes. He sends over a
selection of things at the beginning of each season, spring and fall.'
He took out a pile of shirts and began throwing them, one by one,
before us, shirts of sheer linen and thick silk and fine flannel, which
lost their folds as they fell and covered the table in many-coloured
disarray. While we admired he brought more and the soft rich heap
mounted higher – shirts with stripes and scrolls and plaids in coral
and apple-green and lavender and faint orange, with monograms of
Indian blue.

F. Scott Fitzgerald, *The Great Gatsby*, ch. 5

## Followers of fashion: rich women in Chrysostom's audience

We have already seen the way in which, as part of the construction of
gender roles within late antique society, certain sins took on gendered
associations. And so 'active' sins such as fornication, murder and pride are
readily associated with the male sex, while women are thought of as
performing more passive sinful actions – being seductive, false, vain and
self-indulgent. However one area in which both sexes are seen as more
culpable than any other in Chrysostom's scheme of things is in the misuse
of wealth. In this respect we can read Chrysostom in a very different way
from Peter Brown, who suggested that the preacher's utterings on sex and
gender were simply a side-show to his more real concerns about the gap
between rich and poor in the city. We have already seen how Chrysostom's
attitudes to the sexes and gender roles demonstrate his attempts to alter
society in favour of a Christian model. His discussions of wealth and its
dangers are simply another side of this coin, and the two inform each
other. As will become apparent, Chrysostom believes that a strict monitoring of gender roles will in fact do much towards realising his dream of
closing the social gap between rich and poor.

Discussions of wealth are in fact one of the few areas in which
Chrysostom is less than rigid in his adherence to the guidance of Paul with
regard to the issues that come in for his attention. When preaching,
Chrysostom is generally true to the original sentiments of the Pauline
epistles, and as such much more than the issues of gender and wealth that
we are concentrating on here is covered in the course of his homilies. But

even more so than the issue of gender ambivalence, it is the thorny subject of money which seems to get the preacher most exercised. It is very noticeable when Chrysostom chooses to discuss a theme not first introduced, however slightly, by Paul. He is consistently careful to conduct a thorough exegesis of the chosen text of the day, and while he is prone to embark on tangential ramblings, their origins can generally be found in the content of Paul's writings. Where Chrysostom does digress most substantially, however, is on the topic of the wrongful use of wealth, often allowing it to take over the second half of his sermon, and it is in fact in this context that much of his discourse on either of the sexes is delivered.

The preacher regularly has cause to reprimand his congregation for caring overly much for the trappings of the material world, since they consider the display of possessions to be an affirmation of social standing and honour. Chrysostom wishes rather that their thoughts would be directed towards accruing a more spiritual kind of honour – one which would arise from a lack of wealth rather than an accumulation of it. This general theme will be something to be addressed in the next chapter. But for the purposes of this section we should note that it is often women who Chrysostom believes are responsible for this misguided approach to life, while he regards their husbands as being neglectful in their roles of guidance and control. His argument appears based primarily on traditional opinions of the female sex as being easily influenced when it comes to matters of sin. The failure of all concerned to follow his guidelines is often manifested in their outward appearance, and therefore can easily be highlighted in order to provide examples of behaviour to be shunned and ridiculed. These women fall prey themselves to the sin of vanity, and thus lavish vast sums of money, or worse, encourage their husbands to do so, on the struggle to appear more richly adorned than their neighbours. Of necessity Chrysostom's thoughts on this matter would seem to be addressed to the wealthier portion of his congregation, but we should be aware that this does not preclude the presence of more ordinary folk who may well have enjoyed hearing about the lifestyles and misdemeanours of their richer neighbours. What is most interesting to note throughout these addresses, however, is that in speaking of such matters, Chrysostom appears to be disconcertingly well informed on the minutiae of female dress and make-up, and he is quick to make public examples of those females who seem to him inappropriately adorned for an ecclesiastical setting. On one occasion he asks rhetorically why women have come to church dressed as if they were going to a dance or a theatrical spectacle:

> There such embroidery, such costly clothes, would have been suitable, but here not one of them is wanted. You have come to pray, to entreat pardon for your sins, to plead for your offences, beseeching the Lord and hoping to make Him favour you. Why do you adorn yourself? This is not the dress of a suppliant. How can you groan? How can you weep? How can you pray fervently when you are

dressed in this manner? If you did weep, your tears would be ridiculed by the onlookers. She who weeps should not be wearing gold. It is merely acting, and hypocrisy. For is it not acting to shed tears from a soul overgrown with extravagance and ambition to such a degree? Away with such hypocrisy! God is not mocked! This is the attire of actors and dancers, who live on the stage. Nothing of this sort is suitable for a modest woman, who should be adorned 'with shamefacedness and sobriety' (*Tauta tôn mimôn kai tôn orkhêstôn esti tôn en tais skênais diêmereuontôn: gunaiki de kosmiai ouden toutôn prepei. Meta aidous, phêsi, kai sôphrosunês*).[1]

Here we see both a picture of transgressing females and, by extension, of the ideal woman – one who appears modest, sober and fully conscious of her own inferiority. Chrysostom accomplishes his aim by conjuring up vivid images of both types of woman in the minds of his audience. He seems particularly irate in this passage, leading me to speculate that there were women erring in this very matter visible to him in the church on that occasion. It is possible to argue that the preacher was merely employing a rhetorical mood of anger which happened to suit his theme for the day, but I am more inclined to believe that he was responding to a situation of which he had first-hand experience.

In a homily delivered on another Pauline text we see an entertaining and lively satire of similarly vain women in which Chrysostom attempts to understand why they felt compelled to dress up to the nines to attend church services. In *Homily III on II Thessalonians*, he describes the entrance of a rich woman into church, whose every move is directed at displaying her person and her dress to best advantage, hoping that her wealth and beauty will be seen and enviously appreciated by other women.[2] The trenchant nature of his comments would again lead me to believe that this grand entrance was something he had seen very recently indeed, and had exercised him to the extent that he felt driven to incorporate his disapproval in the homily of the day. This derisive rebuke encompasses not only the preoccupation with public opinion and ostentatious display as a means of retaining a high status among the observing public, but also the sin of foolish vanity which Chrysostom sees as particularly endemic within the female sex. As he says elsewhere 'For the whole race is vain, but especially the female sex.'[3] Such vanity is particularly disturbing to the preacher when he contrasts it with the humility and fortitude of his beloved Paul, who was content to endure iron chains for love of God. Chrysostom hopes that he can persuade the wealthy female members of his congregation to adopt a similar modesty, urging them to lay aside the fashionable thick gold necklaces they wear, since from a spiritual point of view, even this rich jewellery cannot be more beautiful than Paul's chains:

The number of you women who adorn yourselves with trinkets of gold, should long instead for the bonds of Paul. The collar around your neck does not glisten as much as the grace of these iron bonds gleamed about his soul![4]

In fact their own rich trinkets are more of an imprisonment than Paul's bonds ever were, since they enslave the wearer to the fickle tyranny of public opinion, as well as causing considerable mental anxiety about theft and violence.[5] Just because a chain is made of a precious metal rather than dull iron does not make it any the less of a chain, declares Chrysostom, claiming that if someone were to be placed in the desert with no one to see them and how they were dressed, such a golden chain would very quickly seem heavy and irksome, just like more obvious fetters. This is the evil of vainglory, and it is something Chrysostom feels women are particularly prone to, announcing on one occasion that the sex is especially fond of ornament.[6]

Again, however, the concept of mankind being enslaved to riches is drawn from a longstanding cultural heritage, which Chrysostom merely repackages in this instance in order to Christianise the behaviour of his flock. The sense of riches and finery as being indicators of social corruption is evident even in Jewish tradition in the Old Testament. And in the Pentateuch too, such errant behaviour is seen as being predominantly female, while men retain the superior spiritual abilities.[7] Just as harlots and the *subintroductae* were depicted at length and in great detail so as to arouse audience disgust, so too is gold portrayed here in a similarly despicable light. Such is the public fascination with gold as a mark of beauty and status, complains Chrysostom, that women are even entwining trinkets made of the stuff into their hair. He is anxious that this ridiculous behaviour will next lead to their having their eyebrows and eyelashes coated with the metal,[8] while some women already go so far as to have even the faces of the mules or horses pulling their carriages overlaid with it.[9] Here Chrysostom tries to persuade his audience that such lavish expenditure on mere animals might in fact have the opposite effect to that intended, distracting people from the wealthy individuals themselves and leading them to focus instead on dumb beasts and inanimate objects. And of course we cannot forget those women who requested their chamber-pots be made out of silver, such was their preoccupation with honour and appearance.[10] This ostentation is particularly odious when one considers the flawed nature of humanity, the physical mortality and moral corruption that cannot be successfully hidden under any amount of gold or fine perfumes, as Chrysostom is at pains to point out on a separate occasion:

Why, woman, do you lavish perfumes upon a body which is full of impurity inside? Why do you spend on what is offensive, as if you were wasting perfumes on dirt, or spreading balms on a brick. There is, if you desire it, a precious ointment and a fragrance with which you might anoint your soul; not brought from Arabia, or Ethiopia, nor from Persia, but from heaven itself; purchased not by gold but by a virtuous will, and by sincere faith. Buy this perfume, the fragrance of which is able to fill the world.[11]

Here Chrysostom paints the art of physical adornment as a waste of time and energy, hoping to underline the futility of such actions, thus turning his congregation away from the potential to err in this respect. If he can persuade the women who are seated before him that bedecking themselves with gold and silver is in fact a ridiculous, rather than an admirable, pastime, he should be able to manipulate their behaviour along more appropriately Christian lines, even if it is only through an appeal to their fear of being absurd in the eyes of others.

Chrysostom also shows an acute awareness of the bizarre excuses that might be offered in defence of this vainglorious conduct. Those supposedly devout Christian women who wear fine silks and other rich materials, even though they know that their faith should prompt a more muted style of dress, are reported as claiming that they merely wish to air the garments and guard them against moths! In great indignation the preacher dismisses such base excuses, reminding women that the welfare of one garment is inconsequential when compared to the welfare of their own immortal souls, or even the state of those less well off in society. Chrysostom is irritated with the husbands who countenance such frivolity, thus touching on the appropriate roles of each sex within a marriage; the male should guide his wife in decorous behaviour, and she should be obedient in bowing to his recommendations. But Chrysostom also acknowledges another female excuse within the marital union, namely that women must adorn themselves in this manner in order to please and delight these very husbands:

And do not say, 'What can I do? It is not my own desire, but I must do it for my husband. I cannot win his love unless I agree to this.'[12]

Chrysostom proceeds to refute this argument, declaring that a woman who concentrates on artificially augmenting her beauty is at the same time increasing her husband's unease of mind. Such a woman attracts the attention of other men, whether intentionally or not, and on noticing this her husband becomes jealous and unhappy. Chrysostom is also quick to doubt the innocence of women in such matters, bluntly asserting that they take such pains to adorn themselves in order to attract crowds of lovers and admirers, thus forsaking the modesty and humility appropriate to their sex.[13]

This perception of women as temptresses is maintained even within the marriage bond, as Chrysostom entrusts wives with the responsibility of ensuring that their husbands do not entertain lustful thoughts. By dressing decorously and eschewing makeup and jewellery, a wife can 'train' her husband to appreciate such modesty and humility. He will therefore not find anything attractive in the artificial beauty of a prostitute, and so not seek sexual gratification outside of his marriage bed. This is of course is just as much in the interests of the wife's happiness as of her husband's moral welfare:

> Do not teach him to be captivated by laughter, or by a loose dress, in case you prepare a poison against yourself. Accustom him to take pleasure in modesty, and if your own dress is modest you will accomplish this. But if you have a brazen air, or a flighty manner, how can you address him in a serious way? And who will not hold you in contempt and derision?[14]

Such sentiments are in a similar vein to those we saw expressed in the treatises on the *subintroductae*, where the female ascetics were accused of consigning the souls of those men cohabiting with them to eternal damnation by means of their seductive ways.[15] In this respect the preservation of the standard categorisation of the female into whore or admirable virgin is demonstrated.

However, the above passages use the whore/Madonna dichotomy in a context in which women are consistently described as passive objects of the male gaze. The wife becomes something that is 'looked at', and it is through the activity of looking that sin can enter into the man's soul. It is thus the responsibility of the wife to ensure that she presents a properly demure picture to her husband, to avoid corrupting him in this manner. Chrysostom is constantly aware of the dangers arising from this activity of 'gazing', and he is very conscious that the human eye can actually be an agent of evil. This is reminiscent of his teachings in the written tract, *De Inani Gloria*, where he discusses each of the five senses as being a gateway for temptation and wrongdoing to enter the soul. In order to combat this, Chrysostom urges parents to train their offspring to exercise constant restraint in the use of their senses, especially that of sight. Thus, to bring a son to the theatre is to open the gateway to temptation, since the spectacles there foster thoughts that can in turn lead to fornication or adultery.[16] A similar situation is presented in his treatises on the *subintroductae*, when he catalogues the growth of illicit desire simply through constantly being able to look but not touch.[17] In his homilies on the letters to Timothy, Chrysostom displays a similar attitude to women – that they are to be looked at by men. The more artificial additions to their physical appearance they make, the more they resemble those prostitutes or actresses who are the greatest source of danger to the male gazers. This is yet another means of encouraging his female audience into better behaviour, since they are threatened with the shame of being perceived as akin to harlots through their self-adornment. The pejorative opinion of prostitutes held by contemporary society should be an adequate deterrent to those women who considered themselves to be well-bred and appropriately feminine. But this approach also highlights Chrysostom's own, underlying, preoccupation with the state of the boundaries between the sexes in his community. He fears that women are becoming 'harlot-like' in their pursuit of physical and material pleasures, which in turn makes their behaviour more 'masculine' than feminine, since prostitutes have already transgressed the behavioural boundaries that would have delineated them as properly female.

What is ironic about Chrysostom's treatment of this issue, however, is the way in which his own descriptions of errant and obedient females alike conjure up vivid verbal pictures for his audience, the like of which he complains about when found in the secular arena. While warning of the dangers of gazing upon women, Chrysostom makes both himself and the male members of his audience into a new set of gazers as he lingers on the minute details of female dress, cosmetics and body language. We have already seen how even professed ascetics were not immune from his careful scrutiny, and the result can be an extraordinarily graphic account of the female form and its adornment:

> But what virgin, you ask, wears gold, or has decorated hair? But there can be such a careful refinement of a simple dress, that these are nothing to it. You may contrive the appearance of a common garment far more than those who wear gold. For when a very dark coloured robe is drawn closely round the breast with a girdle (as dancers on the stage are attired), with such daintiness that it neither spreads into breadth nor shrinks into scantiness, but is between the two; and when the bosom is shown off with many folds, is this not more alluring than any silken robes? And when the shoe, shining in its blackness, ends in a sharp point, and is as elegant as a painting, so that even the width of the sole is hardly visible – or when, though indeed you do not paint your face, you spend much time and effort washing it, and spread a veil across the forehead, whiter than the face itself – and above that put on a hood, of which the blackness may set off the white by contrast – is there not in all this the vanity of dress? What can one say about the constant rolling of the eyes? About the wearing of the stomacher, so skilfully as to sometimes conceal, and sometimes disclose, the fastening? For they sometimes expose this too, so as to show the exquisiteness of the belt, and they wind the hood entirely round the head. Then like actors, they wear gloves so closely fitted, that they seem to grow upon their hands: and we could mention their walk, and other artifices more alluring than any ornament of gold.[18]

One wonders how such an austere and ascetic man as Chrysostom could have such detailed knowledge of the niceties of female grooming, but I feel it is a tribute to his keen powers of observation that allowed him to understand the daily lives of his flock, even though he did not share them, thus making his preaching more effective. By pouring such undiluted scorn on the many rituals of female dress as enacted by these wayward virgins,

Chrysostom clearly announces to the rest of his congregation that such vanity will not be tolerated in any person – ascetic or otherwise. By displaying such a detailed knowledge of all that is involved, he leaves the rich women of his congregation well aware that he can see through any of the artifices or ruses they might care to employ in the matter of their physical appearance. Here is a preacher who cannot be duped by feminine wiles, however carefully practised.

Chrysostom's allusions to the theatre and to actors in this passage are also ironic. He is unequivocal in his disapproval of dramatic spectacles, here as elsewhere, feeling that they give rise to sinful thoughts and desires, that they are contrary to his vision of the Christian city, and that they distract Christians from the business of devout living. And yet his response is to conjure up a dramatic image of his own, a kind of microcosmic theatre, contained within a sermon. Worrying that his congregation might go astray in the secular theatre, Chrysostom seems to have resolved to provide a Christianised version of the same, safely contained within the verbal boundaries of his homily and the physical boundaries of the church building. By providing his listeners with such vivid pen-pictures Chrysostom ensures that they remain entertained, even during a church service, while they focus on an imaginary female in the same way they would an actress on stage, but this time for ostensibly moral motives. While criticising the men who gaze upon the female, Chrysostom creates a new set of gazers, of which he is one, and while condemning the theatre and dramatic spectacles, he provides a substitution of much the same type. It would seem that Chrysostom felt a keen sense of competition with the attractions of the secular world, and responded by appropriating the rules for Christian ends.

The preacher's creation of such verbal spectacles can also serve another end. Teresa Shaw discusses a number of sermons by Chrysostom in which he attacks female gluttony as a particularly repulsive transgression.[19] Once more this would be a misdemeanour connected largely with the wealthier members of society, and yet to give in to such base desires is to be reduced to the level of slavery. Here Shaw deals extensively with Chrysostom's use of the concept of public shame and guilt as powerful motivators towards more moral behaviour. Physical appearance in the case of gluttony is very obviously an indication of the sin in question, and I believe a similar philosophy can be traced in Chrysostom's attacks on wealthily dressed females. In their case, the extent of their adornments serves as illustrations of their immorality in spite of professing to be devout Christians. The Christian message of love for all members of society is forgotten in the quest to be envied instead by those less financially fortunate within the community. The easiest way to arouse envy is to make a public display of prosperity and fortune, something these women accomplish by means of their dress and their accessories, and which Chrysostom attacks with growing frustration throughout his sermons. By focusing on their physical appearance to the extent he does in such passages as quoted above, Chrysostom makes these women the objects of the male gaze, but also the gaze of the general public, thus hoping to heighten their feelings of guilt and shame. If he can familiarise such errant females with the notion that they are sinning and are clearly perceived as doing so throughout their community, he will then be able to encourage them to mend their ways, if only for the value of their public appearance and status.

Echoes of the above passages detailing female dress as evidence of a corrupt moral state can be found in the writings of Jerome, roughly contemporary with Chrysostom although writing about the Western empire rather than the Eastern, where he too attacks false virgins, decrying their manipulation of the male gaze as a means of drawing attention to themselves, and thereby drawing men into sin:

> As they walk the streets they try to attract attention and with stealthy nods and winks draw after them troops of young men. Of them the prophet's words are true: 'Thou hast a whore's forehead: thou refusest to be ashamed.' Let them have only a little purple in their dress, and loose bandeau on their head to leave the hair free; cheap slippers, and a Maforte [a short cape, usually lilac] fluttering from their shoulders; sleeves fitting close to their arms, and a loose-kneed walk: there you have all their marks of virginity. Such women may have their admirers, and it may cost more to ruin them because they are called virgins. But to such virgins as these I prefer to be displeasing.[20]

Passages such as these have led to speculation that Chrysostom and Jerome may have met at some point in their careers, perhaps while Jerome was at Antioch, and that they exchanged ideas.[21] Certainly there are distinct similarities between Jerome's discussion of cohabiting ascetics in his *Epistle 22*, and the treatises of Chrysostom on the same subject. Even if the two men never met or conversed, there seems to have been a system in operation in the ancient world whereby texts were circulated among church communities in both the Latin and the Greek halves of the empire, and thus opinions on certain matters could be exchanged and shared.[22] Whether we accept this as an explanation for the strong similarities between the two authors, or we consider Jerome as having composed this passage independently, it remains true that both descriptions were included in their respective texts as having been calculated to be most likely to have an impact on the respective audiences. We can see therefore, the effect such vivid imagery was intended to have on its receivers. Both authors felt confident that their portrayals of the errant female were sufficiently shocking to warn off the rest of their audience from emulation. The more graphic the description, the more salutary the warning.

Conversely, however, female dress can also function as a symbol of behaviour more suited to Christian devoutness. According to

Chrysostom, following the lead of Paul, the correct style of dress in a woman is a visible demonstration of her natural inferiority to the male. In his exegesis of the first epistle to the Corinthians he dwells at length on the instructions of the apostle regarding the necessity of women covering their heads while in church:

> Many different symbols have been given to both man and woman; to him symbols of rulership, to her of subjection: and among them this one, that she should be covered, while he may have his head bare. If indeed these are symbols, you see that both sexes do wrong when they disturb the proper order, and transgress the arrangement of God and their own proper limits, with both the man falling into the woman's inferiority, and the woman rising up against the man by her outward appearance.[23]

It is interesting to see Chrysostom here attaching great importance to outward appearance as a measure of appropriate submissiveness on the part of the female, when elsewhere he has been at great pains to decry any emphasising of surface looks. Similarly the female should wear her hair long, as a natural head covering and a badge of her shame, while the male is rewarded for his superior virtue and intellect with permission to go bareheaded and with short locks. Nor is it suitable to exchange garments between the sexes, adopting the appearance of the opposite gender. This calls to mind the decrees of various church councils in which cross-dressing was specifically prohibited.[24] Some of the earliest ascetic females could only succeed in pursuing their chosen lifestyle by adopting the dress and demeanour of a man and retiring to the desert, sometimes assimilated into a male monastic community. Apocryphal stories tell of their true identity only becoming apparent when the women were being laid out for burial.[25] Here, however, Chrysostom is adamant that female dress should be an appropriate badge of their sex, regardless of their asceticism or membership of the laity. He thus demonstrates a dual approach to the question of female dress and appearance, decrying undue concentration on adornment as evidence of vanity and corruption, while nevertheless declaring that it is vital that women at least dress like women in order to avoid the horrors involved in transgressing gender boundaries.

### Wealthy men in Chrysostom's audience

As in the case of women, much of Chrysostom's criticism of the male members of his congregation is directed at their mishandling of the wealth available to them. However, while we saw women reprimanded for frivolity and vanity in their expenditure, in men such rash spending is viewed as a far more serious manner. For a man to delight so much in material riches as to lose sight of all else is for him to become a slave to money and to sin, and to forfeit his innate superiority. It is also to indulge in excess, an affront against disciplined masculinity under any scheme of things. This is a constantly recurring trope in Chrysostom's homilies, and a measure of his irritation on any particular day is the rhetorical extent of the comparisons he uses for such misguided men. Sometimes they are compared to mere slaves or barbarians, on other occasions to women or those outside the Christian fold, while the worst excesses are rebuked through comparison with base animals, thus indicating a distinct hierarchy of wrongdoing in Chrysostom's mind:

> And what is more shameless than those eyes [of an avaricious man]? What is more immodest, more like a greedy dog? For a dog never holds his ground with such shameless impudence as when he is grasping at all men's goods. What is more polluted than those hands? What more audacious than that mouth, gobbling everything down and still not satisfied? No indeed, do not consider the countenance and the eyes as being a man's [human?] (*Mê gar eis to prosôpon kai tous ophthalmous idêis, hoti anthrôpou*). For such looks as these do not belong to the eyes of men ... The eyes of men are accustomed to look upon poor persons in affliction, and to be softened; but at the sight of the poor the eyes of the rapacious man glare like those of wild beasts. The eyes of men do not look on other men's goods as if they were their own, but rather consider their own belongings as others'; and they do not covet what is given to others, but rather exhaust their own means upon others. But these people are not content unless they take the property of all men. For it is not a man's eye which they have, but a wild beast's.[26]

It is possible to argue that Chrysostom here addresses mankind in general, that the word *anthrôpos* is not gender-specific, and that most rhetoric of the later empire was similarly generic in its nature. It has been suggested, however, that these orators regularly used this term when intending to refer to the male sex, in spite of the fact that it was not gender-specific.[27] In any case, I would contend that in this particular instance, Chrysostom is specifically concerned with the distribution and accumulation of wealth within society, which was predominantly a male activity. He therefore addresses those most likely to offend in this respect. What the men targeted in this passage have done is to take their financial activities beyond the appropriate boundaries and so have become more like predatory animals than noble beings created in God's image. They have forgotten the self-discipline appropriate to their sex, and have instead fallen prey to rapaciousness. As we saw in the previous chapter, women who were reprimanded for inappropriate use of wealth transgressed in the way in which they spent their money – on foolish and frivolous items of unnecessary luxury. Here, however, Chrysostom is far more concerned with the illicit means employed to amass this wealth, thus making his discourse more suited to a male audience.

Their errant ways have forfeited them the right even to be described as men, or human beings of any sort, since their greed has outstripped all reason, thus reducing them to, or below, the level of irrational beasts of prey. The qualities of justice and reason are what mark men out as separate from animals, and it is these qualities which those men who abuse their financial role in society have forfeited. Therefore we see the retention of some degree of rationality being as important to male status as a disciplined approach to one's lifestyle. The fact that the implications of such uses of money are far more wide-ranging than the expenditure of females is particularly worrying to Chrysostom, and his interest in transforming the face of the ancient city quickly becomes bound up with these discussions of wealth. It is the male who has most power and influence in this sphere, in secular and divine considerations, since the man has been granted the ability by God to operate in civic matters, while care of domestic concerns, as we have seen, was granted to the females. If a man is to abuse this power therefore, failing to curb his greed and failing to apply the civic virtue of justice to his financial dealings, the consequences of his actions could conceivably be felt throughout the market place, thus impinging on the daily life of the urban community. Chrysostom, in common with most other thinkers of the day, did agree that women possessed a certain measure of justice in their characters, since this was after all necessary for the smooth running of the domestic sphere. The household is regarded as a microcosm of the larger civic unit, therefore requiring similar administrative structures and virtues. But should a housewife fail to demonstrate these abilities the impact need only be felt within the walls of the *oikos*. If such 'malfunctions' can be restricted to a single household, therefore, the damage can be limited and contained. Should a man, however, while operating in the civic sphere, show evidence of a lack of justice or rational control over his emotions, desires and interactions with other citizens, the containment exercise becomes much more difficult. The urban unit depends on the smooth transaction of business among like-minded men, and so any breach in this contract threatens the entire function of the city. It is on this basis that Chrysostom constructs his appeals to the men in his congregation to closely guard and assiduously practice their male attributes.

Elsewhere in Chrysostom's homilies greedy men are accused of actually becoming effeminate, of allowing their covetousness to overthrow the boundaries between the different tasks appropriate to each of the sexes. In laying such a charge against them Chrysostom indicates the gravity of the situation. A lapse in appropriate male behaviour not only threatens the smooth running of the city, but undermines the very fabric of society itself by corrupting the divisions between the sexes. Instead of performing customary and recognisably male duties, therefore, such men have fallen to involving themselves in weaving and associated textile-related duties as part of their quest to amass greater riches.[28] The similarities in such passages with the sentiments expressed in the treatise on the *subintro-*

*ductae* are very clear. It is also interesting to note that effeminacy is a sin frequently included by Chrysostom with other more 'mainstream' transgressions such as adultery, grave robbing and murder, thus underlining the seriousness with which he viewed it.[29] These crimes and misdemeanours were listed among the possible offences that could be cited by a woman who wished to divorce her husband in the late Roman empire.[30] An erosion of one's gender identity seems to have been viewed similarly seriously by Chrysostom, and although he does not go so far as to countenance divorce, his audience would have had a shared knowledge of this legal allusion, and would thus easily understand his anxiety. A man who has abnegated his masculinity to the extent of undertaking traditionally female tasks simply to accumulate more money is by no means a fit husband, since he cannot rightly even be categorised as male in Chrysostom's eyes. The equation of effeminacy with sins that made even a woman legally allowed to seek a divorce clearly highlights the almost unspeakable nature of such behaviour, and it is the abuse of wealth that is the common theme throughout.

The lack of reason in the behaviour of these corrupt and greedy men is further underlined by their misaligned priorities in life. So engrossed have they become in their lust for wealth and the associated life of luxury, that some of them now care more for the welfare of their hunting dogs as symbols of material success, than they do for the poorer members of society. They have also become so accustomed to this selfishness that they are as oblivious to the peril their souls are in as drunkards are to the rank smell of stale wine.[31] Chrysostom feels that much of this prioritisation of wealth comes from a misguided sense of vanity, as these men hope to win the admiration or even the envy of those around them. Paradoxically, however, this shows a willingness to be a slave – either to money or to public opinion. This too leads to strong condemnation from the preacher:

> For just as a prostitute stands at her place and hires herself out to anyone [gives herself away – as if in marriage], so too do those who are the slaves of vanity. Or rather, these are even baser than she is. For this kind of women often treat those who are infatuated with them scornfully. But you prostitute yourself to everybody … .[32]

We have already seen the way in which the prostitute served as the lowest common denominator of behaviour within society, despised on account of her commercial dealings which marked her out as not modestly feminine, and yet not masculine in any of the admirable qualities of courage or virtue. The fact that these men are described as even more promiscuous in their 'hiring out' of their integrity to fickle public opinion, makes this a stern rebuke indeed. Those who boast of being in such a kind of slavery through their love of wealth are in fact turning their backs on the God-given opportunity to be rational and controlled beings, forfeiting the superiority granted to them over females and dumb beasts. Such men show a conceit, and an added lack of reason in their choice not to rise to God's challenge to be superior to those less well endowed with intelligence.[33] Accusations of effeminacy are also a way of revitalising the well-established philosophical trope that love of wealth is akin to slavery, employed by Chrysostom to make his audience sit up and take more notice of a theory they had heard expounded many times before.[34]

Chrysostom's approach to this problem of the male pursuit of wealth and power to the exclusion of all else varies according to his mood or the seriousness of the problem. He frequently adopts the polemical approach such as is seen above, verbally lashing his audience with his cutting sarcasm or his outright contempt. His righteous anger is certainly something to behold. On other occasions, however, he appeals to what reason he hopes these men yet possess, as well as to their pride and vanity, arguing that all the worldly riches they can accumulate will not guarantee them a place in heaven, or even immortality in the minds of others. Fancy houses do not delight even their owners after a certain amount of time:

> And what is the meaning of the gilded ceiling? Does it not fulfil the same purpose as for the person whose house is more moderate in its scale? 'But there is great delight in it,' he says. Yes there is, for the first or second day, but afterwards, there is none at all, and it stands for nothing. For if the sun does not strike us with wonder, since we are accustomed to it, so much more so do works of art fail to awe us, and we only look at them as at things of clay. For tell me, what does a range of pillars contribute to make your dwelling superior to others, or the finest statues, or the gilding spread over the wall? Nothing; instead these come from opulence and brashness, and overwhelming pride and folly; for everything in the house should be necessary and useful, and not superfluous.[35]

So far does the covetousness of some men extend that they refuse to part with their wealth to anyone, under the pretence that they are safeguarding it for their children's inheritance. Chrysostom ridicules such excuses, pointing out that the Old Testament Jacob had twelve children and yet his honesty or generosity was not compromised, just as Abraham with only one child could always show consideration for those in need. The preacher warns his congregation that if they continue to use their children as justification for their miserly ways they might suddenly find themselves deprived of this God-given gift.[36] Here he appeals to the strong belief all Roman citizens had, which was that children were a means of conferring posterity on the family line, and also the future holders of the family wealth.[37]

On another occasion, in his efforts to curtail their lavish spending, Chrysostom appeals to that same vanity he perceives to be part of the character of the wealthy members of his congregation. He rebukes those men who pander to the frivolous desires of their wives to have their carriages and horses bedecked with gold trappings, or those men who allow their wives to commission silver chamber-pots, arguing that such spending will not in fact do anything to increase their standing within society. On the contrary, such lavishly decorated mules and horses will only serve to distract the attention of the ordinary members of the public, leading them to focus on mere beasts of burden rather than on the humans who seek notice in this manner. Thus, Chrysostom logically concludes, they have wasted all their efforts and a considerable amount of money, on effacing their own glory! Elsewhere he speaks of how, ostentatious as the female sex are in their love of ornament, their husbands frequently outdo them in the pride they take in such display on the part of their wives. In this case they are blamed for instigating such frivolous love of luxury on the part of the female, a rare reversal of the way in which Chrysostom viewed the cycle of temptation and sin between the sexes:

> For I do not think that the wife is so pretentious about her own jewels, as her husband is of the ornaments of his wife. He is not so proud of his own golden girdle, as he is of his wife's wearing jewels of gold. So you men are the causes of this too, since you ignite the spark of ostentation and fan the flames. But more importantly, it is not so great a sin in a woman as in a man. You are ordained to regulate her; you claim in every way to have superiority. Show her then through your own attire also, that you have no interest in these spendthrift habits of hers. It is more suitable for a woman to adorn herself than for a man. But if you cannot escape the temptation, how then can you expect her to?[38]

This makes for an interesting connection with the passage cited earlier where Chrysostom scorns a possible excuse for ostentation offered to him by a rich wife. This hypothetical woman claimed that she only adorned herself so lavishly to please her husband, which Chrysostom declared to be doing him harm rather than good. Here, however, we see that such an excuse may well have some validity. These men do indeed require their wives to be lavishly adorned in order to display them to full advantage. The only difference between the two passages may be in a perception of the hypothetical motives. The wife may well have believed that she was gratifying her husband on a personal level by taking such care with her appearance. The husband, however, sees the situation as having broader implications. He may indeed feel privately gratified by his beautiful and well-dressed wife, but he will feel still more affirmed by the admiration and even envy of his peers when they see the style in which he is able to keep her. For Chrysostom, however, the more lavish the display the more heinous the offence, since pride is added to vanity in this type of sinning.

This passage also highlights the approach Chrysostom feels to be particularly effective when trying to manipulate his congregation, and which we have already seen in operation on several occasions, whereby he warns the men that they are being outstripped in virtue by mere women. Thus these women win the public esteem and respect which should rightfully be the preserve of the males within that society, purely because they have been able to control their physical and worldly desires to a greater extent than the men. They have managed to control even those vices with which they have been naturally endowed, while the men who do not have any such excuses manage to sink to lower levels in their luxurious and pride-filled lifestyles. We have seen Chrysostom in *Homily XIII on Ephesians* make it very clear what he was about, as he detailed the spectacular way in which even rich and delicate women rose above their natural limitations to embrace the ascetic lifestyle. Chrysostom declares openly that he does not speak at such length of these women merely to glorify them or praise them, but to shame the male members of his congregation into reassessing their behaviour:

> I have said these things not from any desire to gratify them, but to shame ourselves, to chastise and reprimand ourselves, so that we can regain the authority that belongs to us, not because we are greater in size, but because of our greater foresight, our protection of them, and our virtue.[39]

Thus we see Chrysostom juxtapose the ideal qualities of masculinity with the implications involved in abandoning these natural advantages in favour of baser instincts – the man ceases to be a fit superior to the woman, and sinks to a lower moral level even than the so-called weaker sex. In arguing in this manner, Chrysostom targets a traditional aspect of civic life on the part of the male. In conventional Roman terms, it was vital that a man's economic and social standing be displayed by his conspicuous consumption. Even his very style of dress served to mark him out as separate from those less financially well off than himself, or less influential in civic circles.[40] Chrysostom now wishes to remove this emphasis on dress and lavish spending as markers of personal worth, replacing them instead with conspicuous almsgiving and modest attire as indicators of an inner virtue. And so he directs his attention towards making traditional behaviour appear ridiculous and even effeminate, in order to improve the outlook of his congregation.

*

This variety of approaches, and the flattering appeal to reason on the part of Chrysostom, would seem to indicate a fundamental difference in his treatment of the two sexes on this question of wealth. When discussing the female use and abuse of riches, Chrysostom had an irritated yet simultaneously resigned attitude to the problem. He believed that the vanity and frivolity which prompted female spending was an innate quality in the female sex, and so it is addressed on that level. Nor does he foresee particularly far-reaching consequences of this feminine failing, since most of his discourse is confined to the topic of female dress and appearance. This is what women spend their money on, according to Chrysostom, and while it is dangerous from the point of view of the lustful thoughts it might arouse in the male, and the detrimental effects it has on the woman's own soul, it is largely a private matter and its ramifications confined to the domestic sphere. The male abuse of wealth, however, is seen by Chrysostom as an infinitely more serious matter, hence the comparisons we have seen of covetous and spendthrift men with animals. Again this would fit in with Chrysostom's perception of male activity as being public and active. Thus any flagrant abuses of wealth and power would have more far-reaching implications than the female equivalent which could have little or no impact in the civic arena. The distribution of money among male family members and peers was one of the foundations of civic society, and Chrysostom is concerned that it should transpire with due Christian devoutness. In the next chapter I deal in greater depth with his preaching on wealth and its influence within the city structure, but the division of the sexes in his teaching on the subject is worthy of note here.

# Money and Chrysostom's City

The Vincys lived in an easy profuse way, not with any new ostentation, but according to the family habits and traditions, so that the
children had no standard of economy, and the elder ones retained
some of their infantile notion that their father might pay for
anything if he could. Mr. Vincy himself had expensive Middlemarch
habits – spent money on coursing, on his cellar, and on dinner-giving,
while mamma had those running accounts with tradespeople, which
give a cheerful sense of getting everything one wants without question of payment.

George Eliot, *Middlemarch*, ch. 23

## Introduction

In the preceding chapters, we have had a chance to examine Chrysostom's
attitudes to wealth in connection with specifically gendered uses and
abuses of it. The preacher had a very clear concept as to the division
between the sexes in this matter. Women were generally seen as guilty of
extravagant spending on frivolous items – silver chamber-pots, heavy gold
jewellery, and cosmetic enhancement of their beauty. Men were criticised
for facilitating these vain desires on the part of the women by making the
funds available to them, or even by themselves taking pride in the lavish
appearance of their wives and household attendants. Thus they too were
accused of spending their wealth foolishly. On a much more serious level,
however, men were also accused of becoming avaricious and grasping in
their desire for wealth and social standing, sometimes going to such
lengths that they forfeited their natural superiority of virtue and intellect.
Thus Chrysostom applied his scheme of gendered conduct and wrongdoing
to riches and their distribution and display throughout society.

This discussion of wealth in connection with the appropriate behaviour
of the two sexes, however, occurs within a much broader context. The evils
of excessive riches kept the preacher exercised on an almost constant
basis, as he frequently reprimands his flock for their failure to live up to
the standards of behaviour set them by their faith. In doing so, as well as
Christianising traditional references to wealth, Chrysostom hopes to
remodel the behaviour of his congregation, thus leading to the eventual

transformation of the *polis* that we have already spoken about. A shift in attitudes to money and its uses would lead to corresponding changes in the overall appearance of the ancient city, since wealth was the cornerstone on which society was established, and by which most activities of this community were influenced.[1] Chrysostom's approach to achieving this ambition through his preaching is similar to that employed in trying to guide the behaviour of each of the sexes along more appropriate lines, as will become apparent as we progress. Here, however, Chrysostom becomes even more exercised on the question of misuse of wealth as detrimental to society than he has been on the issue of the transgression of gender boundaries, leading to an even greater level of outspokenness than we have seen in his homilies to date.

Such outbursts on the part of the preacher are set against a social context in which the possession and public display of wealth was a highly important index of status and worth, and where poverty was seen as a simple fact of life. We have already seen the way in which both men and women took active means to enhance their outward appearance of prosperity in order to attract the notice and admiration of their peers and their social inferiors alike. But Chrysostom remains concerned as to the dangers such acquisitiveness poses to the moral well-being of these wealthy people, and to the community as a whole, since conspicuous consumption of this kind is in direct opposition to his proposed Christianised version of the urban unit. To combat its dangers, Chrysostom begins to preach on economic activities and displays as actions on behalf of God, making his congregation stewards of a divine authority rather than simply of their own affairs, thus hoping to arouse a greater sense of responsibility in them on this issue.

A full examination of all Chrysostom's teaching on this thorny subject of wealth and its display is too large a task to accomplish here. Indeed the structure of the ancient economy and the importance of riches as an index of social worth have been thoroughly discussed by many scholars.[2] It is not my intention to repeat, or even substantially add to this work. My aim is rather to demonstrate the way in which the issues of wealth and the construction of Christian gender roles are inextricably entwined in Chrysostom's work, both in approach and in philosophy. His concern with maintaining boundaries between two contrasting modes of behaviour is by no means restricted to gender issues, but extends to all areas of daily life in the ancient city, including the appropriate attitudes to, and disposal of, the available wealth. Money and gender are so closely related because of Chrysostom's belief that if each of the sexes behaves in a Christian manner then wealth will be regulated almost automatically. Similarly the converse is true; if wealth is disposed of in a Christian manner, each of the sexes will be behaving as it ought. Overall, therefore, a general pattern in the preacher's style can be observed, carefully calculated by him to reach the maximum audience possible, and to manipulate their behaviour along more obviously Christian lines.

## The evils of wealth

Just as in his discussions of female vices and virtues, and the corresponding misdemeanours of the male members of his congregation, Chrysostom's favourite approach to condemning the misuse of wealth is to detail at length the evils which can arise from it. Presenting a concrete example of the infraction in question, the preacher can then systematically expose it for the folly it is, carefully subjecting each of its component parts to his characteristic brand of sarcasm and polemic. Thus we have many passages in which the activities and lifestyles of those who count as the rich and famous of this society are detailed in much the same way as Chrysostom lingered over the minutiae of female dress and cosmetic appearance, followed by similar questions as to the possible use of such behaviour. This approach allows Chrysostom to present many of his favourite philosophies to his audience, while simultaneously retaining their attention by the sheer entertainment value of such vivid depictions of the wealthy lifestyle.

The vast majority of these passages are calculated by Chrysostom as best encapsulating the familiar trope that love of material possessions is in fact a form of slavery rather than freedom, and that wealth brings more pains that it does pleasures. This was, of course, by no means innovative thinking on the part of Chrysostom, nor was it unique or attributable to Christianity. We have already seen Chrysostom himself attempt to persuade women that owning and wearing expensive jewellery simply left them anxious as to its safety, or indeed concerned as to the degree of public notice they had attracted by means of this display. Men too, who worked simply to acquire greater wealth, paradoxically increased their unease and insecurity with regard to its safe possession. But in addition to this Chrysostom feels very strongly that this anxiety is further enhanced when the wealth in question is ill-gotten gains. Some people were prone to argue that it was poverty and the fear of it that made them anxious and uneasy, and so they exerted all their energies in trying to avoid it, primarily through what Chrysostom calls 'grasping' behaviour. But he counteracts such feeble reasoning with the claim that wealth so acquired is far from granting security. Indeed it increases vulnerability to outside threats, something Chrysostom demonstrates with his regular portraits of the wealthy cowering in their ornate mansions lest someone try to wrest their possessions from them. He adds to this deliberately ridiculous picture the persuasive argument that if these people wish to have a secure inheritance to transmit to future generations, it is in their own best interests to ensure that these funds are accumulated in a righteous manner:

> So if you really want to be wealthy, you must never be grasping; if you want to be able to pass wealth on to your children, acquire honest wealth, if indeed there is any such thing. Because this kind remains constant and firm, whereas wealth which is not wholesome

quickly wastes and perishes. Tell me, do you intend to be rich and so grasp at the goods of other people? Surely this is not wealth: wealth consists in possessing what is your own. He who possesses the belongings of others, can never be a truly wealthy man; since at that rate even the silk merchants, who receive their goods as a consignment from others, would be the wealthiest and the richest of men.[3]

This passage is strongly reminiscent of the attack we saw launched in the previous chapter, when covetousness was decried on the basis that it eroded the masculinity and even the humanity of those at fault. Here Chrysostom warns against this kind of behaviour by appealing to one of the cornerstones of Roman society – the safe transmission of wealth to future generations. Any threat to this process would be viewed with great anxiety by Chrysostom's listeners, and he is quick to make use of this insecurity in his preaching, claiming that a Christian attitude to wealth will in fact assist them in performing their traditional civic duties.

Within this more generally aimed effort to urge his congregation away from avaricious behaviour, however, we also see something of Chrysostom's ambiguous attitude to wealth as a commodity in itself. He is not entirely sure whether it is possible to acquire 'righteous' wealth, and further on within the same homily he wonders bemusedly why mankind is so eager to amass riches to begin with, since God fashioned humans within certain boundaries, within which all their needs could be met without having to seek elsewhere. The practice of hoarding, therefore, or the custom of having many duplicated possessions, is a deliberate transgression of those natural boundaries installed by God and is symptomatic of what Chrysostom dismisses as mere 'folly, absurdity, and vainglory ... ':

For instance, God told us to clothe our bodies in one, or at the most two outfits, and there is no need of any more than this to cover ourselves. What is the use of ten thousand changes of clothes, especially when they are moth-eaten? The stomach has its set limits, and when anything is taken beyond these limits, it will naturally destroy the person. What then, is the use of all your herds and flocks of animals, and your butchering of their flesh for food? We only need one roof to shelter us, and so where is the need for your vast sites and expensive buildings. Do you deprive the poor, simply so that vultures and jackdaws can have somewhere to nest? And these actions deserve the worst kind of hell. Many people are constantly erecting structures that glisten with pillars and expensive marbles, in locations that they have never even seen for themselves. What scheme is there that they have not tried? But neither they themselves nor anyone else benefits from all of this.[4]

Christianity by no means has the monopoly on such moral outrage, since similar views were held throughout the classical tradition, as can be seen for example in Aristophanes' remarks through the mouth of his heroine Proxagora in *The Assembly of Women*:

> I want all to have a share in everything, and all property to be in common; there will no longer be either rich or poor; no longer shall we see one man harvesting vast tracts of land, while another has not ground enough to be buried in, nor one man surround himself with a whole army of slaves, while another has not a single attendant ...

Plato's ideal state also propounded an idea of common property as best advancing the happiness and productivity of the society. When men are preoccupied with accumulating more wealth than their neighbour, they become corrupt and hostile to the rest of their society. Holding goods in common would avoid this potential decline of moral standards within the community.[5] While Aristotle does not agree with this position, feeling that the variety of the state would be threatened by such conformity, he does argue against excess in any sphere.[6] He believes that those who are too wealthy do not submit to authority, nor learn the habit of obedience, which is similar to Chrysostom's argument when discussing the contribution made by luxurious living to sexual deviancy, as we previously saw.[7]

We have already seen the great importance attached by Chrysostom to the natural order of things as established by God, when discussing the boundaries which exist between the sexes. Here it becomes apparent that he considered every aspect of life in the ancient city to be similarly structured according to a divinely ordained harmony. The needless excess described above is a direct contravention of this system of organisation, hence Chrysostom's bewilderment and irritation at the attitudes of his flock. This passage also serves, however, to illustrate the paradigm of Chrysostom's approach to this topic, a pattern of argument that remains largely constant whenever it is raised within his sermons. He details the type of expenditure or stockpiling of wealth which he regards as particularly dangerous, often demonstrating his by now familiarly keen levels of observation. Chrysostom then proceeds to a dramatic inquiry as to the possible gains or benefits accruing from such activities. The answer is always the same – no good can come of this kind of behaviour, but rather it is indicative of moral instability and should be avoided on that account. Indeed covetousness of this extent is tantamount to idolatry, since these men and women have placed material possessions on a higher level than God, turning instead to what Chrysostom calls a 'cruel tyrant' – this acquisitiveness. He expresses wonder at those people who attend church, claim to acknowledge God as the true divinity and lift their hands in prayer, and yet owe their allegiance to such a harsh master as wealth and the desire to amass it. The fact that these misguided Christians do not physically bow down to money or slay animals for sacrifices to it does not excuse them from these charges of idolatry, since they have turned away from God in favour of Mammon.[8]

Chrysostom also believes that this covetousness is the basic sin that gives rise to others such as lust, since what they both evidence is a desire to have more than one's fair share. This desire is condemned by Chrysostom as a form of arrogance and misanthropy towards the rest of mankind. Again he returns to God's natural order of things, pointing out that in his goodness God has bestowed the whole earth and its bounty on mankind, and yet they still reach out to grasp yet more for themselves, thus insulting the generosity and munificence of their divine master. People who are covetous to such an extent as to want to inherit the world, warns Chrysostom darkly, can have no inheritance in heaven.[9] He urges his congregation to consider the acts of plunder and acquisitiveness they have committed in their careers, and to make reparation by restoring everything fourfold. This then might serve as a plea to God for leniency when they come to be judged. But the preacher laments for those within his community who have become so taken up by their grasping desires that they do not even notice the danger they are in. Here we see Chrysostom compare such prioritising of wealth to a form of madness and blindness, thus emphasising the seriousness of the situation.[10]

Throughout his preaching Chrysostom regards the pursuit of wealth as an illness or dire disease. It attacks the nobility of the human spirit, making the soul abase itself before an inanimate object, and doing much to take away the element of choice with which God endowed mankind. Chrysostom compares those who concentrate on hoarding wealth to the exclusion of all else in their lives, to diseased patients who do not heed the advice of their physicians, thus further inflaming their condition. A similar process is worked on the immortal soul of those who desire to be rich beyond their normal requirements, ignoring instructions to remain content with what they have. And so their craving of wealth is seen as senseless and dangerous. It is also very interesting to note that those who are foolish enough to admire this kind of wealthy person are similarly condemned as sharing in their sinfulness, and are indeed portrayed as ridiculous, since what they applaud is folly rather than any quality worthy of approbation. Throughout one particular passage, Chrysostom discusses this foolishness by using references to various mythical beasts from the corpus of Greek literature. The desire to acquire money to this dangerous extent is called a Scylla by Chrysostom, a Chimaera, or even a hippocentaur. Thus he condemns the avarice of his congregation as a piece of mythical nonsense, indicating the sheer foolishness of these activities as well as simultaneously pouring scorn on the inherited pagan culture of the audience. He is aware that speaking thus strongly on this issue of wealth will make him himself an object of ridicule to some of his audience, but his response is to paint in even greater detail the madness of those whose priorities are so misaligned:

Truly, being wealthy does indeed make people senseless and mad. If their power stretched to such an extent, they would also try to have the earth made of gold, and walls of gold, perhaps the sky and the air too. What insanity this is, what an outrage, what a burning fever! Another person, made in the image of God, is dying of cold; and are you supplying yourself with such things as these? Oh the senseless pride! How could a madman have acted worse than this?[11]

Chrysostom here is at his most irate, unable to comprehend the wilfulness of his congregation in pursuing their path of error. He threatens the worst offenders with expulsion from his church, since he claims to have no need of a distempered audience. Here he takes his responsibility as leader of his flock very seriously, knowing that he will be called to account for their misdemeanours on the Day of Judgement if he fails to exhort them in this fashion, which goes some way towards explaining the strength of his outburst. He is outraged that the wantonness of his community has become so prevalent that the poor stand around the church cold and hungry, while others are perpetually drunk, bloated, and using silver chamber-pots to receive their excrements. Again he condemns it out of hand as madness and brutishness. In *De Sacerdotio* Chrysostom speaks of the necessity of a priest of a community being discreet and tactful, so that he can persuade those who are wealthy to give to the poor generously, but without alienating those who are already active in almsgiving. Such theoretical tact and restraint does not, however, always seem apparent in Chrysostom's practice, and it would be interesting to see how many of his audience did indeed become offended and disgusted by his continuous ranting against the evils of wealth, and the selfishness of the wealthy.[12]

Other Church Fathers held similar views, however, indicating that there was a standard procedure for discussing wealth and the evils it gives rise to in the ancient world. As discussed by J. Gonzalez in *Faith and Wealth*, the Cappadocians were particularly aware of the hardships caused by poverty and hunger, and felt that greed was the reason men were so driven to amass wealth. An interesting contrast in approaches emerges, however, in the more agricultural tone of their writings as compared with Chrysostom's very urban concerns. While Chrysostom worries about town houses reaching lavish proportions, and commercial activities driving the lifestyles of the citizens, the likes of Basil of Caesarea and Gregory Nazianzus are concerned about the large estates that exist in the countryside, on which the poor are forced to labour for their very survival:

One of us oppressed the poor, taking his lands and moving the boundaries ... as if he alone were to inhabit the earth. Another polluted the earth with interests and rents, reaping where he did not sow ... not tilling the soil, but exploiting the sufferings of the needy ... Another had no mercy for the widow and the orphan, and did not feed the hungry ... . It is for these reasons that God's wrath is unleashed upon the children of unbelief ... .[13]

'What will you tell the Judge, you who dress up your walls and leave humans naked? You who groom and adorn your horses and will not look at your naked brother? You whose wheat rots, and yet do not feed the hungry?' demands Basil of Caesarea,[14] while Ambrose gives us another portrait of urban abuses of wealth, markedly similar to remarks we have seen Chrysostom make:

> You strip people naked and dress up your walls. The naked poor cries before your door, and you do not even look at him. It is a naked human being that begs you, and you are considering what marbles to use for paving. The poor begs you for money and gets none. There is a human being seeking bread, and your horses chew gold in their bits. You rejoice in your precious adornments, while others have nothing to eat. A harsh judgement awaits you, o rich! The people are hungry and you close your granaries. The people cry and you show your jewels. Woe to one who can save so many lives from death, and does not![15]

Previously we saw Chrysostom approach the covetousness of the male members of his congregation in a similar manner, also accusing them of forfeiting their natural superiority in the world by failing to maintain a rational approach to life. But often the accusation is levelled at mankind in more general terms, as Chrysostom warns them of the loss of reason and the descent into animal behaviour resulting from their avaricious behaviour. He even provides an example from recent history to support his point, in which he alludes to the Riot of the Statues at Antioch in 387. The response of the emperor in this case was severe, threatening the city with destruction, and Chrysostom believes that this harsh and tyrannous spirit resulted from the immense wealth and status of this king. This wealth conferred power, which in this case manifested itself in extremely negative terms, leading the emperor in question, Theodosius I, to believe that he could dictate the fate of an entire community.[16] It is interesting to note that this is possibly the only time Chrysostom explicitly criticises imperial administration in his homilies, and the emperor in question is now deceased, making it much safer for the preacher to speak his mind.

Chrysostom speaks frequently of wealth itself in pejorative terms, considering it useless for any purpose but to aggravate human passions to dangerous levels:

> For wealth truly is a thorny plant, bearing no fruit, and being both ugly to look at and difficult to use, injuring those that interfere with it, and not only not bearing fruit itself, but also obstructing what fruit had been growing in that area. So too is wealth. Not only does it not bear eternal fruit, but it even hampers those who wish to acquire it. Thorns are the food of irrational camels; since they are good for nothing they are burned and consumed by fire. So too is wealth useful

for nothing but to ignite the furnace, to light up the day that burns like an oven, and to nourish passions which are without reason, such as revenge and anger. For so too is the camel that feeds on thorns. For it is said by those who know about these things, that there is no animal so implacable, so sulky and spiteful, as a camel. So too is wealth. It feeds the unreasonable passions of the soul, but it pierces and wounds the rational emotions, as is the case with thorns.[17]

Here his comparison of wealth with the sulky camel would have struck a chord with his audience, as well as holding their interest throughout this lengthy tirade. This then is the source of Chrysostom's anxiety regarding the pursuit of riches, that it erodes the reason that was God's special gift to mankind. As such therefore, the accumulation of wealth serves as an insult to God, since it marks a turning of one's back on the path to salvation offered by him. The only way to purge the community of this sinful love of material possessions is to burn it out, just as farmers use fire to eradicate thorns. In this manner, Chrysostom urges harsh measures, as befitting the extent of the problem and the danger to the Christian community arising from it.

An example of the terrible danger arising from the thorn of wealth can be seen in the way all strata of society have grown accustomed to paying homage to those among them who possess great riches. Indeed they pay more heed to those with great estates than they do to the representatives of God. When wealthy members of the congregation enter the church, they enter not to worship or to listen to the word of God, but to display their property to those around them. We have already seen examples of this, as Chrysostom criticises those women who parade into church with no consideration but to attract the notice and envy of other women. When the priest or deacon stands to read to this worldly congregation or offer instruction, they pay him no attention but continue to assess the impact of their public display of wealth on those around them. But it would not be so if an earthly ruler were to address them, asserts Chrysostom. For in that case, his superior wealth and corresponding power and influence, demonstrated by his mode of dress, would command instant respect and attention from the rest of the community:

> Tell me then, I beg you, if now, when we are all here, some one entered, wearing a golden girdle, and holding himself upright, with an air of importance said that he was sent by an earthly king, and that he brought letters to the whole city concerning matters of significance; would you not then all turn at once towards him? Would you not, without any command from a deacon, keep an absolute silence? Indeed I think you would.[18]

Why then should they not pay even greater attention to the representatives of their divine ruler – the one who holds their salvation in his hands?

Again we see Chrysostom's frustration with the waywardness of his congregation, as well as some useful insights into the trappings of imperial messengers and fashion statements in contemporary society. Elsewhere Chrysostom makes the disparity of his audience's attitude still more clear:

> And are we not to be ashamed, that men can be overcome in this way by the love of money, but not show proportionate zeal in our love for God, and that we do not honour him so well as we honour gold? For the sake of money men will undertake vigils and journeys, and constant dangers, as well as hatred, hostility, and in brief, all manner of things. But we do not presume to say a single word in favour of God, nor incur any enmity, and if we are asked to assist any of those who are mistreated, we abandon the injured person, removing ourselves from the hatred of those in power, and the danger it implies.[19]

Chrysostom is adamant that it is love of money that is the root of all other evils, since this love is a love of things present, and a granting of a higher value to them than to more lofty, spiritual matters.[20] He details this progression of sinfulness in *Homily II on the Philippians*, declaring:

> From this source springs envy; indeed all evils come from no other source but this, that we are infatuated with the things of this world. For if you considered worldly wealth and glory to truly be nothing, you would not look with negative feelings on those who possessed them. But since you stare at these things, and adore them, and are attracted by them, for this reason envy and vainglory burden you; it all comes from idolising the things of the present life.[21]

Chrysostom struggles to persuade his listeners that the rich man is worthy to be an object of their pity rather than their admiration and their envy, and that they should not shed tears over their own lack of extreme wealth. Indeed those who are envious to this extent are themselves to be lamented, for they are discontented people who believe they lack something, when in fact they are lucky to have everything necessary to them. Why should they feel jealous of the rich man who has after all merely made himself a slave, asks Chrysostom. The wealthy person is bound like a dog and can enjoy no rest, simply on account of his possessions. For in the evening, if he should hear a noise, he is convinced that he is being robbed. Should his neighbour be the victim of theft he is sure that he will be next, and so remains vulnerable and insecure long after the unfortunate neighbour has put the incident to one side and got on with his life. This anxiety reaches such heights that it keeps sleep at bay, and again we see Chrysostom wonderingly muse on the willingness of his congregation to adopt this form of slavery. The tyranny of wealth, by such means, becomes even greater than the force exerted on a human by nature. For God ordained it that sleep be a natural requirement of the human, and that it should overcome the individual when it is necessary, regardless of his or her will. But now, as if through self-hatred, concern for material possessions sets aside this natural control and exerts its own tyranny on the human condition.

Elsewhere Chrysostom expands on the foolish anxieties attendant upon a surfeit of riches:

> Has day dawned? Then such a person dreads informers. Has night fallen on him? He is terrified of thieves. Is death near? Then the thought that he must leave his goods to others disturbs him even more than death. Does he have a son? His aspirations increase; and then he considers himself to be poor. Has he no son? Then his struggles are all the greater.[22]

In this way Chrysostom again calls into question the very foundations of Roman civic society, namely the transmission of wealth through generations. He scorns the concerns a man might have as to how to draw up his final will and testament, and mocks those who consider children to be a drain on their resources, while others lament the lack of heirs to receive their bequests. The concern of society should not be on this movement of wealth from one individual to another, but on the reverence appropriate to God, and the lifestyle suited to the title of Christian. In this way Chrysostom imbues all the customary economic activities of ancient society with a newly Christianised suspicion.[23] He also employs this passage as a means of eroding the false respect his audience have for such rich characters by rendering them ridiculous and pitiable.

In working to emphasise the unenviable position of the rich man, Chrysostom therefore inverts the situation, claiming that such a man is in fact poor in spirit. On many occasions he cites the parable of the rich man and Lazarus to this end, detailing the punishments endured by this wealthy personage after his death. For all his worldly possessions, and the power he was once able to command, once dead he was reduced to the role of begging even for a drop of water to moisten his tongue. By contrast Lazarus, who once had to plead for scraps from the rich man's table for his very survival, achieved true wealth in the kingdom of heaven. Therefore, claims Chrysostom, he who desires many things and works constantly to acquire is the poverty-stricken one, while he who needs nothing is rich indeed.

Here Chrysostom draws a careful distinction between what is merely wished for, and what is actually necessary for survival. He believes that no one is ever destitute in these simple necessities if he puts his trust in the Lord, for God ensures that each of his creatures is cared for. But God did not ever claim to grant all wishes for items beyond these boundaries of necessity, and those who fail to realise this are in fact the ones who have introduced an imaginary poverty into their lives. Similar sentiments are found in the work of the Western preacher Ambrose:

> But the fool does not own even what he thinks he has. Does he possess riches, do you think, if he broods over his wealth day and night and is tormented by a wretched miser's worries? He is actually in need; although he appears wealthy in the opinion of others, he is poor in his own. He makes no use of what he has, but, while grasping one thing, he longs for another. What enjoyment of riches is there when there is no limit to one's longing? No one is rich if he cannot take from this life what he has, because what is left here is not ours but another's.[24]

In this way, Chrysostom believes, rich people voluntarily increase their own unhappiness, while others in the community are led to feel inferior and inadequate on account of this exalting of material goods:

> Why then do you tremble at poverty? You are unable to say. For if you have enough of the necessities of life, why do you tremble at it? Because you haven't a multitude of servants? But this is truly to be free of masters; this is continual happiness, this is freedom from care. Is it because your vessels, your couches, your furniture are not made of silver? And what greater enjoyment than yours has he who possesses these things? None at all. The use is the same, whether they are of this or that material. Is it because you are not an object of fear to many? May you never become so! For what pleasure is it that anyone should stand in dread and fear of you?[25]

Here the importance of working to earn one's position in society is also strongly emphasised, the joy of honest labour being seen as a gift from God and as an end in itself rather than simply a means of accumulating profit. Chrysostom also believes that envy is one of the most dangerous of emotions aroused by wealth, since it is implacable in its quality. Envy will not rest until it has brought low its object, whereas in other cases, feelings of anger or despair can be mitigated after some reflection. Thus he works to render the wealthy less covetous and arrogant, and the poorer members of his congregation less admiring of those who are richer than themselves.

As part of this argument, Chrysostom begins to assert that it is not wealth in and of itself that is evil or good, which is a change from the opinion we saw demonstrated earlier, when he spoke of riches in terms of thorns to be burnt out. Now, however, he claims that it is the use to which the money is put that renders it a negative or positive force.[26] In this way Chrysostom urges his flock to exert a stricter discipline on their attitudes to the possession or the lack of wealth, so that by employing their God-given reason, each one among them can achieve satisfaction. This way they can have an earthly as well as a heavenly reward, not losing out in either respect:

> If we use our wealth properly, nothing will destroy us; but if we do not, all things will bring us down, whether a kingdom, or poverty, or wealth. But nothing will have power to hurt the man who remains on his guard.[27]

At times, however, this philosophising not working to full effect, Chrysostom is still more blatant in his attempts to prove to his congregation that the poor are in fact better off than their richer counterparts on account of their greater ease of living. It is here that his practice of painting vivid pen-pictures is seen to best effect, as he details the contrasting situations of each side in support of his argument:

> For tell me, what is the advantage of those stacks of expensive clothes, and what good do we gain when we are dressed in them? None, but rather, we are in fact losers. How so? Because even the poor man, in his cheap and threadbare clothing, does not feel the burning of the heat any worse than you do; indeed he endures it better, for clothes that are threadbare and worn single offer more comfort for the body, which is not the case with those that are brand new, even though they might be finer than a spider's web. Besides you, out of your excessive self-importance, wear two and often even three inner garments, and a cloak and a girdle, and trousers too, while no one censures the poor man if he only wears one inner garment; so that he is the man that is most at ease. It is because of this that we see rich men sweating, while the poor are in no way subject to this. Since then his cheap clothing, which cost a tiny sum, serves the same, if not better, purpose for him, and those clothes, which cost someone a huge amount of gold, do only the same job, is not this excess a great waste? For it has added nothing on as regards its use and service, while your purse is emptied of all the more gold, all for something which does the same job and fulfils the same purpose.[28]

Here again Chrysostom hopes to appeal both to the vanity and presumed good sense of his audience by arguing economy with them, and by alluding to the negative public image that might be achieved through sweating too much under layers of unnecessary clothing. It is as part of this same passage that we find his allusion to those men who bedecked their wives and horses in a similar manner, believing falsely that they were in this way increasing their own glory. We saw in the previous chapters how Chrysostom counteracted that belief by declaring that the public gaze was distracted by these means from the spender of the money to the dumb beasts adorned in such a foolish manner. The preacher is therefore cunning and manipulative in the way he manages to sow seeds of doubt as to the effectiveness of gross expenditure in the minds of his richer listeners.

It is worth noting, however, that it is not only Christian sources that document this kind of lavish adornment. It is also something that a pagan author such as Ammianus Marcellinus finds distasteful, and which he condemns in a similar manner:

> Others think that the height of glory is to be found in unusually high carriages and an ostentatious style of dress; they sweat under the burden of cloaks which they attach to their necks and fasten at the throat. These being of very fine texture are easily blown about, and they contrive by frequent movements, especially by the left hand, to show off their fringes and display the garments beneath, which are embroidered with animal figures.[29]

Such passages as those alluded to above have been used to support the argument that Chrysostom's audience were predominately wealthy,[30] and indeed he does address most of his remarks on this topic to those in direct possession of the funds he seeks to see redistributed. This, however, rather than precluding a mixed audience, could simply have been a practical measure on the part of Chrysostom, since if he sought the reorganisation of the systems of wealth and commerce in his society, it would make most sense to try to persuade those who had control over the money round to his way of thinking. Aside from this pragmatic approach, however, we do see Chrysostom obliquely address those members of society who were less well off. Just as when he spoke of virtuous women in an attempt to spur the male Christians on to further acts of righteousness, here by ridiculing those who parade their wealth in this ostentatious manner he can reach the entire audience. As the foolish rich are scorned and ridiculed by Chrysostom, the more ordinary audience members are given a clear view of the behaviour they are to avoid if they wish to safeguard their immortal souls and avoid such stinging sarcasm from their preacher.[31] In this way Chrysostom may also have been working to maintain a certain amount of stability within the community as he encourages those who are poor or in need to be content with their lot, since they can hold themselves as safe from the moral danger that those who are wealthy fall into. Here Chrysostom perhaps wished to avoid the lower social classes becoming disturbed or restive, since this would threaten the Christian order of peace he wished to promote in his parish. And so we see him argue that the poor do fulfil a vital social function, since in being available to receive alms they in fact benefit the donors by providing the opportunity for doing good. Thus the two classes of society are drawn together by this mutual need, creating a more egalitarian community to inhabit Chrysostom's Christian city. If this argument of mutual dependence and the greater earthly contentment of the poor is not sufficiently persuasive, Chrysostom can fall back on the promise of more certain spiritual gains for the poor than are readily available to the rich.

It would thus seem likely from this point of view that there were members of all social classes present in Chrysostom's audience whom he hoped to reach through his addresses to the more influential members of the congregation.[32] His use of such vivid imagery can also contribute to this argument, since it would seem to be partly an entertainment ploy on the part of the preacher. A mixed audience, therefore, would all have found something to appreciate in these vibrant passages, whether it be the sight of Chrysostom becoming incensed on the question of the abuse of wealth, his acerbic wit, or for some of the poorer listeners, simply a chance to glimpse the lifestyles of their society's rich and famous. In many cases Chrysostom supplies a voyeuristic preview of the activities and dress of the wealthy inhabitants of the ancient city that fulfilled many functions within his preaching. The upper classes concerned were rebuked for their misuse of funds, the lower classes were warned against envy and similar covetousness, and the congregation as a whole were kept interested, guarding against their distraction by more secular activities. This approach is seen to particularly good effect in *Homily I on Colossians*, when Chrysostom presents his audience with two hypothetical dinner tables. At one table are seated the very dregs of society – the lame, the blind, the diseased, and the hungry. The other table hosts the other extreme – the *crème de la crème*. Chrysostom then embarks on a detailed description of each table, but he lingers especially over the minutiae of the richer table as he calls on his audience to make a choice as to which table they would choose to join if given the chance:

> But there, at the table of the rich, let all the vessels be of silver and gold, and let there be a semicircular table, not one which can be lifted by one person alone, but which requires two young men to move it, and even then with difficulty. Let the wine-jars lie in order, glittering with gold far brighter than the silver, and let the semicircular table be smoothly covered over with soft cloths. Here, again, let there be many servants, in costumes no less finely adorned than those of the guests, and strikingly dressed, wearing loose trousers, men handsome to look at, in the prime of life, plump, and fit ... and let them have expensive foods ... .[33]

Having set the scene with such care, Chrysostom then goes on skilfully to undermine this very picture by pointing out the difference in the degree of pleasure experienced by the two sets of diners. And indeed he comes to the conclusion that those seated at the more moderately arranged table enjoy a better time than their wealthier counterparts. For at that table everyone feels comfortable and at ease, while those seated with the cream of society are constantly anxious as to their appearance, their table manners, and their rank, often feeling considerable discomfort. This serves as a warning to those in Chrysostom's audience who might wish to join this richly provided table, since he speaks of the unease always felt by those who find themselves in situations for which they are not socially suited. Here he upholds the class system within his society, but also demonstrates that there were probably people from all social strata within his audience, some of whom looked longingly at the lifestyle of those above them. Again Chrysostom is eager to show such wishful thinkers that they are in fact better off where they are, since the demands of living among the upper classes actually serve to curtail rather than to bestow freedom. Aside from this, there are physical considerations to take into account:

> But let us look at even the types of foods themselves. For at the rich table it is necessary to drink a large quantity of wine – even to bursting point – against one's will, but at the poor table no one who does not feel like it has to eat or drink. So at the rich table the plea-sure arising from the quality of the food is annulled by the dishonour that goes before, and the physical discomfort which comes after the gorging. For gluttony does not damage the body any less than star-vation; but actually does more grievous damage; and whoever you would like to give me, I will destroy him more easily by bursting him with surplus food than I would by hunger. For hunger is more easily borne than overeating, since a person could indeed endure hunger for twenty days, but overeating for not even two days. And the country people who are constantly struggling with hunger are healthy, and do not need doctors; while no one can endure gorging without always calling on doctors; Indeed its strength has often baffled all their attempts at a cure.[34]

In this manner Chrysostom both works to persuade his audience against such foolish embracing of excessive wealth, as well as entertaining them with his sometimes lurid accounts of the physical effects of eating to bursting point. And not only the guests, but the hosts too are described in vivid detail, as part of Chrysostom's questioning of one of the key activi-ties of civic life – the hosting of lavish entertainments. This time the preacher chooses to point out the great anxieties attendant upon such events:

> Now he who invites them is making preparations days in advance, and has troubles and anxieties and concerns, neither sleeping at night, nor resting by day; but formulates all kinds of plans in his own mind, and converses with cooks, confectioners, and table layers. Then when the actual day is come, you can see him as being more afraid than those who are going to fight a boxing match, in case anything should turn out other than was planned, in case he is looked at enviously, in case he acquires for himself a crowd of begrudgers.[35]

Chrysostom in this way hopes to undermine the importance attached by his congregation to these kinds of public displays of wealth, indicating the loss of freedom thereby experienced, and in this manner he criticises the conventional activities of the ancient civic unit. The Christian alternative to this can be glimpsed from Chrysostom's advice to his hypothetical hosts to introduce God to the feast by offering thanks for the bounties he has bestowed on them. A regularly recurring argument on the part of the preacher was that all things, wealth included, came from God. Therefore, to introduce flute players, singers and dancers to the banquet instead of hymns and prayers to the Lord, is literally to bite the hand that feeds them like some ungrateful dog. This ostentatious display of possessions is also what leads to the introduction of prostitutes to the company, something that we have already seen Chrysostom become quite exercised by. Here he likens consorting with harlots to pigs wallowing in filth, but on this occasion it is not the lustful thoughts or opportunities for fornication which are his primary concerns, but rather the opulent setting which has sponsored such misbehaviour. The end results of each of these dinner parties are set in stark contrast as Chrysostom draws to the close of his demonstration. Those who were seated at the poorer table go home well satisfied and sober, and feel genuine gratitude to their host and to God. The wealthy guests, however, stagger home drunk, clumsy and quarrelsome, while their host is left with the feeling that he has been praised for his money and display rather than out of a genuine liking for himself. This extended narrative complete, Chrysostom declares that he has indeed been speaking in order to change the minds of those in his audience who feel attracted by such activities of conspicuous consumption, and then draws his sermon to a close.[36]

Chrysostom's graphic imagery of the evils wrought on the physique of those who are excessively luxurious in their lifestyles continues elsewhere:

> Just as in the sewers where there is accumulation of refuse, of dung, hay, stubble, stones, clay, frequent blockages occur; and then the stream of filth overflows above the ground: so too does it happen in the stomachs of these people. Since the stomachs are being blocked up below, a large part of these noxious streams spews out up above. But it is not so with the poor, but is more like those fountains that send out pure streams, and water gardens and pleasure grounds, and so too are their stomachs free from the above excesses. But the stomachs of the rich, or rather the opulent, are not pure like this; but they are filled with humours, phlegm, bile, corrupted blood, putrid substances, and other similar matters. And so no one, if he lives constantly in such luxury, can endure it, even for a short time; but he will be constantly ill throughout his life.[37]

Here again Chrysostom draws a careful distinction between simple wealth and luxury. It is the excessive position that bothers him, in alignment with his former stance that it is the use of a commodity that renders it evil or good rather than the commodity in itself. He is anxious to avoid condemning those members of his congregation who are wealthy but still virtuous, while those who are ostentatious and acquisitive with their possessions are comparable to the above sewers. The persuasion of the poor to remain content with their social position is also evident here, as Chrysostom details the nasty illnesses and weakness they avoid by their more moderate style of living. In making such assertions, Chrysostom is, I feel, being consciously disingenuous, since he cannot help but know that those who are really struggling with poverty would be unlikely to agree that they have the advantage over their rich social superiors. Perhaps he feels, however, that by constant repetition, some part of this philosophy will remain with his audience, and that the poor will be more inclined to remain passively, if not necessarily contentedly, in their current positions. Thus they would be less inclined to focus on the gap between themselves and the wealthy with resentment, and rather consider the similar state everyone in this community is in, in the face of God. It is probable, however, that Chrysostom intended most of this message to be heeded by the luxurious offenders, since he presents those they would normally look down on as being superior to them in their moderation, hoping to engage their competitive spirit if not their consciences. This is the same process enacted when discussing the transgression of gender boundaries, as here the poor serve the same process as women did in exhortations directed at under-achieving men.

The vivid descriptions employed by Chrysostom in pursuing these aims also make the wealthy people in question into objects of the audience's gaze, just as we saw women made into passive objects of the male gaze elsewhere in his preaching. Within the comparatively safe verbal confines of the sermon, Chrysostom can present his congregation with views of the wealthy lifestyle, demonstrating the dangers involved and satisfying their curiosity, without imperilling their moral welfare. He thus paradoxically dwells on the very behaviour he condemns in his efforts to hold the attention of his flock. The striking imagery employed by the preacher also sets in motion the cycle of public shame and guilt previously seen in action. Those with distended bellies and ill health as a result of their gluttony make their sin obvious to the rest of society, and on this account should feel ashamed. Chrysostom's dramatic presentations illustrate the behaviour which will set this cycle in motion, thus warning his congregation of the limits they must not transgress.

Chrysostom has words of comfort for those who believe all the advantages in life lie with the rich. They wonder why God rewards those who seem to be unrighteous while others who are obviously virtuous nevertheless struggle with poverty. Chrysostom urges them not to question God's motives in this way, citing the examples of characters from the Old Testament; Abraham was rich, while the no less righteous Jacob lacked enough to eat. Similarly David, although chosen by God to be his anointed king, laboured hard throughout his life, while Solomon reigned for many years in absolute peace and prosperity. If these paragons of virtue were thus served by God, so much more so should Chrysostom's congregation remain content with their lot. He also adds a warning to the errant rich man to the effect that even if things go well with him for a time, his misdeeds merely store up future punishments for himself. Chrysostom takes the view that some of the very activities indulged in by such wealthy men are punishments in themselves:

> What are you saying? Does he commit fornication, and you think, 'he suffers no evils?' Is he drunk, and do you believe that he is in luxury? Is he spend-thrift, and do you consider that he is to be envied? But what can be worse than this kind of wealth which destroys the soul itself? If his body was deformed and maimed, you would say that he had great cause for complaint and yet you see his soul mangled and still consider him to be happy?[38]

Once more the poorer members of society are encouraged to be of good cheer and at all costs to steer clear of the sin of envy, since there may not actually be much for them to feel jealous of under Chrysostom's scheme of things. He is, however, embarrassed that even heathens are more aware from their own philosophies that surface ornamentation and wealth are no indications of inner beauty and worth. The Christians who wilfully regard riches as an index of merit are thus made into a laughing stock when compared with this pagan self-knowledge and common sense. If they accept instead that all riches are transient they should cease their fruitless questioning of God's motives in making some rich and others poor, while if they do not yet have this mature attitude to the organisation of society, Chrysostom peremptorily orders them to go and stand in the church porch, since they are evidently unfit for entrance into the house of God.[39]

Thus we see Chrysostom's opinion of wealth and its users transmitted in a variety of ways. Occasionally he dismisses riches as evil by nature, but for the most part Chrysostom is firm in the belief that it is the uses to which wealth is put that are negative or positive. In this way he is able to avoid completely alienating those members of his congregation who are possessed of wealth, while simultaneously warning them off the abuse of this prosperity and allowing the less fortunate members of the audience to feel contented with their position in the class structure by means of his skilful and dramatic preaching. Chrysostom's presentation of the economic appearance of the ancient city has been somewhat simplistic. He presents his audience with a basic distinction between rich and poor, ignoring the more subtle grades of wealth and social class within the typical Roman community. This suits his preaching purpose, since he is after all trying to modify the behaviour of those who are avaricious and greedy, rather than trying to restructure the traditional organisation of society. If everyone thought more about the welfare of others, and of the teachings of Christ regarding wealth, existing classes could continue to exist as far as Chrysostom was concerned. Unfortunately it seems that few of his listeners were willing to rise to this challenge.[40]

# The Wealthy Road to Redemption

Emma was very compassionate; and the distresses of the poor were as sure of relief from her personal attention and kindness, her counsel and her patience, as from her purse … . In the present instance it was sickness and poverty together which she came to visit; and after remaining there as long as she could give comfort or advice, she quitted the cottage with such an impression of the scene as made her say to Harriet as they walked away: 'These are sights, Harriet, to do one good. How trifling they make everything else appear!'

Jane Austen, *Emma*, ch. 10

In spite of the somewhat bleak outlook presented in the previous chapter, all is not lost. Chrysostom works equally hard to show that there is a further way in which the richer congregants can avoid the evil influences of wealth aside from simply shunning the medium, and this is to actively redistribute some of their funds throughout the community by means of almsgiving and rediscover the joy of honestly labouring for their advantages in life, since opulence can lead to a slide into idleness which in turn can lead to all manner of sinful activities.[1] Through almsgiving and hard work wealthy members of the community can benefit both those less fortunate than themselves, and their own moral well-being, by using their material possessions for good. The generosity of Christ in offering his life for the sake of mankind should be their guide in this respect, since if he was willing to make such a huge sacrifice for an ultimately sinful people, surely they should be prepared to give a little of their time or their wealth to their fellow man. To refuse is to behave in a short-sighted manner, since if they did give alms they would in fact accrue spiritual benefits for themselves that would stand in their stead when it comes to Judgement Day. Chrysostom even issues a threat to the effect that if the rich do not feel inclined to offer their money willingly to those who need it, they might find it suddenly wrested from them by other, less gratifying means:

He did it for our salvation, but we will not do it even for our own good. For He gains no advantage from our love towards our fellow man, but the whole profit goes to us ourselves. For this is the very reason that we are instructed to give away our belongings, that they

may not be forcibly removed from us. For just as a person who gives
a little child money and tells him to hold it tightly, or give it to the
servant to mind, so that no one who would want to could snatch it
from him, so too does God. For He says, 'Give to him that is in need,
lest some one else should snatch it from you, such as an informer for
instance, or a slanderer, or a thief, or, after all these are avoided,
death itself. For as long as you keep it to yourself, you are not keeping
it safely. But if you give it to Me through the poor, I will keep it all for
you exactly, and in due course will return it with great interest.'[2]

Here again, therefore, we see Chrysostom appealing to the insecurity
which he sees as automatically infecting those with any amount of wealth
in their possession. Not confident enough that a single appeal will have the
desired effect in influencing his audience, Chrysostom has hit upon a standard approach, by which he targets his congregation with at least two, if
not more, means of persuasion, ranging from genuine exhortation, to
threats, to flattery, to appeals to the very acquisitiveness he is trying to
stamp out, encouraging his flock to apply it to the hoarding of spiritual
benefits rather than material goods. This variety of angles shows
Chrysostom's keen powers of observation and the knowledge he has as to
where the priorities and weak points of his flock lie, as well as perhaps a
sense that he is fighting a losing battle. His exhortations on the subject of
almsgiving show him at his most earnest, as he struggles to close the gap
between the comparative wealth of the two main social classes in his
parish. In this manner he hopes to realise his Christianised city, in which
rich and poor will enjoy a mutual dependence in their quest for eternal
salvation.

Among the incentives Chrysostom uses to encourage his parishioners
to adopt this policy of almsgiving, is the promise of heavenly rewards and
benefits for future generations. He complains that his flock are patently
unwilling to donate funds to the poor while they are living, in spite of the
advantages of doing so. He therefore desperately pleads with them to
redress the balance when the hour of their death draws near. When they
are considering how to dispose of their wealth after they are gone,
Chrysostom advocates that they donate some of it to the church or
directly to the poor. In this way, he promises, the offspring of the deceased
will have Christ as their fellow beneficiary, and therefore a kind of heavenly sibling, and this will stand in their favour when they are confronted
with the insults or plots of envious begrudgers. It will also mean that God
will be a lenient judge to the soul just come before him, and will take into
account this generosity, however belated, when assessing the quality of
this soul. Alas, Chrysostom laments, there are some who cannot be moved
by any considerations to release the grip they have on their wealth, even
though they have a number of possibilities open to them. They could
aspire to the rank of angels by giving alms over the course of their lifetime, or they could make provisions in their will to redistribute their

wealth, thus benefiting their children as well as the poor, but if even the thought that after death they can have no use for their money does not move them sufficiently, Chrysostom fears that there can be no mercy for them in the end.[3] But if he can persuade his audience to adopt a great spirit of giving, he promises them that nothing else is calculated to bring them closer to God.[4]

As well as claiming that being poor is in fact an essential role to fill within the organisation of society, since the rich gain spiritual advantages from benefiting them, Chrysostom also argues that a relative degree of poverty even equips those concerned for this vital task of almsgiving on their own part:

> We must not then make ourselves miserable because we are poor, since poverty makes almsgiving easier for us (*Ou toinun talanizein heautous khrê dia tên penian: kai gar eukolôteran hêmin poiei tên eleêmosunên*). For the man who has collected many possessions is haughty, as well feeling great ties to what he has. But he who has only a little is safe from both of these domineering passions: and so he finds more opportunities for doing good. For this man will go cheerfully into a prison, and will visit the sick, and will give a cup of cold water where needed. But the other sort of man will not do any of these deeds, since he is puffed up by his wealth. Do not be downcast by your poverty therefore. For your poverty makes your journey towards heaven easier for you.[5]

The ill temperament of the excessively rich is clearly displayed here, serving as a warning to anyone of this status who might be listening that their behaviour has been noted. The public gaze is then directed towards the less well-off individual and his enthusiastic performance of good deeds. This serves as a reversal of the shame and guilt cycle which we saw in operation in the more damning descriptions of wealthy living, since the frugal lifestyle of the poorer individual serves in this case as an index of *his* moral worth, something the audience are encouraged to admire. In this respect it would seem that Chrysostom's definition of poverty was more subjective than we today are used to. There appears to have been a considerable difference between simple poverty and abject beggarliness. Those who classed themselves as poor were still deemed capable of helping those less fortunate than themselves. This is reminiscent of Chrysostom's attack on the shallowness of public opinion when he complains of the vast number of servants the rich carry about with them as a signal of their wealth and status. Even priests and less well-to-do individuals feel compelled to have at least one servant, while a man with only two or three attendants is looked down on by the rest of his society as being obviously in straitened circumstances.[6] Chrysostom exhorts his congregation towards greater moderation in such matters, declaring that an individual with so much pride as to require hordes of servants to keep off the rest of society is in fact lowlier than the meanest of these slaves. He therefore urges his flock towards a greater sense of economy, where low numbers of servants adequately serve their needs, and the demands for public display of status are abolished. In this way Chrysostom subtly redefines poverty for this audience, making it into a spiritually detrimental state, rather than a simple lack of slaves or fancy clothes.

Indeed Chrysostom very rarely addresses the genuinely poverty-stricken directly in the course of his preaching, although many of his references indicate that they were present in his congregation. He prefers instead to speak of such destitution in a metaphorical sense, as evidence of sinfulness and willing enslavement to a tyrannous master such as Mammon. He understands perfectly the terrible fear his wealthy congregants have of sinking to a lower social level through loss of wealth, often citing their hypothetical protests against almsgiving:

> Why then do you tremble at the thought of poverty? And why do you chase after wealth? 'I fear', says one, 'that I might be forced to go to other men's doors and to beg from my neighbour.' And I constantly hear also many people praying to this end, saying, 'Save me from being in need of others at any time.' And I laugh very hard when I hear these prayers, for this fear is childish. For every day and in every way, so to speak, we stand in need of one another.[7]

Such foolish men also claim that the church allowance will adequately suffice for those in need, a suggestion that is ridiculed in the strongest terms by Chrysostom, pointing out that no salvation can be gained through such weak reasoning:

> But what is their constant talk? 'He has,' they say, 'the common church allowance.' And what business is that of yours? For you will not be saved just because I give; nor if the Church donates will you eradicate your own sins. You don't give for this reason – that the Church should give to those in need? Just because the priests say prayers, will you never pray for yourself? And just because others fast, will you always overeat instead? Do you not know that God invented almsgiving not so much for the sake of the poor as for the sake of the people themselves who donate?[8]

One interesting idea regarding this rebuke on the part of Chrysostom is that his congregation may have been expressing reluctance to give the church body financial support on account of his own unpopularity. It is followed by an interesting passage in which Chrysostom justifies the vast wealth of the Church administration, claiming that it is necessary to possess these riches for distribution among the needy in society, since most of the moneyed population consider themselves exempt from almsgiving on this account. In this way the caretaking role of the church transforms the local prelate into a Christian version of the traditional patron, with his client base being the entire population of the poor within the community.[9]

Thus poverty is generally spoken of as something which is feared by the upper classes within society, to such an extent that they are led to grasping behaviour in their efforts to avoid it. Chrysostom is quick to twist this situation to his own ends, making this dependence on money for security, and this extensive misanthropy, into symptoms of a far more serious poverty – one of the spirit. Again this was a favourite philosophical trope of pre-Christian thought, but Chrysostom effectively Christianises his argument by claiming that the poverty that arises from such behaviour is a lack of God's spirit of mercy and compassion, and a loss of his promised salvation.

In this system of argument the poor, for Chrysostom, remain largely faceless beneficiaries of almsgiving, the clients of the Christianised patrons he is working to create. Occasionally they are described in greater detail, as we saw in the description of the two dining tables in the previous chapter, but Chrysostom does not often enter into their world. Instead he prefers to look in on their lives from a remote position, describing as a narrator the conditions endured by them without asking his audience to engage in the description to the same extent as when speaking of the rich. Again this may have been a rhetorical ploy on the part of Chrysostom, since descriptions of life in poverty would not have interested as many people in the audience, and thus their attention would be quickly lost. Discussions of the wealthy lifestyles, however, have already been shown to be fascinating to Chrysostom's audience, thus opening the way for his persuasive arguments. He does, however, encourage the wealthy members of his congregation to refrain from passing judgement on those less fortunate than themselves, showing an uncanny awareness of the arguments used to pacify their consciences and their overall reluctance to offer help – a description which still stings uncomfortably today:

> Not like us, who if we happen to see a stranger or a poor man, furrow our brows, and do not stoop to even speak to them. And if after thousands of pleas we are softened, and tell the servant to give them a trifle, we think we have quite done our duty.[10]

The great pride of such individuals is subtly condemned here, as Chrysostom describes the guilty parties as not even stooping to hand over the money themselves, but rather leaving it to a slave to conduct the transaction. He would rather that his congregation had a genuine generosity of spirit, and a willingness to give alms regardless of the nature of the recipient. For even the Old Testament Abraham acted in this manner, eagerly welcoming strangers into his home to receive his hospitality, in spite of the fact that he knew nothing about them. In stark contrast to this portrait of good will, many of Chrysostom's flock display an unseemly superiority over the beggar in question, passing judgement on his moral standing and using this as an excuse for refusing aid. The preacher is outraged at such arrogance, pointing out that if God had allowed his sun to shine on this impoverished individual, it was not for a mere mortal to decide that he was a thief or a murderer, and with such reasoning deny him a few pence or a loaf of bread.[11]

The less well-to-do members of society are addressed directly elsewhere in Chrysostom's preaching as, in another series of sermons, he declares that all is not lost for those who are in need themselves, since almsgiving need not be about donating money alone. Offering time, help and friendship to others serves just as well as gold. He suggests that those of a particular skill or profession can offer their talents free of charge where needed, thus deferring disease and painful death if not starvation.[12] Even the artisans of the city have the means at their disposal to help others, as Chrysostom urges sandal-makers, leather-cutters and brass-founders to give the first fruits of their profits to those in need – up to a tenth part of the income in question. In Chrysostom's ideal city a clear system of almsgiving would be drawn up in which it would be the first concern of all involved:

> And let us make a little coffer for the poor at home; and let it be put beside the place where you stand at prayer; and whenever you go in to pray, first drop in your alms, and then offer up your prayer; and just as you would not dream of praying with unwashed hands, so do not pray without giving alms: since not even the Gospel hanging by our bed is more important than that you should gather together alms; for if you hang up the Gospel and do nothing, it will not do you much good. But if you have this little chest, you are guarding against the devil, you are giving wings to your prayer, and you are making your house holy, having laid up a store of food for the King. And for this reason also let the little coffer be placed near the bed, and your night will not be troubled with nightmares.[13]

In addition to Chrysostom's emphasis on almsgiving which emerges from these instructions, we also see the organisation of his ideally Christian *oikos*, in which these values will hold prime place. As well as the regular donation of funds to those less fortunate, Chrysostom hopes that the householder will give pride of place to the books of the Gospel – in literal and figurative terms – and that all activities within the home will be guided by these Christian precepts. It is not made explicit here as to who in the household would actually carry out this redistribution of wealth, but it may have been that Chrysostom envisaged a certain division of labour between husband and wife on this account. We have already seen the way in which he believed that the provision of wealth for the household was the task of the male, while the restrained spending of these funds was the part of the female, since she was held responsible for the preservation of the family wealth.[14] If the wife adequately performed this role, foregoing unnecessary luxuries and shunning all excess, greater sums of money would be made available for the task of almsgiving. These would be the funds that were then placed in the bedside coffer, while it was presumably the male who actively transferred them to those in need throughout the city. Thus almsgiving is presented as having a domestic aspect as well as a more public form, while the appropriately devout couple would run their household within these Christianised parameters, turning aside from the more traditional activities of the Roman household with regard to wealth and its display.

It has been pointed out that a 'macro-economic' argument for the distribution of wealth throughout society has been employed by some church fathers, Basil and Ambrose among them.[15] Under this scheme, the rich members of society who hoard their money for fear of losing it are reprimanded for actually slowing down the economic activity of the community. Money should be kept moving is the argument, since when standing still it loses its value and has no opportunity for increase. Presumably the direction of the movement should be towards the poor, in the form of almsgiving. It is interesting to note that nowhere in his homilies on the Pauline epistles does Chrysostom employ a similar tactic. He does not choose to appeal to the civic sense of his congregation, encouraging them to maintain traditional commercial activities by continuing the dispersal of their funds through customary channels. Instead he restricts his advice and manipulation to the level of the individual. Almsgiving is a privately undertaken activity, and affects only the persons concerned, rather than the overall structure of the city. This would be a clear instance of his attempts to redraw the parameters of the ancient *polis*, since he hopes to draw the attention of his audience away from the current order of the urban unit, and refocus it on the smaller unit of the household. What will then happen is that each *oikos* will become a micro-cosmic version of those monastic communities which so impressed Chrysostom in the earlier stages of his career. He is also heard to express on one occasion, that possessions granted by God to humanity should be held in common,[16] and this is how things are in a monastic setting. We have already seen the way in which he hoped that the appropriate organisation of gender relations within the household would emulate the harmony of an ascetic grouping, and now the same hope is extended to the financial activities of that same household. In many ways Chrysostom sees monasteries as examples of perfect social justice, and hopes to encourage their growth within the urban community, rather than monks feeling compelled to flee to the mountains. But of course this would depend on a shift of priorities among the ordinary inhabitants of the city for the ascetics to feel safe from distraction in the midst of the urban community.[17]

The promise of eternal rewards for almsgiving is a continuous refrain of Chrysostom's, and when set against the evils arising from living in opulence, the right path should appear more than clear to his congregation:

In the case of seeds, someone who sows pulse cannot reap corn, for
what is sown and what is reaped must both be of the same kind. So
too is the case with regard to actions, since he that plants in the body
licentious behaviour, drunkenness, or excessive lust will reap the
fruits of these things. And what are these fruits? Punishment, retri-
bution, shame, derision, destruction. For there is no other end than
destruction possible from lavish dining and rich foods, since they
both decay themselves, and destroy the person. But think, have you
sown almsgiving? Then the treasures of heaven and eternal glory
stand ready for you.[18]

Indeed failure to heed this warning will rouse the terrible wrath of God,
since to refuse to give alms is to refuse to succour those who are God's
spiritual children. Even in the Jewish tradition of the Old Testament there
was a system in place whereby everyone who was able contributed tithes
for the support of widows and orphans. To avoid giving tithes was a matter
of great disgrace in this society, and how much more so should it be among
Christians, declares Chrysostom.[19] Here we see him subtly denigrate the
Jewish ancestry of Christianity by using the examples from the Scriptures
as the lowest possible standard one should strive to live up to. If Christians
are surpassed in generosity by mere Jews it is a sad indictment of the
claims of their faith.

Although almsgiving is important, however, it is equally vital that it is
an activity carried out with the right frame of mind. To give assistance to
the needy in a grudging manner is to negate all the good of the action. Nor
should the donor feel an arrogant sense of his own generosity, as if
bestowing a special favour on the receiver, especially when the truth of the
matter is that he himself is benefiting more than the one to whom he gives
simple money. If his congregation cannot give cheerfully therefore,
Chrysostom tells them that they needn't bother, since to give with such
poor grace is to lose instead of to gain.[20] To spur his flock onwards in this
respect, the preacher regularly reminds them of the widow who fed Elias
in the Old Testament, giving cheerfully of her meagre store, or of the New
Testament widow who donated her two mites to the temple collection.
Neither of these women concerned themselves as to the details of where
their money was going, or who the beneficiary might be, which is a point
in their favour according to Chrysostom, since it shows a sincerity in their
generosity rather than a desire to appear pious.[21] Nor is it of any use if the
funds used in almsgiving are ill-gotten, either through theft or fraud, for
then it is not generosity but cruelty, Chrysostom says.[22] The good to be
gained from almsgiving is completely negated unless it proceeds directly
from the owner of the wealth. But sincere generosity is the means by
which a Christian can truly emulate God in his mercy and pity.

From this range of advice it would seem clear that Chrysostom believed
that almsgiving was a route to salvation open to all, regardless of financial
or social standing. This could indicate that the audience he was addressing

was indeed a socially mixed one. Although he rarely addresses the lower classes directly in his preaching, certain of his comments or instructions are designed to be heard and acted upon by them, while he ostensibly does the upper classes the honour of speaking mainly to them. He is similarly reticent when it comes to addressing women on the subject, although we have seen him mention female examples from the Bible. This could imply a belief on the part of Chrysostom that almsgiving was predominantly a male activity, since in its most obvious manifestation it takes place in the civic arena that was the masculine preserve. Regardless of the composition of his audience, however, Chrysostom is adamant that through sincere almsgiving, his congregation can remodel their lives along more overtly Christian lines, thus altering the structure of the ancient city somewhat. Riches now become not something to be acquired and hoarded, or displayed to arouse the envy of others, but the means by which the wealthy can ensure their own spiritual salvation, as well as offer temporal relief for those less well off than themselves.

For the most part it is an activity that is discussed on an individual basis, just as the ostentatious behaviour of the rich was dealt with as manifesting itself in single instances throughout society. Chrysostom's exegesis of the Pauline epistle to the Romans, however, shows an interesting departure from this approach, as he chooses to discuss the conspicuous consumption of a city as a whole. In this respect he is following the initial lead set by Paul. He attacks the luxury in which the previous citizens of this city lived, and their lavish ostentation, evidenced in their building of ornate temples and altars, their military triumphs, and their elevation of mere kings to divine status. These actions were manifestations of the abuse of wealth on a citywide scale, explaining Paul's warning to the early Christians to be on their guard in such a society. It is possible that Chrysostom chose to elaborate on these vices as an oblique means of reprimanding his own audience, without accusing them outright. By criticising a society of the past in this manner, he shows his contemporary congregation the type of behaviour that will not be tolerated in his vision of a Christian city, thus hoping to influence their behaviour in a more subtle manner. We saw in a previous chapter the way in which he saw the Roman love of luxury as the starting point for the heinous crime of homosexuality, a soft style of living leading automatically to an erosion of masculinity. By discussing this vice from a remote point in time, Chrysostom could simultaneously target his own flock, and issue stern warnings without overtly admitting that they were necessary. Here, when discussing wealth, we see the same process enacted on the community as a whole. Thus a passionate denunciation of ancient Rome could serve as a stern warning to contemporary Constantinople – another lavishly decorated capital city, with all the attendant imperial intrigues and demands.

In spite of this regularly offered advice, however, it would seem that Chrysostom's congregation were generally more reluctant to part with their possessions than he would have liked. He tries to persuade them that a little difficulty encountered on the road to Christian living will only enhance the glory that will be theirs at the end of the day, just as scars increase the status of a soldier, since it proves that trials have been undergone for a worthy end. Thus it is only natural for mankind to suffer, and it should not be regarded as an unfair tribulation sent on a whim of God. Chrysostom believes that every day is a battle towards great devoutness in the practice of Christianity, but if his present flock were to be called to take arms, not one of them would emerge victorious: 'For when I see that you do not despise riches even for the sake of Christ, how can I believe that you will despise blows?'[23]

Instead of being armed with generosity and disregard for material wealth, Chrysostom finds his audience all too concerned with hoarding this wealth simply to gloat over it. If thieves strike they are appalled and devastated, even turning to magicians and diviners in an attempt to recover their money. According to Chrysostom, this pleases the Devil enormously, since by mourning for the loss of worldly goods in this extravagant way, they inflict more harm on their immortal souls than the thieves ever could. Chrysostom urges his audience to guard against the Devil's machinations in this regard by taking a leaf out of the nautical book, lightening the load when a storm hits in order to weather it better:

> Put it to the test, I beg you – if you do not believe me perform the test, and you will see the glory of God. When anything dreadful has happened, immediately give alms; give thanks that it has happened, and you will see how much joy will come to you.[24]

In this way, almsgiving is seen as a prelude to greater strengths and virtues on the part of the congregation just as covetousness was the root of all other evils. If his congregation can learn to have sincere interest in lightening the burden of the needy, Chrysostom believes that they will become strong soldiers in Christ's army and better equipped to deal with the difficulties of the outside world. The moral substance they gain from this course of action will enable them to stand firm against their enemies – even blessing those who curse them. Alas, however, it would seem that his audience were reluctant to take arms in this struggle, their good will lasting only the length of Chrysostom's sermon:

> I know that you are entirely warmed up now, and have become as soft as wax, but when you have left here you will throw it all away (*Oida hoti diethermanthête nun, kai khêrou gegonate pantos hapalôteroi. all' anakhôrêsantes apanta apobluxete*). This is why I am sad, that we do not act out what we talk about, even though we are the ones who would have most to gain in doing so.[25]

It is this refusal to put the things of this earth on a lower level of priorities than spiritual concerns that has led to the exodus from the city of those holy men and women who wish to live undistracted lives of virtue. The frugal existence adopted by such devout individuals is currently impossible to achieve in the atmosphere of competitive ostentation found in the cities. But if Chrysostom's congregation were to adopt some of the ascetic guidelines then 'the cities may become cities indeed' he declares, in this way presenting his long-term vision of a Christianised *polis* to his audience.[26]

\*

Chrysostom's attitude to wealth is consistent throughout his preaching. He considers the current use and display of it by his flock to be highly dangerous, since they have invested all their energies in its acquisition and maintenance, or if unable to do so, they retain all their respect and admiration for those who possess it. We have seen the way in which Chrysostom's often savage rhetoric paints the ostentatiously rich and their enthralled followers as ridiculous, insane, diseased and highly immoral. Once this position is made clear, Chrysostom provides his flock with a lifeline in the form of almsgiving. But his exhortations to this end are not solely intended for the salvation of their souls. The preacher also works to gently erode the sharp class division he saw all around him. He does so not by demanding a radical distribution of resources or the abolition of the class system, but by redrawing the relations between rich and poor along more Christian lines. Chrysostom encourages them to view each other as mutually beneficial partners in the quest for spiritual salvation, hoping that if his audience can be persuaded of this fact, the arrogance, pride and resentment attendant upon current divisions of wealth will be obliterated. Thus his new version of the *polis* can be realised simply by altering the priorities of the old. It is a very different approach from Brown's suggested destruction of the city, but Chrysostom does show a sometimes indiscreet passion in his efforts to accomplish its reorganisation. We have so far seen his attempts to this end specifically in relation to the behaviour of both the sexes, the organisation of the Christian household, and the economic activities of the urban unit. In the final chapter I collect these findings in a more general survey as to the success or failure of Chrysostom in achieving this lifelong aim.

# 12

# Conclusions

Miss Thorne made no reply. She felt that she had no good ground on which to defend her sex of the present generation from the sarcasm of Mr Plomacy. She had once declared, in one of her warmer moments, 'that nowadays the gentlemen were all women, and the ladies all men'. She could not alter the debased character of the age. But, such being the case, why should she take on herself to cater for the amusement of people of such degraded tastes? This question she asked herself more than once, and she could only answer herself with a sigh.

Anthony Trollope, *Barchester Towers*, ch. 35

The central task of this book has been to examine the representations of gender in the homilies of Chrysostom preached on the Pauline epistles, and the uses to which the orator put these representations in his pastoral duties. What has become apparent in the course of this discussion is the pivotal role played by gender divisions and their preservation within the overall framework of society. The maintenance of this system of order is one of Chrysostom's key concerns throughout his preaching career, since he sees appropriate gender relations as an index of a properly regulated society. But this concern on the preacher's part considerably widens the scope of his oratory, since such a community would be similarly well ordered in all its aspects. And hence we have the many references to a posited transformation of the city through the medium of Christian rhetoric. While gender considerations remain central in this great project of Chrysostom's, the other cornerstone of ancient society must also come in for a large share of his attention – wealth and commercial activity. This gives us the trilogy of men, women and money as the group of issues most prevalent in Chrysostom's preaching. Unhappy with the state of affairs which met his gaze each Sunday, or came to his attention by other means in the course of his ministry, Chrysostom strove to present his flock with an alternative mode of behaviour, one which would alter their personal lives and the broader life of the ancient city, and which would also ensure spiritual salvation for people and pastor alike. As the spiritual mentor of two of the largest and most important cities in turn in the eastern empire, Chrysostom's sense of responsibility was great indeed, and throughout his work we see the lengths to which he was prepared to go to avoid accusations of neglecting his duties. When he stands before God's throne on the Day of Judgement, Chrysostom wants to feel confident that he can claim to have done his best to lead his flock to salvation. If he can show that through his ministry he has led even some of his congregation to think of themselves as citizens of God's city before the earthly urban unit, then he can console himself that he has done his best to guard their souls.[1]

In *De Sacerdotio* we see Chrysostom's discussion of the greater pressures and responsibilities placed on any prelate, since he is responsible not only for his own soul, but for the souls of the multitude, and failure in his duties is judged more harshly than a similar slip by a member of the laity. Excuses are not acceptable to God, since the bishop or priest has been set over his people as a watchman, instructed to sound a trumpet of warning when danger approaches. When discussing *De Sacerdotio* at the outset of this study we saw the way in which Chrysostom considered public ministry within the church to be a more difficult vocation than the more individual calling of the ascetic. The priest or bishop needed to combine an impressive array of personal qualities and social graces in order to be a truly representative leader of his flock. But the pressure was not only one imposed from within the spiritual hierarchy, but one built on by the expectations of the congregation themselves. It would seem that the prelate was expected to take on the role and function of a patron of the community, with all the attendant duties and responsibilities. There was thus a kind of contract in place between preacher and people, and the Christian audience were entitled, and indeed likely, to complain if they did not see their needs as being adequately met. The work of this final chapter, therefore, will be to collect the conclusions arrived at by Chrysostom as to how gender relations and the use of money are so entwined with this great ambition to transform the living environment of the later Roman empire, and how his efforts were received by those in his care.

## Performance art – spiritual and secular

The conspicuous consumption and public display of wealth and status which we have seen Chrysostom decry in the preceding chapters were of course defining aspects of civic life, as was the patron-client system, or indeed the lavish entertainments hosted by the wealthy for their peers. By means of these events or displays, the citizens of the late empire overtly signalled their willingness to be part of their urban community and to abide by the structures of imperial society. Public spectacles and munificence laid on by the aristocracy were also vitally important as indexes of the health of the civic unit. In smaller urban units the smaller scale of such entertainments could also be an indication of the way in which a shift of focus occurred during late antiquity, so that the public spaces of a town no longer encapsulated the identity of the *polis*. While this perceived decline cannot be pinpointed in time, or attributed to a single cause, it may well be an aspect of the alteration of civic life that could be characterised as decline or destruction. In larger cities of the empire, however, governors and members of the imperial family maintained the provision of these spectacles and amenities that were dying out elsewhere, explaining why such events remained to be a thorn in the side of someone such as Chrysostom and why the ancient city did not simply cease to be, but underwent a more subtle transformation.[2]

Another key aspect of this civic 'calendar' was the performance of theatrical or sporting spectacles at regular intervals. Attendance at such events was the means by which inhabitants of the city showed their allegiance to their civic unit and continued to perpetuate its existence. However, we have seen some instances in which this area of life in the *polis* along with so many others, met with the disapproval of John Chrysostom. His condemnation arose out of a number of factors – the manner in which the female became the object of the male gaze when performing on stage and the ensuing sins of lust and fornication, the distraction of his flock from more spiritual concerns, and even the noise emanating from the arenas that drowned out his own words of wisdom. But whatever the reasons prompting his criticisms of these popular spectacles, in censuring their staging and attendance Chrysostom automatically censured an integral part of the city in the ancient world.

We have already encountered a number of instances in which Chrysostom attacked the theatre and its performances for the lustful thoughts aroused in his congregation as a result of gazing upon indecorous women on the stage. If the eyes were seen as the gateway to the soul, such calculated 'looking at' actresses could not but be a source of grave danger to the male members of Chrysostom's audience, old or young.[3] However, the subject matter of these dramatic displays was also the source of considerable concern to the preacher in his pastoral role. The themes and plots presented on the stage of theatres of the Late Roman empire were drawn from the inherited literary culture of the Graeco-Roman world. There has been much debate as to whether entire tragedies or comedies were performed in full at this time, and it is now generally agreed that dramatic performances would have consisted rather of a series of excerpts from the original works, performed as a kind of anthology of Greek and Roman myth.[4] Thus the ancient tales of Greek drama and epic poetry would have been well known, even to an audience of late antiquity, although not presented in their entire form. This familiarity is evidenced by the way in which Chrysostom could refer to these texts with only the briefest of references and still rely on the comprehension of his audience. The well-to-do segment of this congregation would of course have a detailed knowledge of the literature in question from the conventional education of the day, but it would seem that even those members of society not privileged enough to have access to such a complete education gathered a decent knowledge of this inherited literary culture from the regular performances of the myths and plays on the stage. Unfortunately for them, Chrysostom was in no doubt as to the moral dubiousness of such dramatic spectacles, and regularly denounced the theatres as dens of iniquity:

> In their indecent night-time gatherings, women were admitted to the performance. There you could see the obscene sight of a virgin sitting in the theatre during the night, amidst a drunken crowd of young men madly revelling. The festival was actually the darkness, and the abominable deeds practised by them.[5]

The argument as to whether women would really have been present at such performances or not matters little. What is evident is the way in which Chrysostom uses the behaviour of the Greeks as a negative *exemplum* for his audience, and the strongest indication of their corruption and unsuitability as role models lies in the way in which they promoted the lapse in behavioural boundaries between the sexes. Here the preacher is ostensibly attacking the practices of his Greek forebears, deeming such confounding of gender boundaries to be indicative of the grave corruption of this ancient society. For women to be admitted to these spectacles in such a blasé manner shows the precarious state of the order of this past civilisation. However, as he continues to condemn the Greek theatrical events, Chrysostom very cunningly manages to blur the distinction between past and present performances, and indeed between fact and fiction. Thus his criticism of past dramatic displays functions as a disparagement of a more current state of affairs:

> One man loved his stepmother, and a woman her stepson, and as a result hanged herself.... And would you wish to see a son married to his mother? This too happened among them, and what is most horrible, although it was done in ignorance, the god whom they worshipped did not prevent it, but permitted this outrage against nature to be committed, even though she was a member of the nobility.... The wife of a certain man fell in love with another man, and with the help of her adulterer, killed her husband on his return home. Most of you probably know the story. The son of the murdered man killed the adulterer, and after that his mother, and then he himself went mad, and was haunted by the furies. After this the madman himself murdered another man, and took his wife for himself.[6]

Here Chrysostom gives a whistle-stop tour of some of the greatest plays within the Greek literary corpus: *Hippolytus*, *Oedipus Rex*, and the trilogy of the *Oresteia*. The off-hand way in which he refers to each text, and readily assumes that his audience will understand the references, indicates the familiarity of the inhabitants of the late antique city with this inherited culture. At the same time, Chrysostom's cursory remarks show his dismissal of the Graeco-Roman culture as almost ridiculous in its catalogue of madness and calamity. But his deliberately brief and non-specific allusions to these plays also help to confound the division between performance and reality, thus appearing to disparage Greek society as a whole, rather than merely the mythical heritage of this society. Chrysostom blatantly ignores the more complex plot motivations behind each of the listed events that would have made the deeds more understandable to an audience, presenting them instead as heinous crimes prevalent in this decadent society. This presentation of ancient Greece as a lawless society occurs elsewhere in his preaching, when he claims that the authorities of this era failed to legislate against fornication, gambling, drunkenness, blasphemy or the seduction of a household slave.[7] The epitome of such corruption in Chrysostom's eyes is once again the theatrical events staged by these Greeks:

> Would you also like to hear about another set of things which indicate their foolishness? For just as they do not punish these deeds, so there are other actions which they compel by laws. What are these actions? They gather crowds to fill theatres, and there they introduce choruses of trollops, and prostituted children, the kind of people indeed who trample on the natural order.[8]

By thus censuring past customs, Chrysostom enacts his customary process of warning his current congregation of the behaviour that will not be accepted from them, without always necessitating that he address them directly about the theatrical displays still presented within their own community. Just as men were informed that vanity and ostentation would not be tolerated by means of stern rebukes directed ostensibly at women, so too by witnessing the contempt their preacher has for these lawless Greeks, his current congregation should understand that their behaviour too is being carefully monitored. By making the Greeks seem patently ridiculous and laughable as well as merely censuring their immorality, Chrysostom further compounds the strength of his recommendations to a more sedate and ordered way of life.

This condemnation of the Greek cultural heritage shared by such a large portion of his audience is not confined by Chrysostom to dramatic texts, but also extends to the philosophy of the time. We have already seen instances of the way in which Paul is regularly extolled over the best known Greek philosophers as having more success in the transmission of his message in spite of a relatively meagre education. But Chrysostom is also careful to denigrate these philosophers in more obvious ways, such as refusing to name them, even when quoting their teachings, and also by condemning some of their suggestions and thinking outright:

> One of their lawgivers ordered that virgins should wrestle naked in the presence of men. I congratulate you that you are not able to bear mention of it; but their philosophers were not ashamed of the actual practice. Another, the chief of their philosophers, approves of their

going out to war, and of their being held as common property, as if he were a pimp and they were something to indulge his lusts.... For if those who professed philosophy among them made such laws, what will we say about those who were not philosophers? If these were the decrees of those who wore a long beard, and a serious cloak, what can be said of others?[9]

Thus Chrysostom dismisses the teachings of both Lycurgus and Plato, without naming either of them directly, as he simultaneously undermines the philosophic mode entirely by his offhand reference to the traditional dress of such thinkers. This consistent denigration of the inherited culture of his audience is particularly ironic given the fact that Chrysostom himself is often seen to utter opinions markedly similar to those he professes to despise. His disgust for the dramatic plots discussed above is actually very close in sentiment to the opinions expressed by Plato in his *Republic*, where this philosopher disparaged Greek epic poetry on the account of its portrayal of men and gods performing immoral deeds.[10] The attitudes to wealth and its abuses witnessed in the previous chapters are also little different from standard philosophic approaches to the problem. It is hard to accurately understand Chrysostom's motivation in enacting this process as he does on so many occasions. Is he deliberately sabotaging the intellectual heritage of his audience in order to replace it with a Christianised version of 'philosophy'? Or is he merely employing the rhetorical cliché of simplicity, which proved so effective and popular a weapon in the Christian armoury? It is a problem not easily solved, but it is, once again, worth noting the lack of innovation in the thematic content of Chrysostom's preaching. In the passage quoted above, the most obvious point to take note of is the way in which Chrysostom objects to the gender transgressions advocated by these philosophers, since their recommendations would in fact subvert and collapse the established order of society.

Chrysostom does not go into similar detail as to the dangers inherent in attendance at sporting spectacles in the civic calendar, due perhaps to the fact that he did not see as many opportunities for sexual misconduct arising out of this particular pastime. He is rather more concerned as to the distraction these events posed to his audience, drawing them away from the church services where they would be more greatly benefited by his own instruction. And so Chrysostom dismisses the activities of the hippodrome and other sporting arenas with even greater brevity than that accorded to the plots of Greek drama, simply accusing his flock of caring more for the success of a particular horse than for the welfare of their immortal souls.[11] Thus he argues against this aspect of urban life on a largely superficial basis – it is a competition for attention that he is involved in, but cannot really win. This is because Chrysostom, in spite of all his efforts to entertain his audience, is unable to provide them with an equivalent to these sporting spectacles that would encourage them into his ecclesiastical arena rather than the sporting one.

Dramatic events such as those discussed above, however, were part of a medium in which he was much more at home. It has already been noted how often Chrysostom has resorted to particularly vibrant and theatrical speeches in his effort to grasp and hold the attention of his recalcitrant audience. Just as he condemns the often lurid plots and themes of ancient Greek stage literature, so he too presents his listeners with startling imagery and carefully worked out metaphors. His shocking accounts of the relative lifestyles of both rich and poor by virtue of their sheer vividness and detail become the moral replacements of these aforementioned plots. Thus, as well as serving as exhortations to a better way of life, passages such as his careful description of the wealthy dining table witnessed in a previous chapter, or indeed the gastronomic ills arising from gluttony, also function as weapons in Chrysostom's ratings war against the theatre. His lively and uncensored manner of speaking provided his audience with just the kind of sensationalism he warns them against seeking in the dramatic arenas. While engaging in this form of competition, however, Chrysostom can reassure himself of the comparative safety of his enterprise, since the spectacles he conjures up for his listeners are carefully contained and controlled within the bounds of his discourse and within the larger confines of the church building. The preacher can therefore monitor the impact of his discourse and limit its effects by turning the attention of the audience to other matters before any damage can be done, while at the same time allowing them a necessary outlet for their potentially harmful thoughts and desires. Left to themselves in the secular theatre, on the other hand, audience members carry the insidious images witnessed there away with them, mulling over them in the mind's eye long after the performance has finished, thus compounding the danger involved, and without the necessary self-control to contain the desires thereby aroused. Chrysostom, however, succeeds in both matching and controlling this precarious world of imagery and its presentation, with his unique combination of liveliness and piety.

The preacher also suggests to his congregation that they might wish instead to turn their eyes towards the heavenly version of the theatre, where they themselves become the actors, with God as their divine spectator. Almost prefiguring Shakespeare, Chrysostom here sees all the world as a stage, but it is God and his angels who are the spectators of this play, and so his congregation must do their utmost to win the approval of this divine audience.[12] It is an interesting metaphor to use, given the contempt and disgust he has demonstrated elsewhere for members of the dramatic professions. But, using imagery familiar to, and popular with, his audience, Chrysostom shifts the tenor of their actions and reminds them of the spiritual benefits thereby accruing. And so a theatre of the divine becomes the Christian offering in place of the secular entertainments offered by the benefactors of the city, and an arena in which every person can see themselves as playing an active part, rather than simply watching from the sidelines.

### Men, women and money – the Christianised city

The process that Chrysostom enacts in his battle against the public entertainments of the secular city can be seen throughout his preaching on all areas of life in the later empire. It is the means by which he worked to redefine the civic community according to more Christian parameters, and thus achieve the transformation of the city that I have alluded to a number of times throughout this book. Reared with a conventional education, Chrysostom was more than familiar with the philosophic views of what it meant to be a citizen as well as received notions of what the civic unit comprised. Nor does he substantially depart from these traditions. Aristotle, for example, believed that the city state was made up of individual households which combined to form a community in which a version of the good life would be available to at least some, if not all, of the inhabitants.[13] Out of this conglomeration of *oikoi*, the political and administrative aspects of the civic life would arise, leading in turn to the public symbols of the well-being of this city which have already been discussed in relation to the experience of John Chrysostom; namely lavish building work, public entertainments, and the obvious display of wealth and status. Each of these elements was both a signal of the status of the *polis* and a means of the continued perpetuation of this urban unit. Thus we can see that Chrysostom's own understanding of what a city actually was, is not substantially different from the Aristotelian tradition.

What Chrysostom does do, however, is actively work to Christianise the terms of reference for the ancient city and its inhabitants. Thus the Aristotelian version of the 'good life' becomes the Christian sense of spiritual closeness to God evidenced in a devout style of living. Early in Chrysostom's career, his understanding of asceticism as the philosophic life best calculated to win salvation gave rise to those writings which urged celibacy and self-denial on his readers. In his preaching career, however, his increasing realism and understanding of human nature led him to refine his exhortations to advocating simple moderation and restraint in the daily lives of his parishioners. This would be the new good life of the Christian city-state. Similarly Aristotle's conception of the natural order of things is replaced with the Christianised notion of God's divinely ordained system. The natural urges and instincts of human beings, including those that lead to relations between the sexes, are no longer seen as arbitrary forces of Mother Nature, but as part of a carefully calculated plan on the part of God, directed towards the long-term happiness of his people.

It is this 'gentle' process of redefinition of the shared notions of society on the part of Chrysostom, that leaves me so resistant to Peter Brown's claims that Chrysostom's preaching sounded the death knell of the ancient city. Brown asserts that Chrysostom hoped to destroy the existing civic structure, replacing it with an entirely Christian city of the poor, of which he would be the new ambassador.[14] In fact Brown leaves it somewhat unclear as to whether Chrysostom's 'other' city is the one inhabited by the poor – in which case we must ask how this city could hope to survive without financial assistance from elsewhere – or whether it is the newly modelled city where wealth is shared out on a more common basis, and the citizens demonstrate themselves to be obviously Christian. I am inclined to take the latter interpretation myself, given the tone of Chrysostom's preaching in the homilies on the Pauline epistles. Chrysostom does not speak of an entirely new city where everyone will be poor and humble, but rather a more ordered version of what currently exists, and where there will always be a more well-off group of people who will bestow the alms needed by their poorer counterparts. He does not offer any alternative ways as to how wealth or property will be generated by his other city, seeming rather to assume a certain amount of material possessions will automatically be present. In my reading of the preacher's sermons I have not found striking evidence of such radical ambitions as those claimed by Brown. Indeed Chrysostom, like so many of his fellow Church leaders and his audience, was so much himself imbued with classical culture and perceptions of the world, that an attempt at such subversion or destruction of tradition would have been beyond his comprehension or his abilities. This also runs contrary to Brown's opinion that Chrysostom actually underestimated the strong attachment of his congregation to the classical civic idea.[15] Far from underestimating the urban concept, I feel that Chrysostom was in fact keenly aware of its strengths and weaknesses, and knew how best to work the contemporary notions of the *polis* to his own advantage. Instead of trying to raze the city to the ground, therefore, throughout his preaching career Chrysostom endeavoured to overlay an existing structure with a Christianised lens or world-view. Those aspects of civic life which he disapproved of were now presented with competing attractions from the Christian side as Chrysostom strove to redirect the priorities of his congregation, while the safer aspects of urban living were simply renamed as Christian concepts or structures. In fact Christianity could have done much to preserve the civic unit in something close to its original form, through its church-building programme, the installation of divine services in place of public entertainments, and the advance of alms-giving in place of ostentatious munificence.[16] Far from failing to understand the nature of the 'conflict', as Brown would seem to suggest, Chrysostom showed himself to be highly conscious of the forces he needed to contend with, and how best to engage his audience in this combat.

This then is the key to Chrysostom's approach to the problems of life in the rich and sophisticated cities of the later Roman empire. In the entire body of sermons preached on the Pauline epistles we see no evidence of a general call to secular authorities to complete the work of redrawing the boundaries of the urban unit. Rather, Chrysostom exerts all his energies to work a personal change in each individual member of his congregation. If each person who attended his services on Sundays could be encouraged to approach their own life from a more Christian and spiritual angle than had previously been their wont, the ramifications for the appearance of the *polis* as a whole would be great indeed. And so we see all of Chrysostom's exhortations towards moral behaviour characterised by the specific nature of their aim. Instead of calling for a complete ban on theatrical performances or sporting spectacles, although we know from elsewhere that Chrysostom would have loved to do so, he prefers to lay the responsibility in this matter at the door of the individuals concerned. Those who had been accustomed to regular attendance at these events are shown the ill effects arising from the habit, thus encouraging them to turn away from such a potentially harmful pastime. To forestall any reluctance, Chrysostom uses all of his own rhetorical and dramatic skills in his preaching in order to provide a ready-made alternative to these secular entertainments, which will both enthral and morally benefit his audience. Similarly, rather than working for a radical reorganisation of society in order to achieve a classless community, or indeed a city of the poor, Chrysostom consistently appeals to the individuals comprising his congregation, encouraging each one to administer his own material resources as he sees fit according to his Christian conscience. If the priorities and desires of enough of these people can be redirected, and this redirection manifested in positive action, then the overall appearance of the city will be more Christian than before, while the basic structure of the unit remains untouched. And indeed this makes the most practical sense, since some degree of wealth will be necessary to continue the task of almsgiving, as Chrysostom does not introduce any replacement economic model for the sustenance of his Christianised community.

Chrysostom's consistent appeals to the individuals who go to make up each household within the city show just how Aristotelian his notions of urban living really are. He too is firm in the belief that it is a conglomeration of homes that forms the larger civic unit, and so prefers to approach his redefinition of the city from this point upwards. Each household can be seen as a microcosm of the greater urban community, with the system of order in the one being representative of order in the other. It is largely for this reason that we have seen Chrysostom to be so concerned with gender roles and behaviour. The traditional classical household was formed around the division of labour between the sexes. Any breakdown in this order signalled a grave threat to the overall structure of the *oikos*, with further implications for the state of the *polis*. It was therefore vital in Chrysostom's eyes that this system of order be maintained, with its key being in the hierarchy between the sexes, and the roles assigned to each one. This allows us to understand his regularly recurring concerns as to the behaviour of those members of his congregation who seem to be overstepping the boundaries set in place by God in his ordination of the natural order of things. Those women who try to obtrude themselves in the affairs of men pose an enormous threat to the structure of the household, while the extreme vanity and ostentation so often condemned by Chrysostom marks a failure on the part of such females to be constrained by the sense of shame and modesty deemed appropriate to the sex on account of their natural inferiority. But even more worrying to the preacher is the sight of the male sex forgetting its innate superiority, both in intellect and in virtue. The love of money and of conspicuous consumption on the part of so many in his flock leaves Chrysostom constantly anxious as to the masculinity of these individuals. We have seen him complain that their pursuit of wealth has led them even to adopting the women's work of weaving, while their vanity and pride sees them dressing with even more care than the most frivolous female.

Worse even than gender boundaries being transgressed, then, is this mutation of the male sex into something between the two alternatives. Masculine neither in their virtue nor in their use of reason, such men have willingly adopted an effeminacy of manner without entirely emasculating themselves. The inability to categorise these persons threatens Chrysostom's entire conception of society, and is condemned for that reason. Just as sexual misconduct in the dramatic arena was seen as an index of the corruption of previous Greek and Roman civilisations, Chrysostom regards this 'gender-bending' as a symbol of all that is wrong with the society of his day. He is clear in his avowal that the hierarchy of the sexes was the most basic of societal structures, set in place right from the creation of man, and indeed being the only hierarchy God intended among humans from the beginning. To undermine this system, therefore, is not only to blatantly disregard God's plan for humanity, but also to threaten society as a whole with destabilisation and ultimately with destruction. We have seen Chrysostom consistently work to repair and maintain this crucial aspect of life within the city of the late Roman empire, using his rhetorical ingenuity to cajole, threaten, warn and persuade his congregation of the immense danger posed to their community by any move on their part to ignore or transgress this natural order of things.

Chrysostom's ideal Christian household, therefore, would be one in which these boundaries between the sexes were strictly upheld, with care of the domestic sphere being entrusted entirely to the female party, and civic matters falling to the part of the male. Again, this was by no means innovative teaching or thinking on Chrysostom's part, but his Christianisation of this traditional philosophy is carefully worked out indeed. With the man and woman of the household thus organised, this infrastructure is passed on through the generations by means of the conscientious and diligent rearing of the children, as well as the monitoring of servants and attendants. But the realigned priorities of these Christians will hopefully become evident far beyond the walls of the home. Should the preacher succeed in persuading the members of his congregation to live more frugal, more spiritual lives within the private sphere, the ideas and motivations brought to their activities in the public arena will shift correspondingly. And so the traditional appearance of the civic unit will become overlaid with a set of Christianised values. Ecclesiastical congregations will take the place of secular social gatherings, and preaching such as performed by Chrysostom himself will function as an alternative to public entertainments such as the theatre or sporting events. Almsgiving will take the place of conspicuous consumption and euergetism as a new means of acquiring honour and civic respect, while the poor become the spiritual patrons of their rich clients, since they facilitate the moral salvation of those who are their material benefactors.[17] At the same time, bishops and priests become the new representatives, governors, patrons and ambassadors of the Christian city. As we can see from this roundup of the themes which featured most prominently in this work, little of the basic structure of the ancient city is changed by Chrysostom's preaching or ambitions. It is rather the perspective given to this underlying base that has shifted into a more Christian mode. The preacher has employed his rhetoric to alter the outlook of his congregation rather than the form of the civic unit, perhaps transforming the citizens rather than the city. And approaching his audience on such an individual and subjective basis is best done through appeals to their personal traits and relationships – bringing us once again back to the prominence of gender- and wealth-related issues in his preaching. It is by targeting the smaller unit of the household that Chrysostom can best hope to gain the attention and following of his audience, in order to achieve his larger ambition. Thus he can hope to bring the mood and tenor of the ascetic communities he so admired inside the city walls, for even the more ordinary citizens of Christianity to enjoy and perpetuate.

### The reaction of the preacher's audience

Unfortunately we have no real means of monitoring the success or failure of Chrysostom's city. Church sermons are indeed only one half of a dialogue between preacher and audience, but in most cases it is the only side of the conversation we have available to us today. We have already seen the instances in which Chrysostom's audience reacted with applause or outrage, depending on the exertions required of them by their spiritual leader. But there is no system in place to measure the longer-term attention paid to his words by the congregation once they left the church. Did they take on board Chrysostom's recommendations, striving to run their households in accordance to his Christianised standards? Or did they merely combine the secular and ecclesiastical aspects of civic living in an uneasy mixture, maintaining a superficial approach to the issues involved? It is a question about which we can only speculate at this stage, although we do see Chrysostom and Olympias mutually lament over the bishop's exile while so much of his life's work is left unfinished. Nor does external evidence point to any great change in the appearance or function of the city in eastern empire. With so much of Chrysostom's rhetoric being personal in its nature, its effects can for the most part be measured only on a personal, and therefore unknowable, level. Regardless of the success or failure of his project, however, we have in Chrysostom's preaching a series of themes and concerns directly applicable to the daily life of the later empire. The exegetical openings of his homilies regularly give way to extempore discussions of issues immediately relevant to his congregation, the very spontaneity with which they are introduced by the preacher serving as proof of the pertinence of these themes to the personal lives of his flock. Chrysostom thus shows himself to be an astute observer of those in his charge and a caring pastor in his efforts to safe-guard the moral well-being of each and every one of these individuals. However, the regular bursts of vitriol and astringency that we have seen throughout our study show that sometimes Chrysostom could not restrain himself in his desire to permanently alter the outlook of his listeners. This prioritising of a long-term ambition over the short-term comfort of the audience is characteristic of Chrysostom, but it was prob-ably also what damaged his standing in the eyes of the influential members of this society, leading in turn to his political downfall and ulti-mate exile. His approach to the transformation of the ancient city and its citizens looks on paper to be carefully calculated and subtle. The bolstering of gender roles, along with specific guidance for the running of a Christianised household, should have led to a new model of the city in late antiquity, with a corresponding shift in the uses to which civic wealth was put. In reality, however, the personality of the preacher, coupled with his own ascetic zeal, meant that what could have been a finely honed tool for change was often a blunt sledgehammer.

# Abbreviations

*Adv. Eos = Adversus Eos qui apud se habent subintroductas virgines*
*AJP = American Journal of Philology*
*ATR = Anglican Theological Review*
*CP = Classical Philology*
*HTR = Harvard Theological Review*
*JECS = Journal of Early Christian Studies*
*JRS = Journal of Roman Studies*
*JTS = Journal of Theological Studies*
PG = Patrologia Graeca
PL = Patrologia Latina
NFPNF = Nicene Fathers and Post Nicene Fathers, Series 2
*NTS = New Testament Studies*
*Quod Reg. = Quod Regulares Feminae Viris Cohabitare non Debeant*
SC = Sources Chrétiennes
*Stu. Patr. = Studia Patristica*
*VC = Vigiliae Christianae*

# Notes

## 1. Pagan and Christian Cities

**1**. Socrates, *Hist. Eccl.* VI.3, PG 67.668.

**2**. Liebeschuetz (1993), 151-63.

**3**. Liebeschuetz (1972) and (1984), 85-111; S. Elm (1998), 68-93. See D. Raynor (1989), 165-9, for a partial rehabilitation of the character of Theophilus, so often painted as irredeemably black in accounts of Chrysostom's downfall.

**4**. Jones (1969) I.vi-vii.

**5**. Allen (1991), 1-5.

**6**. Leyerle (2000). I am grateful to Blake for allowing to me to read this work while still in manuscript form.

**7**. Leyerle (1993), 159-74, (1994), 29-47 and (1997), 243-70.

**8**. Wilken (1983).

**9**. See Brown (1972), (1982) and (1986) for a comprehensive introduction to the ascetic phenomenon and some of its leading exponents. See also, among others, Cameron (ed.) (1989), Elm (1994), Rousseau (1978).

**10**. See Libanius' *Oration* 15 for some of the clashes between pagan and Christian sensibilities in the city of Antioch prior to and during the reign of Julian.

**11**. Libanius, *Oration* II.55, *Oration* XI.227.

**12**. Libanius, *Julian Misopogon* 362d.

**13**. Libanius, *Oration* II.26-8.

**14**. Ibid., 38.

**15**. Ammianus Marcellinus, Book 28.4.5-9.

**16**. Id., Book 28.4.25-31.

**17**. Brown (1988), 306.

**18**. Palladius, *Dialogus* V, PG 47.20.

**19**. Wylie (1992) offers such an esoteric interpretation of Chrysostom's work.

**20**. Gleason (1990), 390-1 and (1995), ch.1.

**21**. M. Satlow (1996), 19-40.

**22**. D. Roark (1994) also argues that any search for change in late antique society must begin with the family as the basic unit of that society.

**23**. For example Clark (1979) on the *subintroductae*, and (1983) on the treatises *On Virginity* and *Against Remarriage*. Also Leyerle (2001) on the *subintroductae*.

**24**. Aristotle, *Politics* 1.1.

**25**. See for example Cameron (1989) and (1991), Brown (1992) and (1995), Lim (1995).

**26**. See Parvey (1974), 117-49, and Schussler Fiorenza (1983), ch. 6 on this subject.

**27**. Chadwick (1954), 261-75.

**28**. Introduction to Palladius' *Dialogus*, viii.

**29**. Palladius, *Dialogus* V, PG 47.18-21. Also Carter (1962), 357-64.

**30**. Socrates, *Hist. Eccl.* VI.3, Sozomen, *Hist. Eccl.* VIII.2, and more recently Jones (1953), 171-3 and Kelly (1995), ch. 1.

**31**. Hunter (1988), 525-31 and (1989), 129-35.

**32**. Sozomen, *Hist. Eccl.* VIII.2; ['he was] a man of noble birth, and of exemplary life, and possessed of such wonderful powers of eloquence and persuasion, that he was declared, by Libanius the Syrian, to surpass all the orators of the age'.

**33**. *De Sacerdotio* I.5, PG 48.624.

**34**. *De Sacerdotio* I.6, PG 48.626.

**35**. Palladius, *Dialogus* V.

**36**. Ibid., PG 47.19.

**37**. Sozomen, *Hist. Eccl.* VIII.2.

**38**. Palladius, *Dialogus* V, PG 47.19.

**39**. Ibid., PG 47.19-20.

**40**. See for example Liebeschuetz (1991), ch. 19, or Kelly (1995), 159ff.

**41**. Holum (1982), ch. 2.

**42**. The sermon in question now appears to be spurious, but the attack on Eudoxia is reported in Palladius, *Dialogus* VIII, PG 47.30; Socrates, *Hist. Eccl.* VI.15; Sozomen, *Hist. Eccl.* VIII.16.

**43**. Liebeschuetz (1984).

**44**. Socrates, *Hist. Eccl.* VII.25; Liebeschuetz (1984), 100.

## 2. *Nolo Episcopari* and the Transformation of the City

**1**. Brown (1971), 98.

**2**. *Homily XIV on I Timothy*, NFPNF 13.456-7, PG 62.575-7.

**3**. Dudley (1991), 162-5.

**4**. See further Urbainczyk (2001).

**5**. See Downey (1962), 70; Liebeschuetz (1972), 144-8; Pack (1935), 61-3.

**6**. See for example Veyne (1976), ch. IV.

**7**. *De Sacerdotio* III.16-17, PG 48.654-60.

**8**. A. Wallace Hadrill (1989).

**9**. *Homily I on Titus*, NFPNF 13.523, PG 62.669; *houtos de pantakhou perielketai, polla kai tôn huper dunamin apaiteitai. an mê eidêi legein, polus ho goggusmos. an de eidê legein, palin katêgoriai, kenodoxos estin. an mê nekrous anistai, oudenos logou axios, phêsin. ho deina eulabês estin, outos de ou. An apolauêi summetrou trophês, palin katêgoriai. Edei auton apêgkhonisthai, phêsin. an louomenon idêi tis, pollai katêgoriai. Holôs oude ton hêlion horain opheilei, phêsin.*

## 3. Christian Preaching and its Audience

**1**. A.N. Couratin (1969), Cunningham (1990), 30-1 and Liebeschuetz (1990), 177.

**2**. As noted by E.A. Clark (1990), 19.

**3**. Cameron (1991), 19.

**4**. Allen & Mayer (1993), 262.

**5**. Paul, I Corinthians 1:22-5.

**6**. Augustine, *De Doctrina Christiana* IV.4, Fathers of the Church series vol. 2, 172.

**7**. *De Sacerdotio* IV.5, NFPNF 9.66, PG 48.663.

**8**. Basil of Caesarea, *Homily* 327.2, PG 31.492.

**9**. Basil of Caesarea, *Address to Young Men on What Profit may be Derived from Pagan Literature*, Loeb trans.

**10**. See *On Vainglory and Advice to parents on the right way to bring up children*, trans. M. Laistner.

**11**. *De Doctrina Christiana* IV.2, 169.

**12**. Ibid., IV.15, 198.

**13**. Deferrari (1922), 97-124; 193-220.

**14**. Allen (1991), 1.

**15**. *Homily VIII on Ephesians*, NFPNF 13.92, PG 62.66.

**16**. *Homily V on Romans*, NFPNF 11.367, PG 60.431.
See also *Homily IX on Ephesians*, NFPNF 13.94, PG 62.69; 'But now the chain is dragging me away still further from my subject, and pulling me back again, and I cannot bear to resist it, but am drawn along willingly – yes indeed, with all my heart; and I wish it could always be my task to be speaking about Paul's chain.'

**17**. *Homily XIV on I Corinthians*, NFPNF 12.22, PG 61.40.

**18**. *Homily XIII on I Corinthians*, NFPNF 12.74, PG 61.110. See also *Homily XXX on Acts of the Apostles*, NFPNF 11.193, PG 60.226.28 and *Homily II On the Statues*, NFPNF 9.347.

**19**. Miles (1997).

**20**. *De Sacerdotio* V.1, NFPNF 9.70, PG 48.672.

**21**. *Homily VIII on Ephesians*, NFPNF 13.94, PG 62.69.

**22**. This was the occasion his audience reacted with excitement at a reference made to Plato in *Homily XXVI on I Corinthians*, NFPNF 12.156, PG 61.224; 'Did you let out a great shout [at hearing of this philosopher]? Why, I at this moment am in deep mourning, when heathens prove better lovers of wisdom than we.'

**23**. *Homily VII on Colossians*, NFPNF 13.292, PG 62.349.

**24**. *Homily VIII on Colossians*, NFPNF 13.293, PG 62.351.

**25**. Goodall (1979), 71.

**26**. Gregory Nazianzus, *De Baptismo*.

**27**. Young (1983), 156.

**28**. Kelly (1995), 58. The biographer in question was George of Alexandria.

**29**. *De Doctrina Christiana* IV.25, 191.

**30**. Goodall (1979), 264; J. Kelly (1995), 94.

**31**. Socrates, *Hist. Eccl.* VI.4, PG 67.672.

**32**. See for example Liebeschuetz (1991), 172; J. Kelly (1995), 132-5.

**33**. *Homily VI on Ephesians*, NFPNF 13.78, PG 62.48.

**34**. For example, *Homily I on II Thessalonians*, NFPNF 13.379, PG 62.467.

**35**. A summary of their ideas and work to date can be found in Allen (1991) and (1995).

**36**. Carter (1999).

**37**. Mayer (1999).

**38**. *Homily III on Colossians*, NFPNF 13.270, PG 62.317. See also *Homily XXIV on Ephesians*, NFPNF 13.167, PG 62.167 and *Homily V on I Corinthians*, NFPNF 12.25, PG 61.43.

**39**. MacMullen (1989), 503-11.

**40**. *Homily XL on I Corinthians*, NFPNF 12.248, PG 61.353.

**41**. *Homily V on Genesis*, PG 54.602-3.

**42**. See for example *Homily VIII on I Timothy*, NFPNF 13.433, PG 62.542, *Homily III on II Thessalonians*, NFPNF 13.387, PG 62.483 and *Homily X on Colossians*, NFPNF 13.307, PG 62.371.

**43**. Basil, *De Hexaemeron* III.1, SC 26.190.

**44**. Rousseau (1994), 42 and (1998).

**45**. Liebeschuetz (1991), 173.

**46**. Mayer (1999). See also G. Clark (1999) for similar arguments in relation to Augustine's preaching.

**47**. Leyerle (1994), 29-47.
**48**. *Homily XVII on II Corinthians*, NFPNF 12.361, PG 61.520.
**49**. The vast majority of Chrysostom's preaching was ostensibly exegetical in nature, with homilies on all the Pauline epistles, the letter to the Hebrews, Acts, the Gospels of John and Matthew, and the Book of Genesis. Other surviving sermons were preached on particular feast days such as that of St Babylas, but they are greatly outnumbered by those preached on specific scriptural texts.
**50**. Ruether (1969), 43ff. Also Meredith (1995).
**51**. Gleason (1995), 73.
**52**. Cameron (1991), 86.
**53**. *Homily XXXIV on I Corinthians*, NFPNF 12.207, PG 61.294.
**54**. H. Hubbell (1924), 263.
**55**. Kecksemeti (1989), 136-47.
**56**. Liebeschuetz (1991), 178.
**57**. Cunningham (1990), 44-7.
**58**. Ryan (1982), 12.
**59**. Deferrari (1922), 220; Bailey (1999).
**60**. Liebeschuetz (1972), 96.
**61**. *Contra Iudos et theatra I*, PG 56.263-5.
**62**. *Codex Theodosianus* II.8.23.
**63**. *Homily XXXVI on I Corinthians*, NFPNF 12.221, PG 61.315.
**64**. See for example *Homily IV on I Corinthians*, NFPNF 12.16-22, PG 61.32-40 and *Homily V on Titus*, NFPNF 13.535-40, PG 62.687-96.

## 5. Role Models for the Christian City

**1**. See McLynn (1994), 305-9.
**2**. For example Holum (1982), ch. 2.
**3**. *De Sacerdotio* I.5, NFPNF 9.34.
**4**. *Homily VI on I Thessalonians*, NFPNF 13.351, PG 62.433.
**5**. *Homily VII on II Timothy*, NFPNF 13.503, PG 62.641. See also *Homily XIV on I Timothy*, NFPNF 13.454, PG 62.573.
**6**. See for example Malingrey (1968), E. Clark (1968), 209-28, Rousseau (1995), 116-47.
**7**. Kelly (1995), 113.
**8**. *Life of Olympias*, trans. E. Clark, 127-42.
**9**. Sozomen, *Hist. Eccl.* 8.9.
**10**. Broc (1991), 150-4.
**11**. See Mayer (1999) for a much needed survey of these wealthy and influential women.
**12**. Brown (1961), 1-11, and Yarbrough (1976), 149-64.
**13**. *Hom. II cum imperatrix media nocte in magnam ecclesiam venisset*, PG 63.469, cited in Holum (1982), 57.
**14**. Palladius, *Dialogus* VIII, PG 47.30. The historian Zosimus 5.23.2 also indicates that Eudoxia had already been long wearied by Chrysostom's habit of reprimanding her in front of his general congregations.
**15**. Socrates, *Hist. Eccl.* VI.11.
**16**. Kelly (1995), 211.
**17**. Palladius, *Dialogus* IX, PG 47.30.
**18**. *Homily XI on Ephesians*, NFPNF 13.108, PG 62.87.
**19**. *Homily III on Colossians*, NFPNF 13.274, PG 62.324.
**20**. Holum (1982), ch. 2.

**21**. See further Young (1989), 192.

**22**. See for example *Homily X on II Timothy*, NFPNF 13.516, PG 62.659.

**23**. *Homily XXX on Romans*, NFPNF 11.552, PG 60.667.

**24**. *Homily XXXI on Romans*, NFPNF 11.554, PG 60.668-9; *Semnunometha men gar, hoti toiautai par' hêmin gunaikes. aiskhunometha de, hoti sphodra autôn apolimpanometha hoi andres. All' ean mathômen pothen ekeinai kallôpizontai, takheôs kai hêmeis autas katalêpsometha. pothen oun kallôpizontai; Akouetôsan kai andres kai gunaikes. ouk apo tôn melliôn, oude apo tôn harmiskôn, oude apo tôn eunoukhôn, kai tôn therpainidôn kai tôn khrusopastôn himatiôn, all' apo tôn huper tês alêtheias hidrôtôn.*

**25**. See further Malingrey, (1975), 199-218.

**26**. Clark (1999).

**27**. *Homily IV on I Thessalonians*, NFPNF 13.343, PG 62.421. See also *Homily X on Colossians*, NFPNF 13.308, PG 62.372.

**28**. *Homily III on II Corinthians*, NFPNF 12.292, PG 61.416. *Hotan men gar hê gunê phtheggêtai tou Iôb, diabolos energei*: See *Homily IV on I Thessalonians*, NFPNF 13.340, PG 62.417 and *Homily XV on Romans*, NFPNF 11.454.

**29**. *Homily XIII on Ephesians*, NFPNF 13.115, PG 62.97.

**30**. *De Sacerdotio* I.1-5.

**31**. Kelly (1995), 27.

**32**. Ibid., 110, 150.

**33**. *Homily VII on Colossians*, NFPNF 13.291, PG 62.347.

**34**. *Homily IV on I Thessalonians*, NPFNF 342-3, PG 62.421.

**35**. *Homily V on Philippians*, NFPNF 13.204, PG 62.215.

**36**. *Homily III on II Corinthians*, NFPNF 12.292, PG 61.416.

**37**. *Homily XX on Ephesians*, NFPNF 13.149, PG 62.144.

**38**. See *On How to Choose a Wife*, 100-4, trans. Roth and Anderson.

**39**. *Homily X on I Thessalonians*, NFPNF 13.369, PG 62.459, *Homily XXI on Ephesians*, NFPNF 13.156, PG 62.153-4 and *Homily XXXIV on I Corinthians*, NFPNF 12.207, PG 61.294-5.

**40**. *Homily II on Galatians*, NFPNF 13.18, PG 61.640.

**41**. *Homily XXXVIII on I Corinthians*, NFPNF 12.230, PG 61.327.

**42**. See for example *Homily IV on Philippians*, NFPNF 13.198, PG 62.206, *Homily I on Colossians*, NFPNF 13.257, PG 62.304 and *Arg. to Homilies on Romans*, NFPNF 11.335, PG 60.391.

**43**. See for example *Homily I on Colossians*, NFPNF 13.258-9, PG 62.301-2. Also Mitchell (1998), 93-111.

**44**. See Wilken (1983), 95; Cameron, (1999) , 697.

**45**. Kelly (1995), 106, citing the record of Chrysostom in the office-books for feast of saints in the eastern church, PG 29.391i-ii.

**46**. *Homily IX on II Timothy*, NFPNF 13.511, PG 62.652-3.

**47**. *Argument to Homilies on Romans*, NFPNF 11.335, PG 60.391.

**48**. Cameron (1998), 670.

**49**. Coleman-Norton (1930), 305-17.

**50**. Coleman-Norton (1931), 85-9.

**51**. *Homily II on Titus*, NFPNF 13.525, PG 62.673; *Hôste ou khreia kompou rhêmatôn, alla phrenôn, kai Grafôn empeirias, kai noêmatôn dunameôs. Oukh orais Paulon trepsamenon tên oikoumenên hapasan, kai meizonôs iskhusanta kai Platônos, kai tôn hallôn apantôn.* See also *Homily IV on I Corinthians*, NFPNF 12.18, PG 61.33 and *Homily II on Romans*, NFPNF 11.347, PG 60.407; 'The tentmaker has converted all of Greece and all the barbarian lands. But Plato, who is so applauded and admired among them, on coming a third time to Sicily with the verbosity of his speech, and with his brilliant reputation, did not even get the better of a single king, but came off so wretchedly, that he even lost his liberty.'

## 6. Construction of Gender

**1**. See for example E. Clark (1977) and (1986). For more general studies of the Church Fathers and questions of femininity see for example G. Clark (1993) and Cloke (1995) among others.

**2**. See further Hartney (1999).

**3**. Socrates *Hist. Eccl.* VI.3.

**4**. Palladius, *Dialogus* V. See also Dumortier (1955), Bailey (1959), 33ff. and E. Clark (1977), 171-85.

**5**. Harris (1989) and Marrou (1956) for discussions of rates of literacy in the Roman empire.

**6**. Leyerle (2000).

**7**. E. Clark (1977), 173 and Reynolds (1968), 547-66.

**8**. *Quod Regulares Feminae Viris Cohabitare non Debeant* 1, PG 47.515, trans. Clark (1979), 211 (hereafter *Quod Regulares*); *hê gar ekeinou mania son ergon esti*.

**9**. *Adversus Eos qui apud se habent subintroductas virgines* 10, PG 47.510, trans. Clark (1979), 197 (hereafter *Adv. Eos*).

**10**. *Adv. Eos* 1, PG 47.496, trans. Clark (1979), 166.

**11**. Ibid., 6, PG 47.503, trans. Clark (1979), 180; *Dia touto laimargôn kai parasitôn kai kolakôn kai gunaikodoulôn pantakhou doxan lambanomen, hoti khamai tên eugeneian hapasan rhipsantes tên anôthen dotheisan hêmin, antikatallattometha tên apo tês gês douloprepeian te kai euteleian*.

**12**. Ibid., 9, PG 47.507, trans. Clark (1979), 191.

**13**. Ibid., 9, PG 47.508, trans. Clark (1979), 192-3.

**14**. Ibid., 10, PG 47.509, trans. Clark (1979), 194.

**15**. Ibid., 7, PG 47.506, trans. Clark (1979), 187.

**16**. Homer, *Iliad* VI.311-53.

**17**. Tougher (1997), 168-84.

**18**. *Homily XIII on Ephesians*, NFPNF 13.115-6, PG 62.98.

**19**. Leyerle (1994).

**20**. Cox Miller (1993), 21-45.

**21**. See also Shaw (1997), 591.

**22**. *Life of Melania the Younger* 31-2, trans. E. Clark (1984).

**23**. Jerome, *Epistle* 138. See also Perkins (1995), ch. 8.

**24**. Roark (1994), 76-81.

**25**. *Homily XII on Colossians*, NFPNF 13.318, PG 62.387.

**26**. *Homily VIII on I Timothy*, NFPNF 13.434, PG 62.543. See *De Virginitate* VII, PG 48.537-8, for further descriptions as to how a true virgin should appear – untidy and even dirty, with eyes always downcast in acknowledgment of her inferiority.

**27**. See for example Jerome, *Epistle 22* and Gregory of Nyssa, *On Virginity*.

**28**. *Homily VIII on I Timothy*, NFPNF 13.434, PG 62.543. See also *Homily XIX on I Corinthians*, NFPNF 12.110, PG 61.159-60.

**29**. *Homily XXX on Acts of Apostles*, NFPNF 11.192.

**30**. *Homily V on I Thessalonians*, NFPNF 13.347, PG 62.427.

**31**. See for example E. Clark (1981), 240-57, Ruether (1974) and Cameron (1989), 181-205.

**32**. Aristotle, *Politics* 1.1260a.

**33**. Satlow (1996), 19-40.

**34**. See Gleason (1990), 390-1 and (1995) on this issue as played out in second-century Roman society.

## 7. Gendered Sins

**1**. *Homily VII on Colossians*, NFPNF 13.292, PG 62.349.

**2**. Ibid., NFPNF 13.293, PG 62.350.

**3**. *Homily IV on I Timothy*, NFPNF 13.422, PG 62.524.

**4**. *Homily XVII on Romans*, NFPNF 11.476, PG 60.570.

**5**. *Homily XI on Romans*, NFPNF 11.410, PG 60.486.

**6**. See for example *Homily X on Philippians*, NFPNF 13.230.

**7**. *Homily XX on Romans*, NFPNF 11.500, PG 60.601.

**8**. *Homily III on II Thessalonians*, NFPNF 13.387, PG 62.484.

**9**. Ibid.

**10**. *Homily V on I Thessalonians*, NFPNF 13.345, PG 62.425.

**11**. *Homily XIX on I Corinthians*, NFPNF 12.105, PG 61.152.

**12**. *Homily XXXVII on I Corinthians*, NFPNF 12.224, PG 61.318.

**13**. *Homily IV on I Timothy*, NFPNF 13.422, PG 62.524.

**14**. *Homily XXVI on I* Corinthians, NFPNF 12.153, PG 61.218; *Deutera hautê huperokhê palin, mallon de kai tritê kai tetarê. Prôtê, hoti kephalê hêmôn ho Khristos, hêmeis de tês gunaikos. deutera, hoti hêmeis doxa Theou, hêmôn de hê gunê. tritê, hoti oukh hêmeis ek tês gunaikos, all' ekeinê ex hêmôn. tetartê, hoti oukh hêmeis di' autên, all' ekeinê di' hêmas.*

**15**. Ibid., NFPNF 12.156, PG 61.222. See also *Homily XX on Ephesians*, NFPNF 13.149, PG 62.144; 'Neither, however, let the husband, when he hears these things, with the claim of having supreme authority, take to reviling her or to blows; but let him encourage her, let him admonish her, as being less perfect than he, let him persuade her with arguments. Let him never raise his hand to her – for this is far from a noble spirit – no, nor give insult to her, or taunt her, or revile her; but let him regulate and direct her as one being wanting in wisdom.'

**16**. *Homily XXXVII on I Corinthians*, NFPNF 12.222, PG 61.316.

**17**. *Homily V on II Thessalonians*, NFPNF 13.397, PG 62.499.

**18**. *Homily XIII on I Timothy*, NFPNF 13.452, PG 62.569.

**19**. *Homily VII on Phillippians*, NFPNF 13.218, PG 62.257.

**20**. *Homily VI on II Corinthians*, NFPNF 12.308, PG 61.439.

**21**. See Romans 1:26.

**22**. *Homily IV on Romans*, NFPNF 11.356, PG 60.417.

**23**. Ibid; *hoper eskhatês estin apôlêias deigma, hotan ekateron ê to genos dieph-tharmenon, kai o te didaskalos tês gunaikos einai takhtheis, hê te boêthos tou andros keleustheisa genesthai, ta tôn ekhthrôn eis allêlous ergazontai.*

**24**. Ibid., NFPNF 11.358, PG 60.420.

**25**. Boswell (1980), 156-159.

**26**. Tanner (1979), 1185-95.

**27**. *Homily XII on* Romans, NFPNF 11.425, PG 60.506.

**28**. *Homily XVII on Romans*, NFPNF 11.475, PG 60.568.

**29**. *Homily VI on II Corinthians*, NFPNF 12.308, PG 61.440.

**30**. *Homily XXVI on Romans*, NFPNF 11.533, PG 60.644. See also *Homily VI on Ephesians*, NFPNF 13.78, PG 62.47-8; 'But see how great the present disorder is. They, who were living virtuously, and who under any circumstance might feel secure, have now taken possession of the tops of the mountains, and have escaped out of this world, separating themselves as if from an enemy, and an alien, and not from a community to which they belonged.' *Hora goun anômalia nun hosê. Hoi men gar orthôs biountes, kai hopôsdêpote parrhêsian ekhontes, tas koruphas tôn oreôn kateilêphasi, kai ek mesou gegonasin, hôsper polemiou kai allotriou, all' oukhi oikeiou sômatos apospômenoi.*

**31**. *Homily XXIII on II Corinthains*, NFPNF 12.384, PG 61.555.

## 8. Natural and Social Order in the *Oikos* and *Polis*

**1**. *Homily XXVI on I Corinthians*, NFPNF 12.150-2, PG 61.215.

**2**. *Homily XXXIV on I Corinthians*, NFPNF 12.205, PG 61.291.

**3**. *Homily XX on Ephesians*, NFPNF 13.143, PG 62.136. See also *Homily V on Titus*, NFPNF 13.539, PG 62.694; *Homily III on II Thessalonians*, NFPNF 13.397, PG 62.499.

**4**. Ibid., NFPNF 13.149, PG 62.144.

**5**. *Homily X on II Timothy*, NFPNF 13.516, PG 62.659; *Oude gar mikron tês pasês dioikêseôs anadedektai meros hê gunê, to oikouron*: *all' ekeinês khôris, oude ta politika dunêsetai sustênai pote. Ei gar melloi thorubou kai tarakhês empeplêsthai ta kata tên oikian, hekastos tôn politeuomenôn emellen oikoi kathêsthai, kai ta kata tên polin kakôs an diakeisetai. Hôste oude en ekeinois to elatton ekhei, oude en tois pneumatikois.*

**6**. *Homily XXVI on I Corinthians*, NFPNF 12.154, PG 61.220 and *Homily XXXIV on I Corinthians*, NFPNF 12.205, PG 61.291.

**7**. Arjava (1996), 130-2.

**8**. *Homily XXVI on I Corinthians*, NFPNF 12.156, PG 61.222.

**9**. *Homily V on I Thessalonians*, NFPNF 13.345, PG 62.425.

**10**. *Homily XXIX on I Corinthians*, NFPNF 12.105, PG 61.152. See Arjava (1993), 6-9 for the legal context of such instructions.

**11**. *Homily V on Titus*, NFPNF 13.538, PG 62.693; 'In their indecent nocturnal assemblies, women were admitted to the spectacle. There was seen the abomination of a virgin sitting in the theatre during the night, amidst a drunken multitude of young men madly revelling. The very festival was the darkness, and the abominable deeds practised by them.' Again in *Homily V on I Thessalonians*, NFPNF 13.347, PG 62.427; 'When you see women displayed in the context of their physical bodies, and see spectacles and songs containing nothing but deviant loves, as when such a woman it is said, loved such a man, and not being able to have him hanged herself; or unlawful loves which are felt for mothers; when you hear of these things as well as seeing them … tell me, how can you possibly remain chaste afterwards?'

**12**. *Homily XII on I Corinthians*, NFPNF 12.69, PG 61.103.

**13**. Ibid., NFPNF 12.70, PG 61.105.

**14**. *Homily IX on I Timothy*, NFPNF 13.435, PG 62.544.

**15**. *Homily XXXVI on I Corinthians*, NFPNF 12.221, PG 61.315. Elsewhere he refers to the sex as 'somewhat talkative', *Homily IX on I Timothy*, PG 62.544.

**16**. See Cooper (1996), 3 and also Esler (1997), 121-49.

**17**. *Homily X on Colossians*, NFPNF 13.304, PG 62.366.

**18**. See *On How to Choose a Wife*, trans. Roth & Anderson, for further examples of this sentiment, with an extended comparison to the way Abraham organised his son Isaac's marriage to Rebecca.

**19**. *Homily XX on Ephesians*, NFPNF 13.150, PG 62.145.

**20**. Cooper (1996), 145.

**21**. *Homily XX on Ephesians*, NFPNF 13.151, PG 62.147. See also *Homily V on II Thessalonians*, NFPNF 13.397, PG 62.499, for further advice as to how to hurry home to educate the family in appropriate devoutness; 'Extend your hand in spiritual matters. Whatever useful things you have heard, carry them back and give them to the mother and little ones, just like a swallow carries food in its mouth. For is it not absurd, in other things to think yourself worthy of superiority, and to occupy the place of the head, but in teaching to desert your post?'

**22**. E. Clark (1999), 159-62.

**23**. *Homily V on I Thessalonians*, NFPNF 13.346, PG 62.426.

**24**. See further French (1998), 293-318.

**25**. *Argument to Homilies on Philippians*, NFPNF 13.183, PG 62.181-2.

**26**. *Homily XXI on I Corinthians*, NFPNF 12.124, PG 61.179.

**27**. *Homily XVII on II Corinthians*, NFPNF 12.361, PG 61.520.

**28**. Aristotle, *Politics* 2.1269b.

**29**. *Homily XIII on Ephesians*, NFPNF 13.116, PG 62.99. See also *Homily V on II Thessalonians*, NFPNF 13.397, PG 62.499.

**30**. *Homily IV on I Corinthians*, NFPNF 12.22, PG 61.38-9. See also *Homily VII on I Corinthians*, NPFNF 12.39, PG 61.62.

**31**. *Homily V on Titus*, NFPNF 13.539, PG 62.694.

## 9. The Sins of the Wealthy

**1**. *Homily VIII on I Timothy*, NFPNF 13.433, PG 62.541.

**2**. *Homily III on II Thessalonians*, NFPNF 13.387, PG 62.484.

**3**. *Quod Reg.* PG 47.527.

**4**. *Homily X on Colossians*, NFPNF 13.307, PG 62.371.

**5**. *Homily VII on I Timothy*, NFPNF 13.432, PG 62.539-40.

**6**. *Homily XIII on Ephesians*, NFPNF 13.116, PG 62.100.

**7**. See further Coon (1997), 30.

**8**. *Homily VII on Colossians*, NFPNF 13.293, PG 62.350.

**9**. *Homily XI on Romans*, NFPNF 11.415, PG 60.493.

**10**. *Homily VII on Colossians*, NFPNF 13.292, PG 62.349.

**11** *Homily II on I Timothy*, NFPNF 13.415 PG 62.513.

**12**. *Homily IV on I Timothy*, NFPNF 13.422, PG 62.524.

**13**. Ibid.

**14**. Ibid., NFPNF 13.423, PG 62.526. See also *Homily V on I Thessalonians*, NFPNF 13.346, PG 62.426.

**15**. *Quod Reg.* 1, trans. Clark (1979), 211, PG 47.515; 'Prostitutes hide the bait at home but you carry the snare everywhere; you stroll around the marketplace spreading the wings of pleasure. Granted you have not engaged in conversations, you have not spoken the words of a harlot, 'Come! Let us roll up together in love!' You have not pronounced them with your tongue, but you have spoken them with your demeanour; you have not uttered them with your lips, but with your gait you have loudly proclaimed them; you have not called with your voice, but you have spoken them more clearly with your eyes than with your voice.'

**16**. *De Inani Gloria*, SC 188, trans. Laistner (1951).

**17**. *Adv. Eos* 1, trans. Clark (1979), 166, PG 47.496.

**18**. *Homily VIII on I Timothy*, NFPNF 13.434, PG 62.542.

**19**. Shaw (1998), 131-9.

**20**. Jerome, *Epistle* 22.13 ad Eustochium, Loeb trans., 81.

**21**. For this debate see Baur (1906), 430-6 and (1907), 249-65, Courcelle (1969), and Kelly (1995), ch. 5.

**22**. Kelly (1995), 49.

**23**. *Homily XXVI on I Corinthians*, NFPNF 12.151, PG 61.216.

**24**. See for example *Canon XV* of Council at Gangra; 'If any woman, under pretence of asceticism, shall change her apparel, and instead of a woman's accustomed clothing, shall put on that of a man, let her be anathema.' Also Laeuchli (1979). The declaration of someone to be anathema would be one of the most severe punishments handed down by Church authorities, thus illustrating the importance attached by the church to the maintenance of appearance boundaries between the sexes.

**25**. See further Anson (1974), 1-32, Patlegean (1981) and Clark (1993), 128-9.

**26**. *Homily IX on I Corinthians*, NFPNF 12.52-3, PG 61.80.

**27**. See G. Clark (1999), (1998), 171 and (1998), 13-22.

**28**. *Homily XXXIV on I Corinthians*, NFPNF 12.205, PG 61.291.

**29**. See for example *Homily VII on Philippians*, NFPNF 13.218, PG 62.257.

**30**. *Codex Theodosianus* III.16.1.

**31**. *Homily XI on Romans*, NFPNF 11.414, PG 60.490. See also *Homily VI on Philippians*, NFPNF 13.210, PG 62.225; 'A grievous tyrant indeed is the love of gold, and terrible in putting the soul beside itself. A man is not so beside himself through drunkenness as through love of money, not so much from madness and insanity as from love of money.'

**32**. *Homily XVII on Romans*, NFPNF 11.476, PG 60.570; *Kathaper gar etairizomenê gunê kai epi tou stegous hestôsa pasan heautên ekdidôsin, houtô kai hoi kenodoxias douloi. mallon de kai ekeinês aiskêious houtoi. Ekeinai men gar pollakhou katephronêsan tinôn erasthentôn autôn. su de hapasi sauton prouthêkas … .*

**33**. *Homily VII on Philippians*, NFPNF 13.217, PG 62.236.

**34**. See Leyerle (1994)

**35**. *Homily X on Philippians*, NFPNF 13.232, PG 62.260.

**36**. *Homily X on I Thessalonians*, NFPNF 13.360; PG 62.459.

**37**. See further Dixon (1992), 111, Rawson (1986), 9-10 and Treggiari (1991), 8-13.

**38**. *Homily XIII on Ephesians*, NFPNF 13.116, PG 62.100.

**39**. Ibid., NFPNF 13.117, PG 62.100.

**40**. Coon (1997), 57.

## 10. Money and Chrysostom's City

**1**. Meggit (1998), 3.

**2**. See for example Gordon (1987), 108-20, Karayiannis (1994), 39-67 and Leyerle (1994), 29-47 for discussions of Christian attitudes to wealth. For a sample of the more general discussions of the economy and society of late antiquity see Brown (1978), Veyne (1987) and Cameron and Garnsey (eds) (1998).

**3**. *Homily II on Ephesians*, NFPNF 13.58, PG 62.21-2.

**4**. Ibid., NFPNF 13.59, PG 62.22.

**5**. Plato, *Republic* 417b.

**6**. Aristotole, *Politics* 1295ff.

**7**. See further Gonzalez (1990) ch. 1.

**8** . *Homily XVIII on Ephesians*, NFPNF 13.134, PG 62.124.

**9**. Ibid., NFPNF 13.135, PG 62.125.

**10**. Ibid., NFPNF 13.136, PG 62.126.

**11**. *Homily VII on Colossians*, NFPNF 13.292, PG 62.349.

**12**. Ibid., NFPNF 13.293, PG 62.352; *De Sacerdotio* III.13, SC 272.215. See also Greeley (1989), 127.

**13**. Gregory of Nazianzus, *Oration* XVI.18.

**14**. Basil of Caesarea, *Homilia in Divites* 4.

**15**. Ambrose, *De Nabuthe* 56.

**16**. *Homily VII on Colossians*, NFPNF 13.291, PG 62.347.

**17**. *Homily III on II Thessalonians*, NFPNF 13.386-7, PG 62.483.

**18**. Ibid., NFPNF 13.387, PG 62.484.

**19**. *Homily VII on II Timothy*, NFPNF 13.502, PG 62.639.

**20**. See further Gordon (1975) for a discussion of the tradition behind this philosophical trope.

**21**. *Homily II on Philippians*, NFPNF 13.191, PG 62.194; *Oudamothen allothen ho phthonos, all' ek tou prostetêkenai tois parousi, mallon de panta ta kaka. Ei gar mêden enomizes einai ta khrêmata, kai tên doxan tou kosmou toutou, ouk an tois ekhousin ebaskêas. All' epeidê kekênas, kai thaumazeis auta kai eptoêsai, dia touto soi kai ta tê baskanias enokhlei, dia touto kai ta tês kenodoxias: kai panta apo toutou ginetai, apo tou thaumazein ta tou parontos biou.*

**22**. Ibid., NFPNF 13.192, PG 62.195. This is strongly reminiscent of sentiments contained in the Old Testament. See for example Ecclesiastes 5:10-15; 'Whoever loves money never has money enough; whoever loves wealth is never satisfied with his income. This too is meaningless. As goods increase, so do those who consume them. And what benefit are they to the owner except to feast his eyes on them? The sleep of a labourer is sweet, whether he eats little or much, but the abundance of a rich man permits him no sleep. I have seen a grievous evil under the sun: wealth hoarded to the harm of its owner, or wealth lost through some misfortune, so that when he has a son there is nothing left for him. Naked a man comes from his mother's womb, and as he comes, so he departs. He takes nothing from his labour that he can carry in his hand.'

**23**. Gordon (1975), 91.

**24**. Ambrose, *De Nabuthe* 28.

**25**. *Homily II on Philippians*, NFPNF 13.193, PG 62.197. See also Basil of Caesarea, *In Divites* 56c-57b; 'You say you are poor, and I agree with you; for anyone who needs a great many things is poor, and you have a great many needs because your desires are many and insatiable ... .'

**26**. See also Ambrose, *Epistle* 2.15.

**27**. *Homily XII on Philippians*, NFPNF 13.241, PG 62.274.

**28**. *Homily X on Philippians*, NFPNF 13.232, PG 62.259.

**29**. Ammianus Marcellinus, *History of the Later Roman Empire* 24.6. See also 28.4; 'When they leave the bath of Silvanus or the spa of Mamaea, each of them as he emerges from the water dries himself with a fine linen towel. Then he has his presses opened and makes a careful inspection of his shimmering robes, of which he has brought enough with him to dress eleven people. Finally, he makes his choice and puts them on, takes back from his valet the rings which he has left with him to avoid damage from the water, and goes his way.'

**30**. MacMullen (1989), 504.

**31**. See further Gonzalez (1990), 181.

**32**. Allen (1995), 12.

**33**. *Homily I on Colossians*, NFPNF 13.260, PG 62.304.

**34**. Ibid., NFPNF 13.261, PG 62.306. See also Grimm (1996) and Shaw (1997), 579-96 on the concept of the linkage of food with sexual incontinence or other forms of impurity.

**35**. Ibid.

**36**. Ibid., NFPNF 13.262-3, PG 62.307-8. In *Homily XXIV on Romans*, NFPNF 11.520, PG 60.626 he goes into more graphic detail as to the physical effects of such unrestrained feasting; 'And so far, I have said nothing of the problems it leads to, but up to now I have only been speaking to you of the pleasure that fades away so quickly. For the party is no sooner over than all that passed for enjoyment is completely gone. But when I come to mention the vomiting, and the headaches, and the innumerable disorders, and the soul's captivity, what have you got to say to all this? ... And in saying this I do not try to stop you from gathering together, or eating your meals together, but try to prevent you acting in an unseemly manner, since I would like indulgence to be really a matter of indulgence, and not a punishment, or a vengeance, or drunkenness and revelling (*tauta de legô, ou kôluôn sunienai oude koinêi sundeipein, alla kôluôn askhêmonein, kai boulomenos, tên truphên einai truphên, alla mê kolasin mêde timôrian kai methên kai kômon*).'

**37**. *Homily XII on II Corinthians*, NFPNF 12.341, PG 61.489-90. See also *Homily XIII on Philippians*, NFPNF 13.243, PG 62.278; 'You were given a belly, so that you could eat, not bloat it, so that you could control it, not be controlled by it; so that it could serve you for the nourishment of the other parts of your body, not that you should serve it, and not that you could exceed its limits.'

**38**. *Homily XXX on I Corinthians*, NFPNF 12.174, PG 61.247.

**39**. Ibid.

**40**. Jones (1966), chs 20 & 21 and Garnsey & Cameron (eds) (1998), chs 10 & 12, for a more detailed analysis of the social and economic structure of the ancient city.

## 11. The Wealthy Road to Redemption

**1**. *Homily IX on Romans*, NFPNF 11.400, PG 60.472. See also Basil, *Homilia in Divites 4*.

**2**. *Homily VII on Romans*, NFPNF 11.382, PG 60.450.

**3**. *Homily XVIII on Romans*, NFPNF 11.485, PG 60.582.

**4**. *Homily XIX on Romans*, NFPNF 11.495, PG 60.594.

**5**. Ibid.

**6**. *Homily XL on I Corinthians*, NFPNF 12.248, PG 61.353.

**7**. *Homily XVII on II Corinthians*, NFPNF 12.361, PG 61.520.

**8**. *Homily XXI on I Corinthians*, NFPNF 12.124, PG 61.179.

**9**. Brown (1992), 101.

**10**. *Homily XXI on Romans*, NFPNF 11.504, PG 60.605.

**11**. Ibid., NFPNF 11.505, PG 60.606. This advocating of indiscriminate charity is often in direct contrast to other church fathers who advise more care in the act of almsgiving. See for example Basil, *Epistola* 150.3, Ambrose, *De Officiis* 1.15.73 and Augustine, *Enarrationes in Psalmos* 102.12.

**12**. *Homily XXV on Acts of Apostles*, NFPNF 11.166, PG 60.196; see also *Homily XXI on Romans*, *NFPNF* 11.502, PG 60.600.

**13**. *Homily XLIII on I Corinthians*, NFPNF 12.262, PG 61.372-3.

**14**. *Homily V on II Thessalonians*, NFPNF 13.397, PG 62.500.

**15**. Gordon (1987), 115.

**16**. *Homily 12 on I Timothy*, PG 62.563.

**17**. See further Ritter (1989), 170-80.

**18**. *Chapter VI on Commentary on Galatians*, NFPNF 13.45, PG 61.676-7.

**19**. *Homily IV on Ephesians*, NFPNF 13.69, PG 62.36. See also *Homily XXIV on Ephesians*, NFPNF 13.172, PG 62.175-6.

**20**. *Homily I on Philippians*, NFPNF 13.187, PG 62.188.

**21**. Ibid., NFPNF 13.188, PG 62.189. See also *Homily XV on Philippians*, NFPNF 13.251-2, PG 62.291-2.

**22**. *Homily VI on II Timothy*, NFPNF 13.498, PG 62.634.

**23**. *Homily III on I Thessalonians*, NFPNF 13.335, PG 62.411.

**24**. Ibid., NFPNF 13.338, PG 62.415.

**25**. *Homily XXII on Romans*, NFPNF 11.509, PG 60.612.
**26**. *Homily XXVI on Romans*, NFPNF 11.533, PG 60.644.

## 12. Conclusions

**1**. See *De Sacerdotio* VI.
**2**. See Liebeschuetz (1991), 2 and Ward-Perkins (1998), 380-2.
**3**. See also *On Vainglory* 77, trans. M. Laistner, 117; 'First then let us guide it [the soul] away from shameful spectacles and songs. Never let a free-born boy enter the theatre. If he yearn after the pleasure to be found there, let us point out any of his companions who are holding back from this, so that he may be held fast in the grip of emulation.'
**4**. Kelly (1979), 21-44. Also Easterling and Miles (1999), 95-111.
**5**. *Homily V on Titus*, NFPNF 13.538, PG 62.693.
**6**. Ibid., NFPNF 13.538-9, PG 62.693. See also *Homily V on I Thessalonians*, NFPNF 13.347, PG 62.427 (translated above, Chapter 8 n. 11).
**7**. *Homily XII on I Corinthians*, NFPNF 12.68, PG 61.102. Also *Homily V on Titus*, NFPNF 13.538, PG 62.692; 'For nothing was worse than the brutality of mankind before the coming of Christ. They all behaved towards each other as if they were enemies and at war. Fathers killed their own sons, and mothers behaved insanely against their children. There was no order ordained, no natural or written law; everything was upside down ... And naturally, since they worshipped a god of such base character (*ouden ên hestêkos, ou phusikos, ou graptos nomos, alla anatetrapto hapanta ... kai eikotôs, hopou ge kai theon poiouton esebon*.)'
**8**. *Homily XII on I Corinthians*, NFPNF 12.68, PG 61.102; *Boulei kai hetera palin akousai deiknunta autôn tên anoian; tauta men gar ou kolazousin, hetera de kai nomothetousin autoi. Tina oun eisin ekeina; Theatra sunagousi, kai pornôn ekei gunaikôn khorous eisagogtes kai paidas peporneumenous kai eis tên phusin autên enubrizontas.*
**9**. *Homily V on Titus*, NFPNF 13.539, PG 62.694.
**10**. Plato, *Republic* 2.378-83, 3.387-93.
**11**. *Contra Iudos et theatra* 1, PG 56.263-5.
**12**. *Homily II on Titus*, NFPNF 13.526, PG 62.674.
**13**. See Aristotle, *Politics* 1.2 for the stages in forming a city state, with the gendered couple of husband and wife being regarded as the natural starting point for any such community. Books 7 and 8 join together to present a possible picture of what the best possible life within such a state might be.
**14**. Brown (1988), 306-9.
**15**. Ibid., 319.
**16**. See Ward-Perkins (1998), 392-403, Garnsey (1998), 327, 332 and Natali (1975), 41-59.
**17**. Natali (1979), 1176-84.

# Bibliography

## Primary sources

Ambrose, *De Nabuthe*, PL 14.766-92.

—— *Epistles* PL 126.913-1342, trans. in *Fathers of the Church*, vol. 26.

Ammianus Marcellinus, *The Later Roman Empire, AD 354-378*, trans. W. Hamilton (London, 1986).

Aristotle, *Politics*, Loeb Classical Library vol. 264.

Augustine, *De Doctrina Christiana*, trans. in *Fathers of the Church*, vol. 2.

Basil of Caesarea, *In Homilia Divites*, PG 29.

—— *Ad adulescentes*, PG 31.563-590, *Address to Young Men on What Profit may be Derived from Pagan Literature*, trans. R. Deferrari & M. McGuire, Loeb Classical Library.

—— *De Hexaemeron*, PG 29.4-208, SC 26, trans. A. Clare Way, *St Basil Exegetical Homilies* in *Fathers of the Church*, vol. 46.

*Codex Theodosianus*.

Gerontius, *Vita Melaniae Iunioris*, SC 90, trans. E. Clark (New York, 1984).

Gregory of Nazianzus, *Orations* PG 35.395-1252, NFPNF 8.

Gregory of Nyssa, *De Virginitate*, PG 45.317-416, NFPNF 5.

Jerome, *Epistles*, trans. Loeb Classical Library.

John Chrysostom, *Homiliae XXIV in Epistolam ad Ephesios*, PG 62, Nicene Fathers and Post Nicene Fathers Series 2 (hereafter NFPNF), 13, ed. P. Schaff.

—— *Homiliae XV in Epistolam ad Philippenses*, PG 62, NFPNF 13, ed. P. Schaff.

—— *Homiliae XII in Epistolam ad Colossenses*, PG 62, NFPNF 13, ed. P. Schaff.

—— *Homiliae XI in Epistolam primum ad Thessalonicenses*, PG 62, NFPNF 13, ed. P. Schaff.

—— *Homiliae V in Epistolam secundam ad Thessalonicenses*, PG 62, NFPNF 13, ed. P. Schaff.

—— *Homiliae XVIII in Epistolam primam ad Timotheum*, PG 62, NFPNF 13, ed. P. Schaff.

—— *Homiliae X in Epistolam secundam ad Timotheum*, PG 62, NFPNF 13, ed. P. Schaff.

—— *Homiliae VI in Epistolam ad Titum*, PG 62, NFPNF 13, ed. P. Schaff.

—— *Homiliae III in Epistolam ad Philemon*, PG 62, NFPNF 13, ed. P. Schaff.

—— *Homiliae LV in Acta Apostolorum*, PG 60 NFPNF 11, ed. P. Schaff.

—— *Homiliae XXXII in Epistolam ad Romanos*, PG 60, NFPNF 11, ed. P. Schaff.

—— *Homiliae XLIV in Epistolam primam ad Corinthios*, PG 61, NFPNF 12, ed. P. Schaff.

—— *Homiliae XXX in Epistolam secundam ad Corinthios*, PG 61, NFPNF 12, ed. P. Schaff.

—— *Commentarius in Epistolam ad Galatas*, PG 62, NFPNF 12, ed. P. Schaff.

—— *De Sacerdotio*, PG 48, NFPNF 9 SC 272.

—— *De Virginitate; De non iterando conjugio*, trans. S. Shore, *On Virginity and Against Remarriage*, *Studies in Women and Religion* 9 (New York, 1983).

—— *Ad viduam juniorem*, PG 48.599-610, SC 138.

—— *Comparatio Regis et Monachi*, PG 47.387-392.

—— *Adversus Eos qui apud se habent subintroductas virgines*, PG 47.495-514, trans. E. Clark *Jerome, Chrysostom and Friends* (New York, 1979).

—— *Quod Regulares Feminae Viris Cohabitare non Debeant*, PG 47.514-52, trans. E. Clark *Jerome, Chrysostom and Friends* (New York, 1979).

—— *Homiliae XXI de Statuis ad populum Antiochenum habitae*, PG 49.15-222, NFPNF 9.

—— *Homilies on Genesis*, PG 54.

—— *On How to Choose a Wife*, in *On Marriage and Family Life*, trans. C. Roth and D. Anderson (New York, 1997).

—— *On Vainglory and Advice to parents on the right way to bring up children*, SC 188 trans. M. Laistner *Christianity and Pagan Culture in the Later Roman Empire* (Cornell, 1951).

—— *Contra Iudos et theatra* PG 56.

—— *Letters to Olympias* SC 13.

Palladius, *Dialogus Concerning the life of Chrysostom*, PG 47, trans. H. Moore (London, 1921).

Plato, *Republic*, trans. D Lee (London, 1955).

Socrates Scholasticus, *Historia Ecclesiastica*, PG 67, NFPNF 2.

Sozomen, *Historia Ecclesiastica*, PG 67, NFPNF 2.

*Vita Sanctae Olympiadis Diaconissae* SC 13, trans. E. Clark in her *Jerome Chrysostom and Friends* (New York, 1979).

## Secondary works

Allen, P., 'Homilies as a source for social history', *Stu. Patr.* 24 (1991), 1-5.

—— 'John Chrysostom's homilies on 1 & 2 Thessalonians; the preacher and his audience', *Stu. Patr.* 31 (1995), 3-21.

—— 'Severus of Antioch as pastoral carer', *Stu. Patr.* 35 (2001), 353-68.

Allen, P. & Mayer, W., 'Computer and homily: accessing the everyday life of early Christians', *VC* 47 (1993), 260-80.

—— 'Chrysostom and the preaching of homilies in series: a re-examination of the 15 homilies *In Epistulam ad Philippenses*', *VC* 49 (1995), 270-89.

Anson, J., 'The female transvestite in early monasticism: the origin and development of a motif', *Viator: Medieval and Renaissance Studies* 5 (1974), 1-32.

Arjava, A., 'Women in the Christian empire: ideological change and social reality', *Stu. Patr.* 24 (1993), 6-9.

—— *Women and Law in Late Antiquity* (Oxford, 1996).

Attwater, D., *St John Chrysostom* (London, 1959).

Bailey, D.S., *Sexual Relation in Christian Thought* (New York, 1959).

Bailey, L., 'Preacher and audience: the sixth century west', presented at the 13th International Conference on Patristic Studies (1999).

Baker, D. (ed.), *The Church and Wealth*, Studies in Church History, vol. 24 (Oxford, 1992).

Baldovin, J., *The Urban Character of Christian Worship: the origins, development and meaning of stational liturgy* (Rome, 1987).

Barnes, T., 'The funerary speech for John Chrysostom', presented at the 13th International Conference on Patristic Studies (1999).

Baur, C., *Saint John Chrysostom and his Time* (Maryland, 1959).

—— 'S. Jérôme et S. Chrysostome', *Revue Benedictine* 23 (1906), 430-6.

—— 'L'entrée littéraire de S. Chrysostome dans le monde Latin', *Revue d'Histoire Ecclesiastique* 8 (1907), 249-65.

Beckwith, R.T., 'The Jewish background to Christian worship' in C. Jones, G. Wainwright, E. Yarnold (eds), *The Study of the Liturgy* (London, 1978), 39-51.

Boswell, J., *Christianity, Social Tolerance, and Homosexuality: gay people in western Europe from the beginning of the Christian era to the fourteenth century* (Chicago, 1980).

Brakke, D., 'The problematization of nocturnal emissions in early Christian Syria, Egypt and Gaul', *JECS* 3:4 (1995), 419-60.

Broc, C., 'Le rôle des femmes dans l'Eglise de Constantinople d'après la correspondance de Jean Chrysostome', *Stu. Patr.* 27 (1991), 150-4.

Brooten, B., *Love Between Women: early Christian responses to female homoeroticism* (Chicago, 1996).

Brown, P., 'Aspects of the Christianization of the Roman aristocracy', *JRS* 51 (1961), 1-11.

—— *Religion and Society in the Age of St Augustine* (London, 1972).

—— *The Making of Late Antiquity* (London, 1978).

—— *Society and the Holy in Late Antiquity* (London, 1982).

—— *The Body and Society: men, women and sexual renunciation in early Christianity* (New York, 1986).

—— *Power and Persuasion in Late Antiquity: towards a Christian empire* (Wisconsin, 1992).

—— *Authority and the Sacred: aspects of the Christianisation of the Roman world* (Cambridge, 1995).

Burnell, P., 'The functions of the family and of civil society in Augustine's *City of God*', *Stu. Patr.* 33 (1997), 35-9.

Cameron, A., 'Virginity as metaphor: women and the rhetoric of early Christianity' in A. Cameron (ed.), *History as Text* (London, 1989), 181-205.

—— *Christianity and the Rhetoric of Empire* (Berkeley, 1991).

—— *The Later Roman Empire*, Fontana, (London, 1993).

—— *The Mediterranean World in Late Antiquity* (London, 1993).

—— 'Early Christianity and the discourse of female desire' in L. Archer, S. Fischler, M. Wyke (eds), *Women in Ancient Societies: 'An Illusion of the Night'* (London, 1994), 152-68.

—— 'Sacred and profane love: thoughts on Byzantine gender' in L. James (ed.), *Women, Men and Eunuchs: gender in Byzantium* (London, 1997), 1-23.

—— 'Education and literary culture' in A. Cameron & P. Garnsey (eds), *Cambridge Ancient History*, vol. XIII (Cambridge, 1998), 665-707.

Cantarella, E., *Pandora's Daughters: the role and status of women in Greek and Roman society* (Baltimore, 1987).

Carter, R., 'Saint John Chrysostom's rhetorical use of the Socratic distinction between kingship and tyranny', *Traditio* 14 (1958), 367-71.

—— 'The chronology of Saint John Chrysostom's early life', *Traditio* 18 (1962), 357-64.

—— 'The chronology of eighteen homilies of Severian of Gabala', presented at the 13th International Conference on Patristic Studies (1999).

Chadwick, H., ' "All things to all men": a study in Pauline inconsistency', *NTS* 1 (1954), 261-75.

Clark, E., 'John Chrysostom and the *subintroductae*', *Church History* 46 (1977), 171-85.

—— *Jerome, Chrysostom and Friends* (New York, 1979).

—— 'Ascetic renunciation and feminine advancement: a paradox of late ancient Christianity', *ATR* 63 (1981), 240-57.

—— 'Introduction' to *On Virginity and Against Remarriage, Studies in Women and Religion* 9 (New York, 1983).

—— *Life of Melania the Younger* (New York, 1984).

—— *Ascetic Piety and Women's Faith*: essays on late ancient Christianity, *Studies in Women and Religion* 20 (New York, 1986).

—— 'Early Christian women: sources and interpretation' in L. Coon, K. Haldane, E. Sommer (eds), *That Gentle Strength*: historical perspectives on women in Christianity (Virginia, 1990).

—— 'Ideology, history, and the construction of 'woman' in late ancient Christianity', *JECS* 2:2 (1994), 155-84.

—— *Reading Renunciation*: asceticism and scripture in early Christianity (New Jersey, 1999).

Clark, G., *Women in Late Antiquity*: pagan and Christian lifestyles (Oxford, 1993).

—— 'Adam's engendering' in Swanson (ed.), *Gender and Christian Religion* (Suffolk, 1998), 13-22.

—— 'The Old Adam: the Fathers and the unmaking of masculinity' in L. Foxhall (ed.), *Thinking Men* (London, 1998), 170-82.

—— (1999) 'Pastoral care: town and country in late-antique preaching', presented at the third Shifting Frontiers conference.

Cloke, G., *This Female Man of God*: women and spiritual power in the Patristic age, AD 350-450 (London, 1995).

Coleman-Norton, P., 'St John Chrysostom and the Greek Philosophers', *CP* 25 (1930), 305-17.

—— 'St Chrysostom's use of Josephus', *CP* 26 (1931), 85-9.

Coon, L., *Sacred Fictions*: holy women and hagiography in late Antiquity (Philadelphia, 1997).

Cooper, K., *The Virgin and the Bride*: idealized womanhood in late Antiquity (London, 1996).

Couratin, A.N., 'The Liturgy' in R.P.C. Hanson (ed.), *The Pelican Guide to Modern Theology*, vol. 2 (London, 1969).

Courcelle, P., *Late Latin Writers and their Greek Sources* (Massachusetts, 1969).

Cox Miller, P., 'The blazing body: ascetic desire in Jerome's Letter to Eustochium', *JECS* 1:1 (1993), 21-45.

Cunningham, M.B., 'Preaching and the community', in R. Morris (ed.), *Church and People in Byzantium* (Birmingham, 1990).

Davidson, I., 'Social construction and the rhetoric of ecclesial presence: Ambrose's Milan', *Stu. Patr.* 38 (2001), 385-93.

Deferrari, R.J., 'St Augustine's method of composing and delivering sermons', *AJP* 43 (1922), 97-124 and 193-220.

Dixon, S., *The Roman Family* (Baltimore, 1992).

Downey, G., *Antioch in the Age of Theodosius the Great* (Oklahoma, 1962).

Dudley, M., 'Danger and glory: priesthood in the writings of John Chrysostom', *Stu. Patr.* 27 (1991), 162-5.

Dumortier, J., *S. Jean Chrysostome*: les cohabitations suspectes (Paris, 1955).

Elm, S., *Virgins of God*: the making of asceticism in late Antiquity (Oxford, 1994).

—— 'The Dog that did not Bark; doctrine and patriarchal authority in the conflict between Theophilus of Alexandria and John Chrysostom of Constantinople', in L. Ayres & G. Jones (eds), *Christian Origins*: theology, rhetoric and community (London, 1998), 68-93.

Esler, P., 'Family imagery and Christian identity in Gal. 5:13 to 6:10' in H. Moxnes (ed.), *Constructing Early Christian Families*: family as social reality and metaphor (London, 1997), 121-49.

Ettlinger, G., 'Some historical evidence for the date of St John Chrysostom's birth in the treatise *Ad viduam iuniorem*', *Traditio* 16 (1960), 373-80.

Festugière, A.J., *Antiochene paienne et chrétienne* (Paris, 1959).

Fiorenza, E. Schussler, *In Memory of Her*: *a feminist theological reconstruction of Christian origins* (New York, 1983).

French, D., 'Maintaining boundaries: the status of actresses in early Christian society', *VC* 52:3 (1998), 293-318.

Gardner, J., *Women in Roman Law and Society* (London, 1986).

Garnsey, P. & Cameron A. (eds), *Cambridge Ancient History XIII* (Cambridge, 1998).

Garnsey, P. & Whittaker C., 'Trade, industry and the urban economy', in A. Cameron & P. Garnsey (eds), *Cambridge Ancient History XIII* (Cambridge, 1998).

Gleason, M., 'The semiotics of gender: physiognomy and self-fashioning in the second century CE', in D. Halperin, J. Winkler, F. Zeitlin (eds), *Before Sexuality*: *the construction of erotic experience in the ancient Greek world* (Princeton, 1990).

———— *Making Men*: *sophists and self-presentation in ancient Rome* (Princeton, 1995).

Gonzalez, J., *Faith and Wealth*: *a history of early Christian ideas on the origin, significance, and use of money* (San Francisco, 1990).

Goodall, B., *The Homilies of St John Chrysostom on the Letters of St Paul to Titus and Philemon, Prolegomena to an Edition* (Berkeley, 1979).

Gordon, B., *Economic Analysis Before Adam Smith*: *Hesiod to Lessius* (London, 1975).

———— 'The problem of scarcity and the Christian Fathers: John Chrysostom and some contemporaries', *Stu. Patr.* 22 (1987), 108-20.

Greeley, D., 'St John Chrysostom: prophet of social justice', *Stu. Patr.* 17 (1979), 1163-8.

———— 'John Chrysostom, *On the Priesthood*: a model for service', *Stu. Patr.* 22 (1989), 121-8.

Gregory, D., *The Shape of the Liturgy* (Westminster, 1943).

Grimm, V., *From Feasting to Fasting*: *the evolution of a sin* (London, 1996).

Hanson, R., 'The achievement of orthodoxy in the fourth century AD' in R. Williams (ed.), *The Making of Orthodoxy*: *essays in honour of Henry Chadwick* (Cambridge, 1989), 142-56.

Harris, W., *Ancient Literacy* (Harvard, 1989).

Hartney, A., 'Manly women and womanly men: the *subintroductae* and John Chrysostom' in L. James (ed.), *Desire and Denial in Byzantium* (London, 1999), 41-8.

Hill, R., 'The spirituality of Chrysostom's commentary on the Psalms', *JECS* 5:4 (1997), 569-79.

Holum, K., *Theodosian Empresses*: *women and imperial dominion in late Antiquity* (California, 1982).

Hubbell, H., 'Chrysostom and rhetoric', *CP* 19 (1924), 261-76.

Hunter, D., 'Borrowings from Libanius in the *Comparatio Regis et Monachi* of St John Chrysostom', *JTS* n.s. 39 (1988), 525-31.

———— 'Libanius and John Chrysostom: new thoughts on an old problem', *Stu. Patr.* 22 (1989), 129-35.

Jones, A.H.M., 'John Chrysostom's parentage and education', *HTR* 46 (1953), 171-3.

———— *The Later Roman Empire*, vols 1 & 2 (Oxford, 1969).

Kannengiesser, C. (ed.), *Jean Chrysostome et Augustin. Actes du Colloque de Chantilly 1974* (Paris, 1975).

Karayiannis, A.D., 'The eastern Christian Fathers (AD 350-400) on the redistribution of wealth', *History of Political Economy* 26:1 (1994), 39-67.

Kecksemeti, J., 'Exégèse Chrysostomienne et exégèse engagée', *Stu. Patr.* 22 (1989), 136-47.

Kelly, H., 'Tragedy and the performance of tragedy in late Roman antiquity', *Traditio* 35 (1979), 21-44.

Kelly, J.N.D., *Jerome: his life, writings, and controversies* (London, 1975).

——— *Golden Mouth: the story of John Chrysostom – ascetic, preacher, bishop* (London, 1995).

Kennedy, G., *Classical Rhetoric and its Christian and Secular Tradition from Ancient to Modern Times* (London, 1980).

——— *Greek Rhetoric under Christian Emperors* (New Jersey, 1983).

Konstan, D., *Friendship in the Classical World* (Cambridge, 1997).

Laeuchli, S., *Power and Sexuality: the emergence of Canon Law at the Synod of Elvira* (Philadelphia, 1979).

Laistner, M., *Christianity and Pagan Culture in the Later Roman Empire* (Cornell, 1951).

Lawrenz, M., 'The Christology of John Chrysostom', *Stu. Patr.* 22 (1989), 148-53.

Leyerle, B., 'John Chrysostom on the gaze', *JECS* 1:2 (1993), 159-74.

——— 'John Chrysostom on almsgiving and the use of money', *HTR* 87:1 (1994), 29-47.

——— 'Appealing to children', *JECS* 5:2 (1997), 243-70.

——— *Displays of Holiness: John Chrysostom's attack on spiritual marriage* (Berkeley, 2000).

Liebeschuetz, J., *Antioch: city and imperial administration in the Later Roman Empire* (Oxford, 1972).

——— 'Friends and enemies of John Chrysostom' in A. Moffat (ed.), *Maistor: Classical, Byzantine and Renaissance studies for Robert Browning* (Sydney, 1984), 85-111.

——— *Barbarians and Bishops: army, church and state in the age of Arcadius and Chrysostom* (Oxford, 1991).

——— 'The end of the ancient city', in J. Rich (ed.), *The City in Late Antiquity* (London, 1991), 1-49.

——— 'Ecclesiastical historians on their own times', *Stu. Patr.* 24 (1993), 151-63.

Lim, R., *Public Disputation, Power, and Social Order in Late Antiquity* (Berkeley, 1995).

MacMullen, R., 'The Preacher's audience', *JTS* n.s. 40:2 (1989), 503-11.

Malingrey, A., 'Introduction' to *Lettres à Olympias* SC 13 (Paris, 1968).

——— 'Les sentences des sages dans la prédication de Jean Chrysostome' in C. Kannengiesser (ed.), *Jean Chrysostome et Augustin. Actes du Colloque de Chantilly 1974* (Paris, 1975), 199-218.

Mann, M., *The Sources of Social Power*, vol. 1: *A History of Power from the Beginning to AD 1760* (Cambridge, 1986).

Markus, R., *The End of Ancient Christianity* (Cambridge, 1990).

Marrou, H., *A History of Education in Antiquity* (London, 1956).

Mayer, W., 'Who came to hear John Chrysostom preach? Recovering a late fourth-century preacher's audience', submitted to *Ephemerides Theologiae Lovanienses* (1999).

——— 'At Constantinople, how often did John Chrysostom preach?', presented at the 13th International Conference on Patristic Studies (1999).

——— 'Constantinopolitan women in Chrysostom's circle', *VC* 53 (1999).

McLynn, N., *Ambrose of Milan* (Berkeley, 1994).

Meggit, J., *Paul, Poverty and Survival* (Edinburgh, 1998).

Meredith, A., *The Cappadocians* (New York, 1995).

Miles, R. & Easterling, P., 'Dramatic identities: tragedy in late Antiquity', in R. Miles (ed.), *Constructing Identities in Late Antiquity* (London, 1999), 95-111.

Mitchell, M., 'A variable and many-sorted man: John Chrysostom's treatment of Pauline inconsistency', *JECS* 6:1 (1998), 93-111.

Natali, A., 'Christianisme et cité à Antioche à la fin du IVe siècle d'après Jean Chrysostome', in C. Kannengiesser (ed.), *Jean Chrysostome et Augustin. Actes du Colloque de Chantilly 1974* (Paris, 1975), 41-59.

———— 'Eglise et éuergétisme à Antioche à la fin du IVe siècle d'après Jean Chrysostome', *Stu. Patr.* 17 (1979), 1176-84.

Oesterley, W.O.E., *The Jewish Background to the Christian Liturgy* (Oxford, 1925).

Pack, R., *Studies in Libanius and Antiochene Society under Theodosius* (Michigan, 1935, dissertation).

Parvey, C., 'The theology and leadership of women in the New Testament', in R. Radford Ruether (ed.), *Religion and Sexism* (New York, 1974).

Patlegean, E., *Structure sociale, famille, chrétienté à Byzance IVe-XIe siècle* (London, 1981).

Perkins, J, *The Suffering Self: pain and narrative representation in the early Christian era* (London, 1995).

Quasten, J., *Patrology*, vol. III (Maryland, 1964).

Rawson, B., *The Family in Ancient Rome: new perspectives* (Oxford, 1986).

Raynor, D., 'The faith of the *simpliciores*: a patriarch's dilemma', *Stu. Patr.* 22 (1989), 165-9.

Reynolds, R., '*Virgines subintroductae* in Celtic Christianity', *HTR* 61 (1968), 547-66.

Ritter, A., 'Between theocracy and simple life: Dio Chrysostom, John Chrysostom and the problem of humanizing society', *Stu. Patr.* 22 (1989), 170-80.

Roark, D., *Urban Family Structure in Late Antiquity as Evidenced by John Chrysostom* (Ohio State University, 1994, dissertation).

Rousseau, P., *Ascetics, Authority and the Church* (Oxford, 1978).

———— *Basil of Caesarea* (Berkeley, 1994).

———— 'Learned women and the development of a Christian culture in late Antiquity', *Symbolae Osloenses* 70 (1995), 116-47.

———— 'The preacher's audience: a more optimistic view', in T. Hillard, R. Kearsley, C. Nixon, A. Nobbs (eds), *Ancient History in a Modern University II* (Cambridge, 1998).

Ruether, R.R., *Gregory of Nazianzus: rhetor and philosopher* (Oxford, 1969).

———— 'Misogynism and virginal feminism in the Fathers of the Church' in R. Ruether (ed.), *Religion and Sexism* (New York, 1974).

Ryan, P.J., 'Chrysostom – a derived stylist?', *VC* 36:1 (1982), 5-15.

Satlow, M. 'Try to be a man: the Rabbinic construction of masculinity', *HTR* 89:1 (1996), 19-40.

Shaw, T., 'Creation, virginity and diet in fourth-century Christianity: Basil of Ancyra's *On the True Purity of Virginity*', *Gender and History* 9 (1997), 579-96.

———— *The Burden of the Flesh* (Philadelphia, 1998).

Tanner, R.G., 'Chrysostom's Exegesis of Romans', *Stu. Patr.* 17 (1979), 1185-95.

Tougher, S., 'Byzantine eunuchs: an overview, with special reference to their creation and origin' in L. James (ed.), *Women, Men and Eunuchs: gender in Byzantium* (London, 1997), 168-84.

Treggiari, S., *Roman Marriage: iusti coniuges from the time of Cicero to the time of Ulpian* (Oxford, 1991).

Urbainczyk, T., 'Cloth and sackcloth in Theodoret's *Religious History*', *Stu. Patr.* 35 (2001), 167-71.

Veyne, P., *Bread and Circuses* (London, 1976).

———— *A History of Private Life*, vol. 1 (Harvard, 1987).

Wallace Hadrill, A., *Patronage in Ancient Society* (London, 1989).

Wallace Hadrill, D.S., *Christian Antioch: a study of early Christian thought in the East* (Cambridge, 1982).

Ward-Perkins, B., 'The Cities' in A. Cameron & P. Garnsey (eds), *Cambridge Ancient History*, vol. XIII (Cambridge, 1998), 371-410.

Wilken, R., *John Chrysostom and the Jews: rhetoric and reality in the late fourth century* (Berkeley, 1983).

Wylie, A.L.B., *John Chrysostom and his Homilies on the Acts of the Apostles: reclaiming ancestral models for the Christian people* (Princeton, 1992, dissertation).

Yarbrough, A., 'Christianization in the fourth century: the example of Roman Women', *Church History* 45 (1976), 149-64.

Young, F., *From Nicaea to Chalcedon: a guide to the literature and its background* (Philadelphia, 1983).

———— 'The rhetorical schools and their influence on patristic exegesis', in R. Williams (ed.), *The Making of Orthodoxy: essays in honour of Henry Chadwick* (Cambridge, 1989), 182-99.

# Index

alms and almsgiving 10, 43-5, 71, 106, 127-8, 148, 157, 164, 171-81, 191, 192, 194

Ammianus Marcellinus 8, 9, 164

Ambrose 10, 44, 67, 68, 80, 158, 162, 177

animals 105, 111, 114, 120, 136, 143-4, 147, 149, 154-5

Anthousa 16, 17, 69

Antioch 1, 2, 6-9, 16-20, 24, 25, 29, 30, 41, 42, 48, 79, 89, 141, 158

anti-Semitism 4

Arcadius 21, 78, 79

Aristotle 14, 15, 82, 102, 119, 128, 155, 190

asceticism 4, 5, 7, 11, 17-18, 23, 24, 26, 28, 78, 87-8, 90-4, 99, 100-2, 117, 126, 129, 138-9, 141-2, 177, 190

Augustine 2, 10, 26, 28, 36, 37, 40, 46, 47, 50

Basil of Caesarea 10, 35, 36, 44-6, 50, 157, 158, 177

Basil (friend of John) 17-18, 26, 78

bestiality 114

Cappadocians, the 28, 40, 46, 48, 50, 157

Classical tradition, the 12, 16, 18, 29, 30, 33, 35-7, 43, 45, 46, 50, 93, 154, 191, 192

clergy 10, 17, 25, 26, 27, 30, 31, 34, 35, 37, 173, 174, 184, 194

Constantinople 3, 6, 9, 19, 20-2, 28, 30, 41, 42, 48, 49, 71, 72, 79, 89, 179

dinner parties and entertaining 8, 64, 99, 126, 165-7

dress 3, 9, 44, 75, 95-6, 98, 99, 100, 106, 121, 123, 130, 134-43, 147-9, 153, 159, 163-5, 193

education 5, 7, 12, 15, 16, 18, 24, 36-7,

43, 45-6, 47, 50, 58, 120, 125, 185, 187, 190

Eudoxia 21, 67, 72, 73, 74, 78, 79

euergetism 8, 194

eunuchs 75, 88, 92, 112, 116, 120

Forum, the 6, 125

gender 12-16, 33, 43, 49, 53, 58, 68, 71, 79, 81, 85-102, 103, 106, 108-16, 118, 126, 127-34, 142, 143, 145, 151, 152, 168, 177, 183, 184, 186, 188, 192, 193, 194, 195

Greeks 34, 47, 82, 129, 130, 186, 187

heresy 30, 62, 115

hippodrome, the 6, 19, 29, 49, 188

homosexuality 108, 112, 113, 114, 122, 179

Jerome 2, 26, 27, 28, 36, 37, 97, 98, 141

jewellery 75, 135, 137, 151, 153

Jews 4, 34, 80, 105, 129, 130, 178

Libanius 6, 7, 8, 16, 77

marriage 27, 28, 53, 56, 59-70, 98, 100, 107, 112, 118, 119-28, 132, 137

monks 7, 17, 21, 41, 126, 177

Olympias 70, 71, 194

Palladius 3, 18, 25

pagans 6, 10, 14, 16, 30, 34, 36, 43, 46, 47, 50, 77, 81, 98, 111, 122, 131, 156, 164, 169

pagan religion 8, 9, 155, 179

Paul 15, 16, 34, 41-2, 53, 54, 56-70, 74-5, 80-2, 112-14, 118-19, 122, 128, 129, 133-6, 142, 179, 187

Plato 15, 82, 155, 188

precious metals 21, 25, 39, 54, 56-7, 73,